DANGEROUS
IDEAS

DANGEROUS IDEAS

A BRIEF

HISTORY OF

CENSORSHIP

IN THE WEST,

FROM THE

ANCIENTS

TO FAKE NEWS

Eric Berkowitz

BEACON PRESS, BOSTON

BEACON PRESS
Boston, Massachusetts
www.beacon.org

Beacon Press books
are published under the auspices of
the Unitarian Universalist Association of Congregations.

24 23 22 21   8 7 6 5 4 3 2 1

This book is printed on acid-free paper that meets the uncoated paper
ANSI/NISO specifications for permanence as revised in 1992.

Text design and composition by Kim Arney

Page 142: *Luxury or the Comforts of a Rumpford*, London.
© The Trustees of the British Museum. Used with permission.

Library of Congress Cataloging-in-Publication Data

Name: Berkowitz, Eric, author.
Title: Dangerous ideas : a brief history of censorship in the West, from
    the ancients to fake news / Eric Berkowitz.
Description: Boston : Beacon Press, [2021] | Includes bibliographical
    references and index.
Identifiers: LCCN 2020057089 (print) | LCCN 2020057090 (ebook) |
    ISBN 9780807036242 (hardcover) | ISBN 9780807036259 (ebook)
Subjects: LCSH: Censorship—Western countries—History. | Freedom of
    speech—Western countries—History.
Classification: LCC Z658.W46 D36 2021 (print) | LCC Z658.W46 (ebook) |
    DDC 363.31—dc23
LC record available at https://lccn.loc.gov/2020057089
LC ebook record available at https://lccn.loc.gov/2020057090

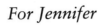

For Jennifer

CONTENTS

DANGEROUS
IDEAS

INTRODUCTION

During the Chinese fever dream known as the Cultural Revolution (1966–76), Mao Zedong's Red Guards marauded through the country destroying the "Four Olds": old ideas, old culture, old customs, and old habits. Central to that campaign was the annihilation of ancient religion, leading to the destruction of millions of books, images, and objects related to Confucius and Tibetan Buddhism. Scholars of the ancient philosopher were deemed "reactionary" and tortured, as Confucian texts and statues were extirpated. Buddhist monks were forced to trample their books and use what remained as toilet paper, and Tibet's holiest temple was repurposed as a place to keep and slaughter pigs.[1] Secular schools and universities were also closed, their books destroyed—again by the millions—as "poisonous weeds." Red Guards invaded homes to destroy family photographs ("feudal" relics) and replace them with images of Mao, before which citizens were required to confess their sins.[2]

Yet even as Mao eliminated China's "backward elements" to make himself the beginning, middle, and end of Chinese thought, he publicly aligned himself with the "First Emperor"—Qin Shi Huang (259–10 BCE), who also burned books and used violence to unify the region's seven major states and create the centralized kingdom that became China. Despite his considerable achievements, the First Emperor was disliked, to say the least. As long as people's thoughts remained out of his control, he knew his power was not entirely secure. As he traveled the empire, he seethed upon hearing of Confucian and other scholars who compared his regime unfavorably to the golden ages of the past. He decided to immolate that past.

The events referred to as "The Burning of the Books and the Burying of the Philosophers" took place in 213–12 BCE, when countless poetry, history, and philosophy texts (mostly silk rolls and bamboo and wooden tablets) were destroyed, particularly Confucian texts and those of the so-called Hundred Schools of Thought. Most private book ownership became forbidden. Qin kept copies of the books he burned, but those who knew the texts best were not spared: hundreds of scholars were buried alive. From that point forward, anyone who criticized Qin's regime with examples from the past—or even discussed the ideas in the banned books—was executed along with their relatives.

Like most political censorship throughout history, observes the scholar Lois Mai Chan, Qin's book burning "proved to be, rather than a condemnation, a recognition of the power of knowledge."[3] For Qin, security meant dominance not only of the wheels of state but also of the ideas darting through the minds of the governed. Intellectuals in particular were empowered by the forbidden books, which bred seditious thoughts that challenged the First Emperor's absolute rule.[4] As the twentieth-century Chinese writer Lu Xun observed:

> The statesman hates the writer because the writer sows the seeds of dissent. What the statesman dreams of is to be able to prevent people from thinking; and thus he always accuses the artists and writers of upsetting his orderly state.[5]

Soon enough, however, Qin's paranoia brought him to the same end that he had meted out to his critics. As assassination attempts increased in frequency, he spent his days in tunnels with a sword on his lap and became consumed with forestalling death.[6] Just three years after he burned the books, according to legend, he drank what he hoped was an elixir of immortality and died. He was buried with a massive terracotta army to protect him in the afterlife, but the Qin dynasty—from which China derives its name—fell into chaos and collapsed.

Mao found much in Qin to emulate, except the First Emperor had not gone far enough. In 1958, nine years before the Cultural Revolution began, Mao bragged in a speech:

> [Qin] buried 460 scholars alive—we have buried 46,000 scholars alive. You [intellectuals] revile us for being Qin Shihuangs. You are wrong. We have surpassed Qin Shihuang a hundredfold.[7]

When Mao died in 1976, it was said that the glow of his thought would shine into future generations. Yet despite the crowds who visit his mausoleum and the presence of his image on Chinese currency, Maoism is as vital today as Qin's clay soldiers.

Apart from Pol Pot's Cambodia, where the ability to read could be a capital offense, no modern society has so pillaged its own culture and history as China during the Cultural Revolution. But while the scale of the devastation was unique, the impulse behind it was not. When a regime's power rests on force rather than consent, its legitimacy requires constant manhandling of the past—in effect, making history an instrument of ideology and power. In China, as in the totalitarian superstate described in George Orwell's *Nineteen Eighty-Four*, history was a palimpsest, to be "scraped clean and re-inscribed" as often as necessary.[8] In any such system, Orwell wrote elsewhere, "history is to be created rather than learned."[9]

History has always been a form of practical literature, useful for sanctifying institutions and providing people with a sense of destiny. But for authoritarians, history is a matter of urgent necessity: to make their presence appear inevitable and welcome, to legitimate their actions, and to undermine their adversaries. "Warring authorities," explains the historian J. H. Plumb, "mean warring pasts."[10] This is why totalitarian regimes give historians no freedom, why Donald Trump vehemently denied irregularities in his election and advanced a false, contrary narrative, and why the sixteenth-century Spanish invaders in Mesoamerica destroyed the Maya civilization's most sacred and ancient texts. It also explains why the Guatemalan government targeted the Maya for renewed cultural extermination during that country's 1960–96 civil war. For the sin of supporting anti-government elements, Mayan elders, who were responsible for transmitting accumulated cultural knowledge to younger generations, were "murdered with exceptional cruelty in order to destroy the people's links with their past," according to one investigation.[11]

It has been said that "any old man who dies is a burning library." Indeed, one of the more odious forms of censorship is the destruction of the people and texts that give a culture cohesion and collective memory. However, the past can also be forcibly curated in the service of truth, as attested by multiple laws across the West criminalizing Holocaust denial. These rules are meant (among other things) to quell the vicious claim that Jews use a genocide myth to extort money from Christian nations. By guarding the factuality of the Holocaust, lawmakers hope to prevent a hideous form of hate speech and the violent extremism that is nourished by it. What could be wrong with that? Quite a bit, it turns out, because even such well-intentioned censorship is not readily squared with a commitment to freedom of speech and inquiry, at least not in the context of American and Canadian law.

In 1985, one Ernst Zündel was put on trial in Canada for publishing a pamphlet called *Did Six Million Really Die?*, which claimed the Holocaust was a Zionist hoax. Canada didn't have a specific Holocaust-denial law, and he was charged under a statute criminalizing the publication of false news causing "injury or mischief to the public interest." Zündel arrived at the courthouse each day wearing a hard hat emblazoned with the words "freedom of speech." Not wanting to shortcut the prosecution's duty to prove guilt, the court required the state to demonstrate that the Holocaust had in fact occurred, and allowed rebuttal evidence that it had not: exactly what Zündel hoped for. During the lengthy, circus-like trial, he and his "experts" spewed the same calumnies that were in the pamphlet, but on a bigger, more legitimate platform than he had ever enjoyed. Newspapers featured headlines such as "Women Dined and Danced at Auschwitz, Expert Witness Says."[12] Zündel was found guilty, but the conviction was thrown out on appeal—in part, because a documentary film used as evidence of the death camps' reality was rejected as hearsay.

Zündel was tried and convicted again in 1988. But this time he won a much bigger victory on appeal. The Supreme Court of Canada held that the law against spreading false news unconstitutionally abridged speech. The law's vague prohibitions could have totalitarian effects, the court held, because it allowed convictions "for virtually any statement which does not accord with currently accepted 'truths,'" and could be used "to permit the prosecution of unpopular ideas." To freeze history into one acceptable narrative, the court reasoned, would repeat the errors of the Nazi and Communist regimes, as well as the racist slanders regarding Native Canadians and African Americans that were once taught as fact.[13] In its attempt to protect truth, the Canadian legal system had, in the end, protected the free-speech right of Zündel to spread falsehoods. Zündel's troubles were far from over—he was later deported from Canada and imprisoned in Germany for inciting hatred—but the longstanding tension remained between the ideals of free speech and the urge to prevent the harms that words can cause.

The compulsion to silence others is as old as the urge to speak, because speech—words, images, expression itself—exerts power. Many in the Judeo-Christian tradition believe that the world was created with words and that words can also cause its destruction. Speech influences people's hearts and minds, and affects their actions. Indeed, in many ways, speech *is* action. Dissent disturbs, and those who rattle norms often do so in obnoxious ways. It takes a lot of self-possession to endure jarring ideas that call one's beliefs into question, and most of us are inclined to suppress opposition. For governing authorities, tolerating speech that challenges the status quo implies approval of that challenge, which in turn subverts the myths on which their power is based. If such speech goes unpunished, others are encouraged to follow, and society's stability can be put at risk. Even in countries where free expression is cherished, we often forget that forgoing censorship requires the embrace of discord as a fair price for the general good. Tolerance is risky. Suppression, on the other hand, is logical—and, across history, it has been the norm.

This is the paradox: censorship violates our natural rights, yet it has always been a pervasive element of social reality—in the psyches of individuals no less than of dictators. The US Supreme Court correctly recognizes that "those who begin coercive elimination of dissent soon find themselves exterminating dissenters,"[14] yet this has not always stopped the court from endorsing repression, particularly during conflicts with enemies real or imagined. And while most in the West agree that the function of freedom of expression is to encourage robust, sometimes acrimonious debate, some of us seek "safe spaces" where we are shielded from views that disturb us. We yearn to make ourselves known, to yell on a soapbox, just as we try to block the voices of others. It's an unresolvable conflict.

Just what *is* censorship, anyway? There is no agreement on a single definition. Nor are those in the business of censorship often willing to admit to censoring. Napoleon censored even the subject of censorship, the Soviet Union claimed to guarantee freedom of speech, and Facebook restricts access to more than one million pieces of content per day yet fervently presents itself as a platform for free expression. The word "censor" derives from the Latin *censeo* or *censere*, to judge, determine, or assess—which is as good a place as any to start for a definition. Censorship generally involves the use of coercive power to prevent, suppress, or punish expression. Typically, that has meant a government's efforts to control its citizens' speech: on one side, an operative such as a judge, police official, or postal inspector imposing force under the law; on the other, a person or group is compelled to submit to that power.

Considering these dynamics, the targets of censorship have usually been outliers—dissidents, radicals, heretics, artists, nosy members of the press, and the like—who are vulnerable to the force of authority. This is the process at play throughout much of this book: protections of speech have almost always represented a gain for the powerless at the expense of the governing classes. However, developments of late have complicated this two-sided contest. Nongovernmental actors in the form of Internet and social media platforms have achieved raw power over speech beyond the aspirations of even the most repressive governments. Facebook alone operates what the journalist Susan Benesch calls "the largest system of censorship the world has ever known."[15] In many cases, the platforms answer only to their own self-interest, and their employees' decisions as to whose speech to permit or suppress traverse borders. Never before have ordinary citizens had the power to silence their own president, or the rulers of other countries, or, for that matter, sub-Saharan shopkeepers. And while censorship was always the work of sentient people, much online suppression is performed by algorithms—the unsubtle workings of which are largely unknown. Given the fluctuating value each of the billions of online postings have as vehicles for targeted advertisements, censorship decisions are also tied to money as never before.

In addition to the advent of Internet companies as global speech arbiters, a shift in outlook has taken place toward censorship itself. Censorship was something right-thinking people regarded as evil, a species of power abuse by the likes of Mao or Joseph McCarthy against society's best interests. But many on the left have come to look to governments to *impose* censorship—against pornography and sexism; against racist, hate, and otherwise offensive speech; against fake news; and against the excesses of the wealthy and of industry. The Harvard professor Henry Louis Gates Jr. found it difficult to imagine such an agenda being pushed by these leftists' "activist counterparts in the sixties, who defined themselves through their adversarial relations to authority and its institutions." Now, writes Gates, "the aim is not to resist power, but to enlist power."[16] It is not just governments that are being asked to censor. As of early June 2020, many Facebook employees were in revolt against their CEO, Mark Zuckerberg, for not removing Donald Trump's inflammatory postings.[17]

This misplaced trust in institutions to censor in the public interest has received an assist from a "What's the big deal?" outlook emerging from some of the more rarified confines of the ivory tower. Starting with the work of Michel Foucault and followed up by a stream of academics, the idea is that censorship is not merely something enforced by authorities; it's also hardwired into the oppressive power dynamics of everyday life, communication, and thought formation—including what Frederick Schauer calls "the ways some discourses marginalize others by displacing them" and what Ruth Gavison identifies as "self-restraint by speakers themselves, a variety of market devices [and] social implementation of norms of unacceptability."[18] That does not leave much out. The scholarship is wryly summarized by Rae Langton:

> Nothing you say is really free. Whatever you try to say is silenced before you even begin. . . . Culture, discourse, perhaps even language itself, all breathe down your neck with their threats and orders. . . . You are a prisoner in an invisible cage, invisibly gagged,

allowed to say one thing, prevented from saying others. . . . The very idea that *you* say what *you* want to say is a joke. What is this *you*? . . . Censorship is everywhere.[19]

This view, while compelling, glides over important distinctions between different exercises of censorious power—the cold concrete of the jail cell versus market forces, for example. If institutional censorship is no different from the restrictions laced through life itself—if being for or against censorship is "to assume a freedom no one has," as Michael Holquist puts it, and if censorship is "the norm rather than the exception," as Robert Post explains—then institutional repression is normalized.[20] This helps to explain why so many people are now ready to enlist governments to bar the objectionable speech or "silence" the conduct of others. The state is seen less as a censor than a gatekeeper, or a censor of censors.

This scholarship gives a textured perspective on the power dynamics at play around us—and there is no questioning the pain that, for example, racist hate speech can cause—yet I remain unconvinced that government speech restrictions or—God help us—Mr. Zuckerberg can protect us against social ills. Indeed, one of the key points of this book is that *censorship doesn't work*. The ideas animating suppressed speech remain in circulation and, in the end, can become more effective for being forbidden. Will Durant's conclusion about the First Emperor's destruction of unapproved texts applies to most censorship: "The only permanent result was to lend an aroma of sanctity to the proscribed literature."[21] Given censorship's dismal record, and the extraordinary suffering it has caused, it is ill suited to address the harms arising from quotidian power inequalities. That has not stopped many governments or social media platforms from trying, though, and the results so far have been mixed. In many cases, efforts to bar hate speech have been used to suppress legitimate dissent, as have rules against the spread of fake news.

Much political censorship over the centuries has been directed at small aggressions against institutional authority: speech that in some way challenges or denigrates a government or its personnel. Such aggressions pose no tangible risk to a regime. Rather, they chip at the brittle veneer of infallibility it strives to maintain. "Authority requires a mask," observes the sociologist F. G. Bailey, to conceal its failings and shield it from contempt.[22] Thus Machiavelli counseled his prince to preserve his grandeur above all else, and a London printer was chopped into four pieces in 1664 for publishing a pamphlet arguing that the king was accountable to the people. It's why a New Jersey drunkard was jailed for sedition in 1800 for voicing his hope that a flying cannonball land in President John Adams's "arse," and why members of governments have been consumed with suppressing even accurate statements that question their actions. When speech held rulers up to derision, it was criminalized under British and early American law, and the speakers or publishers were often jailed, bankrupted, and/or mutilated.

"No government can subsist" unless those who cause people to have an "ill opinion" of it are punished, said England's lord chief justice in 1704 about a pamphlet accusing public officials of corruption. Even autocratic power requires a measure of popular faith, and all faith is fleeting.[23] Authority must be constantly reaffirmed, and one way to do so is to make the elimination of forbidden texts a spectacle of power. This was the case with the depredations of Qin, Mao, and the Spanish conquistadors, and it has been repeated up to the present day. The public destruction of offending materials, particularly with fire, asserts a ruler's sole prerogative to command the public discourse and, more essentially, to erase the ideas the targeted texts express. That the thoughts or opinions remain in people's minds is beside the point (and copies of such texts usually evade destruction in any case). Their very existence is an affront, and visible corrective action must be taken, even if it is transparently futile. The destruction is, in fact, a confession by the authorities that they cannot coexist with nonconforming ideas. Censorship is always, by varying degrees, a display of weakness.

The drive to censor is especially charged when texts or images are seen as having their own independent agency, apart from what they signify. Almost everywhere, words, writing, and imagery were believed to have originated with the divine. They evoked spirits—in many cases, they *were* spirits that could give and destroy life, and were approached with awe, fear, and often hatred. Hence the biblical ban on "graven images" and idols, which were thought to be infested with malignant spirits; the claim by many anti-porn advocates that pornography itself, no less than what it depicts, constitutes the violent subordination of women; and the radioactive effect that displays of swastikas or Nazi imagery have in modern Germany, even when used, as one German court put it, only as "eye-catching devices" to attract attention on the Internet and not to promote Nazi ideology. In each case, the object is toxic in itself, apart from context.[24]

By the same token, forbidden materials have been likened to poison for those consuming them, as well as to the body politic, and their destruction to a purification rite. This was the case with many secular works—Voltaire, among the most censored of all authors, saw his works repeatedly compared to arsenic and excrement, which his readers were considered to "swallow"—but in the premodern age such conflation was mostly applied to nonconforming religious or oracular texts. In Rome, the ritualized destruction of books was often meant to purify the state of unclean beliefs and, not coincidentally, the political menace their adherents represented. Poison was also the main point of comparison for the first forbidden translations of the Bible into vernacular languages, the works of hated Christian missionaries in Japan and China, and the writings of Protestants, Jews, and other nonestablished religious groups.

Similar metaphors were applied to obscenity, once it became a target for censorship. Sexual materials were framed as poison, pollution, filth, satanic. The modern era of obscenity suppression started when England's lord chief justice, John Campbell, expressed horror at the sale of deadly "acid"—that is, pornography—on London's Holywell Street, and the resulting Obscene Publications Act of 1857. To destroy sexually arousing materials was to cleanse the streets and those who walked on them of soul-destroying infection. American anti-obscenity enforcers used the same language in their destruction of pornography, information on birth control and reproduction, and a thick dollop of some of the best (and worst) of modern literature.

But then, what is venomous for persons in one social class is often nourishment for those in another, and class questions pervade most censorship issues. From the beginning, censorship has been an exercise not just in suppressing speech but also in channeling it. Censorious elites almost invariably deem themselves worthier of expressing themselves or receiving information than others, and those others have usually been the poor, women, and the young. Before mass printing began, even dubious materials were often thought to pose little danger, because they were usually confined to upper-class men. But once printing gave all strata of society access to words and images, modern censorship began in earnest. The Catholic Church issued its *Index of Forbidden Books (Index Librorum Prohibitorum)* in 1559; pornography, an instant sensation among the unwashed, was proscribed; and much of the key learning of the Renaissance was banned, as were the plain-spoken pamphlets of Martin Luther and other religious nonconformists. As for reports about the workings of government, the seventeenth-century English censor Roger L'Estrange summed up official attitudes when he wrote that public newspapers must be suppressed because they "make the multitude too familiar with the actions . . . of their superiors."[25]

The apogee—although far from the end—of Western class-based censorship was in nineteenth-century Europe, where agitation from the lower and working classes for political and economic reforms, coupled with periodic revolutions, drove the upper orders to a state of near desperation. No effort was spared to keep anything that might aggravate discontent out of general circulation, including low-priced newspapers, caricatures, political content in theatrical works, books that discredited religion or otherwise risked challenging social norms, or even, in Austria, the very word *liberté* when imprinted on household items. Most of these materials were available, if expensive or otherwise directed to the established or wealthy, but they were barred when cheap versions risked stirring people on the wrong side of society's tracks.

Class-based censorship continued into the twentieth century, particularly of the new and first truly mass medium of cinema. The degree of concern over how impecunious audiences might respond to political, sexual, or criminal messaging in movies would be laughable, had it not been so harmful. But restrictions on cinema were soon folded into a more complex global matrix of censorship, lies, and selective truth telling that took shape amid the propaganda-soaked cataclysms of two world wars and the rise of broadcast communications. As political censorship became associated with the regimes of industrialized murder and dissent came to be viewed as a positive attribute of a free society rather than the seed of its downfall, and as the West remade itself after World War II, the commitment to a truly free press and unconstrained self-expression expanded as never before. At least in the US, the accepted remedy for harmful or false speech came to be more speech rather than suppression.

Recently, however, this ideal has been constricted in several critical respects. European fascism was defeated at war, but its hateful precepts were never erased from the collective consciousness. To guard against a resurgence of murderous intolerance and protect human dignity, many European democracies imposed speech limitations that the US adamantly rejected. These contrasting approaches to racist and hateful speech ran on roughly parallel tracks until the Internet forced a collision, the results of which are still being sorted out. The Internet's upending of mass communications has also served the malign ends of jurisdictions that reject freedom of speech. It has been a godsend for China, for example, allowing its government to surveil its citizens, control their speech, and influence foreign companies to an unprecedented degree. Other authoritarian regimes have followed suit, often under China's tutelage. Rather than acting as an unqualified engine for the promotion of global democracy and political freedom, as was initially hoped, the Internet has also been a widely used tool for hindering them.

The Internet has put the value of speech itself under review. In many ways, the marketplace of ideas envisioned a century ago by US Supreme Court justice Oliver Wendell Holmes has materialized, but in badly mutated form. Individual voices have indeed multiplied by the billions, but instead of sitting neatly on the market's shelves waiting to be purchased, they are weaponized against each other and combined with bots to drown out and denigrate the ideas various antagonists wish to suppress. And far from ideas being presented equally to be judged on their own merits, the Internet platforms running the marketplace have made the profitable junk-food viewpoints cheap and plentiful, while nutritious fare is harder to find. As such, speech itself has become, in one of the bitterest ironies in the history of communications, a tool of censorship.

In 1946, Orwell published a trenchant essay about censorship titled "The Prevention of Literature." After the waves of lies during the war, and with corporate and political ideologies still conspiring against truth, he observed a public that was indifferent to being told fact or falsehood, who "do not care about the matter one way or the other" so long as what was said fit their political orthodoxy. Yet even in an environment in which truth was undervalued, he saw no menace to the "exact sciences." Bombs and airplanes still needed building, and for that even Hitler could not deny that "two and two have to make four."[26] Had Orwell lived in the present day—when the science of global warming has been subject to unprecedented censorship, the phrases "climate change" and "greenhouse gases" were purged from US government publications, and when critical information regarding its existence and effects has been buried—he would have had to adjust his thinking. If controversies over censorship concern, at bottom, what Orwell called "the right to report contemporary events truthfully," then addressing these controversies is more urgent than ever—even in a time with unprecedented freedom of speech.

HELPING GOD ALONG

Speech Suppression in the Ancient World

The Babylonian Talmud describes the final moments in the life of Rabbi Hanina ben Tradion, sentenced by Rome to burn to death in public for teaching Jewish law despite a strict ban. The Romans meant to make an example of him, so they placed wet wool on his body to prolong the pain of the fire, then wrapped him in a Torah scroll. As the flames grew, his students asked him what he saw. He replied: "The parchments are being burned, but the letters are flying away." This would not have been surprising to the students, who believed fervently in the Torah's divinity, but for the Roman executioner it was transformational. He offered to remove the wool to reduce the rabbi's suffering, if he would take him along to heaven. The rabbi agreed, and the executioner leaped onto the flames. A heavenly voice then boomed down, announcing that the two men were indeed on their way to the World to Come.[1]

Rabbi ben Tradion and his executioner took their flight in the second century CE, but the key element of this account—the ascent of the Torah's words—is rooted in the origins of language. From the beginning, words have been understood as more than mere sounds or dabs of pigment denoting something else. Rather, they were products of the divine, wrapped in awe and laden with taboos. Words were endowed with mystical powers, "a sort of primary force in which all being and doing originate," in the words of the philosopher Ernst Cassirer. In all mythical cosmogonies, "as far back as they can be traced, this supreme position of the Word is found."[2]

Cassirer explains that in the creation accounts of most religions, the *word*—language itself—is allied with the spiritual forces of creation, either as a device that the creator(s) use to forge the cosmos or, more fundamentally, as the source from which all existence is derived. The holy texts of the Uitoto people of Peru and Colombia tell us: "In the beginning, the word gave origin to the Father."[3] The Gospel of John starts with "In the beginning was the Word, and the Word was with God, and the Word was God." In Hebrew scripture, God creates the world with words. Later, those who denied that the Torah was God's handiwork forfeited their place in the World to Come. The poet John Milton may not have had all this in mind when he wrote, in his *Aereopagitica* (1644), that "books are not absolutely dead things, but do contain a potency of life in them," but the message was there: words carry their own power.

The gods of the ancient world were nothing if not terrifying, and given the divinity of words, it followed that they could also carry a dreadful force. The names of deities often packed the mightiest charge, which is why even knowledge of them was frequently concealed. For example, when the Egyptian goddess Isis compelled the sun god Ra to disclose his secret name to her, she gained power over him and all the other gods.[4] And a century before Rabbi ben Tradion and his Torah left this earth, pronouncing the Hebrew god's true name was a high offense for all but the high priest, and then in restricted circumstances.

More broadly, words or word combinations were believed to contain magical and often demonic properties, whether spells, incantations for health or success in hunting or battle, or curses against enemies. Such words needed to be controlled, as their unauthorized or improper application posed serious risks—not only to the individuals who misused them, but to all of society.

Ancient civilizations also saw the supernatural in images. The archaeologist V. Gordon Childe points to Neolithic carvings of animal images or symbols on precious stones, which were then imprinted onto clay that was used to seal containers of high-value items. The process involved multiple layers of magic: the stones themselves possessed "magic virtue," which was then enhanced by the power that came with the images—say, of bulls or swastikas. When the seals' images were transferred to the clay, they carried the same magical quality and brought curses on those who broke into the containers.[5] As civilizations developed, taboos attached as much to images as to words. They were considered volatile, and their use was often restricted, if not suppressed entirely.

At its core, censorship is rooted in the fear of words and pictures; restrictions on them were imposed to avoid the calamities they might trigger. The ancients believed that some word combinations or images were so venomous that their very existence could contaminate society. This dread was no less during the early Christian era, when pagan astrological texts were condemned as "poison that creeps inside . . . [society's] silent marrow"; nor had such trepidation abated by the mid-nineteenth century, when England's lord chief justice characterized sexually arousing materials as "prussic acid" for the body politic.[6] And when the contemporary feminist scholar and anti-pornography advocate Catharine MacKinnon argues that pornography *is* violent sex, "no less an act than the rape and torture it represents," she means exactly what she says.[7] Words and images can wield destructive potential; to suppress them is to prevent harm.

Faced with stakes that high, the elimination of offending materials in the ancient world—particularly through fire—was necessary to appease the divine and cleanse the collective soul of pollution. Just as the smoke from animal sacrifices linked worshippers to their gods, so the fumes of smoldering forbidden texts propitiated the gods. And just as the immolation of texts destroyed the wickedness they embodied, so the destruction represented the deaths of the writers who produced them. An author's books were living extensions of their persons; burning them was akin to killing the author in effigy. There was no choice in the matter, as the consequences of allowing errant speech were fearsome.

BANNED IN THE BIBLE: WORDS AND PICTURES AMONG THE HEBREWS

For the Hebrews, compliance with God's precepts on what to say or not say was not optional. Deuteronomy 30:17–18 warns, "If you are not obedient, . . . you will certainly be destroyed." Jewish law is rife with rules and warnings about deviant speech, some dictated by God Himself—starting with the commandment against taking His name in vain. The punishment was being stoned to death by the entire tribe, a sacrifice of the sinner to avert divine punishment of the collective.[8]

The examples in Scripture of this form of blasphemy expand on the point. On the direct instruction of heaven, Moses orders the execution of a foreigner who "blasphemed the Name [i.e., God] with a curse."[9] In the book of Isaiah, when Assyrian invaders besiege Jerusalem, their general mocks God's capacity to protect the city and its Jewish inhabitants from destruction, and further denigrates God by comparing Him to the deities of other peoples the Assyrians had steamrolled. For that, God sends an angel—a plague, according to a tradition that places the event in 701 BCE—thus ending the lives of 185,000 Assyrian soldiers overnight and causing the decimated army to retreat.[10] Quite a penalty, considering that the general, for all his bravado, hadn't even technically damned God or taken His name in vain, but merely expressed skepticism (albeit in insulting terms) about His power. From roughly this point forward, the concept of blasphemy would expand to include words and practices that were merely disrespectful of the deity.

No less forbidden under Jewish law are figurative images, which include depictions of God, idols, and pictures "of any shape, whether formed like a man or a woman, or like any animal on Earth or any bird that flies in the air, or like any creature that moves along the ground, or any fish in the waters."[11] The reasons for this broad form of censorship are subject to scholarly dispute, but it likely rested first on the conviction that God was both unknowable and reflected in everything on earth, and thus could not be represented without sinful distortion. More prosaically, banning images allowed the Jews to distinguish themselves from the surrounding cultures, whose religions were profoundly visual. Restricting images showed "that they were different, that their God was not a part of the dominant culture," explains the scholar Philip Alexander.[12]

Even though the ban is set in uncompromising terms, it has been followed inconsistently, as the basic human need to create and interact with images was no less compelling for Jews than for others.

Throughout antiquity and into modern times, Jewish attitudes toward images have oscillated between strict and liberal. King Solomon himself erected altars to pagan gods for some of his many wives, and God was worshipped in various visual forms well after the Hebrews left Mount Sinai. Jewish law also bent the rules by making fine distinctions between images for purposes of worship and for decoration; three-dimensional figures versus flat pictures; and exact versus inexact images. In the first century CE, there was almost no figurative imagery in Jewish life. Matters loosened a couple of centuries later to the point where the walls of at least one synagogue, the ancient synagogue in Dura-Europos, present-day Syria, were covered with paintings. Decorative images were also used in synagogues during the Middle Ages, as well as in books—most notably a thirteenth-century German Passover book (Haggadah) known as the Bird's Head Haggadah.[13] It contains illustrations of Jews with the heads of birds; since bird-people did not exist, the rule against representations of nature was not violated.

Pagan idols in all their forms were to be avoided whenever possible and sometimes were attacked, in no small part because, like visual representations of God himself, they were understood to be infused with malign spirits. Jewish law set precise and often bizarre instructions for neutralizing and interacting with them, however they manifested themselves. For example, to desecrate trees venerated by pagans, Jews were told to remove the leaves but not the branches; to defuse the spirits lurking "behind" a stone idol, they were to remove the tip of its ear, nose, or fingers, or simply hack at it with a tool. Spitting or urinating on it or dragging it in the dirt was not considered effective, however tempting it might have been to do so.[14]

When not desecrating idols, Jews were to interact with them using extreme caution. If some debris fell from an idol's shrine onto a Jew's property, they were commanded to discard it with the contempt they would show to a "menstruous cloth." Should the Jew's house happen to collapse, the structure was not to be rebuilt unless it could be erected at least four cubits away from the shrine. The shade of a pagan holy tree was to be avoided unless the tree hung over a road, in which case no defilement would occur by merely passing under it. Vegetables could be grown under such trees, but only if they were planted during the rainy season. Lettuce, however, could be planted under such trees during any season.[15] And so on.

Unsurprisingly, the ancient Jews were also not keen on theatre. The sages sharply disapproved of the plays, circuses, and similar entertainments of the Hellenistic-Roman world, and theatres in Palestine were targeted for destruction during the 167 BCE revolt of the Jewish Maccabees against the Hellenistic Seleucid Empire. The hostility was warranted: pagan sacrifices were offered in theatres, and the public mistreatment of Jews was often considered entertainment. Several centuries later, in Roman Syria, Jewish women were forced to eat pork onstage, and the emperor Vespasian once slaughtered 1,200 Jews in the stadium in Tiberias.[16] It was not until the early Renaissance that some forms of Jewish drama began to emerge, and the Purim play, depicting the story of Esther, gradually became a counterpart to the Christian carnival.

Early Jewish restrictions on speech and idol worship produced an inward-looking culture that was uneasy with the vibrant intellectual, literary, and religious ferment that surrounded it. There was simply too much risk of running afoul of one or another restriction on blasphemy, and the price of missteps was too high. In the first century CE, the sage Rabbi Akiva warned that the reading of *any* writings outside the Jewish canon was forbidden, on pain of being barred from the World to Come[17]—a drastic form of censorship still observed by ultra-Orthodox sects today. While such insularity arguably contributed to the longevity of the Jewish religion, it placed Jews in a world apart. The eventual influence of the Old Testament on censorship was enormous but would wait until the spread of Christianity carried many of its precepts forward. Until that took place, another set of traditions took hold in the Mediterranean that would shape attitudes toward speech suppression no less profoundly.

INSULTS, IMPIETY, AND THE BAD EXAMPLES OF GODS IN ANCIENT ATHENS

Ancient Athenian attitudes toward censorship fall roughly into three contexts: daily life on the streets and in the city's assemblies; times of war and stress, when there was powerful uneasiness toward anything that might offend the gods; and the constellation of restrictions Plato imposed on the hapless inhabitants of his imagined republic, which have hung like a stench over discussions about censorship for two millennia. The considerations were different in each situation, as were the law's targets.

"It's a slave's lot not to say what one thinks," moans Jocasta in Euripides's *The Phoenician Women*. In lamenting her own circumstances, the doomed queen also highlights a key characteristic of everyday Athenian life: liberty of expression was the privilege of the elite. Slaves, women, foreigners—about two-thirds of the population—did not have the rights accorded to the poorest male citizens. But even with that important limitation, the Athenian citizenry had more latitude than other Greeks enjoyed, not just to participate and speak freely in civic discussions, but also to ridicule leaders and even shout down the most respected citizens at public assemblies.

In the agora, where people congregated to debate and make decisions for the polis, all male citizens were free to speak their minds. It was sometimes (reluctantly) acknowledged that even the least prominent citizens might have better ideas to offer than professional statesmen. This liberty of equal participation in public debate was called *isegoria*, and it was put to good use. Between 355 and 322 BCE, for example, more than one thousand citizens made formal proposals in the assembly. But *isegoria* was just one aspect of Athenian speech rights. The contours of what one could say in public, how it might be said, and about whom, is covered in part by *parrhesia*.

Parrhesia gave one license to be ridiculous, as in the case of Diogenes the Cynic, the philosopher who lived in a barrel, masturbated in public, and had the temerity to tell Alexander the Great to stop blocking his sunlight—all, he said, to expose (among other things) the arbitrariness of Greek customs. It also permitted citizens to insult senior statesmen, as when Dinarchus called the august Demosthenes a "beast" and said that he was "open to bribes" and "a person to be spit upon." Aristophanes repeatedly criticized Athens's war against Sparta in plays performed from the public purse, and also lampooned the city's leaders with obscene irreverence. The playwright also took his chances by calling a politician a coward in battle—one of few impermissible accusations, unless it was true (he appears to have gotten away with it).[18] With the right to disrespect power also came the prerogative to engage in an early form of no-platforming, whereby citizens, during assemblies and trials, heckled, shouted down, or laughed at speakers when they disapproved of what they were saying. On more than one occasion, they dragged Plato's brother, Glaucon, off the speaker's platform, claiming he was "ignorant of what was said there."[19] Thus, while open debate was in theory protected, how much debate occurred was subject to the moods of the crowd being addressed.

Most paradigmatically, *parrhesia* allowed philosophers and teachers to ply their trades in the agora and at private drinking parties called symposia. Self-styled "lovers of wisdom" such as Socrates and Diogenes would confront citizens and tell them what was on their minds, even if what they said was unwelcome and they offended society's bedrock social and religious foundations in the process. They weren't always particularly liked, but they were tolerated. Socrates, for example, hated Athenian democracy and spoke against it regularly, but he never left the city, for it was there that he was free to speak in the open and without deadly consequence—until, finally, he wasn't.

Taken together, *isegoria* and *parrhesia* conferred liberty upon citizens to speak in public, participate in civic debate regardless of wealth or position, and say what they wished, including vicious insults or parodies of leaders. But if, as Pericles announced with such pride, free and open discussion was a key element of Athens's good governance, that did not mean there was an inviolate right of free expression or religious dissent. Sharp limits were imposed when the polity was under stress, particularly during times of war. When irreligious speech was understood to cause the city misfortunes or defeats, *parrhesia* gave way to paranoia, and the most dearly held ideals were jettisoned as so much harmful ballast. During the city's disastrous conflict with Sparta and its chaotic aftermath, several intellectuals who had long been tolerated found themselves condemned for insulting the gods.

Religious observance was the main means by which the city ensured social cohesion and good fortune. Aside from a few outliers, no one questioned the gods' existence or whether it was necessary to stay in their good graces by participating in rituals required by the gods' cults. That political officials also managed important religious affairs only made sense, as the collective welfare depended in large part on a meticulous concern for cult-related matters.[20] There were many rites to oversee: religious ones attached to every important stage of individual and civic life, from birth through initiations, marriages and deaths, and those related to war, commerce, agriculture, theatre, and athletic contests. According to the scholars Giulia Sissa and Marcel Detienne, to shun such observances was "to exclude oneself from the human community, to sink into madness and abandon oneself to violent excess." Even worse for the polis, to shirk one's duties to offer sacrifices or to frequent altars was "to strike a blow against the city, against its principles, against its very being."[21]

Religious belief, then, was much the same as practice, and faithful practice meant the gods would bring the city stability or at least not punish it with calamity. That is why Plato maintained that ensuring the gods' favor through an official cult was the beginning of any civic order. Religious rituals also preserved continuity with the past, linking the city's populace to its ancestors and divine beginnings. "Annually, the mythical heroes reappeared at the great religious festivals in tragedy and choral ode," explains the historian M. I. Finley, "and they recreated for their audiences the unbroken web of all life, stretching back over generations of men to the gods. . . . All this was serious and true, literally true."[22] When the Athenians listened to a public recitation of the *Iliad*, made a sacrifice to Athena, or partook in the mysteries of Eleusis, they embraced time-tested interpretations of human destiny and its dependence on the gods. Religious observance was reality ordered.

To call these truths into question during times of peace and prosperity was an irritation, but the good general welfare was evidence that the gods neither noticed nor cared much. To do so in troubled times was another matter, and nothing caused more trouble for Athens than the war with Sparta and its allies, which started in 431 BCE and lasted until the final defeat of Athens and its allies nearly three decades later. Soon after the conflict began, a gruesome epidemic decimated the city's fighting forces and its inhabitants at home. Everywhere one looked, people were covered with pustules and suffering from uncontrollable diarrhea. They bled from the throat, retched violently, and died in excruciating pain. The streets and temples filled with untended corpses. In the panic, the city's social order nearly collapsed. According to Thucydides, "No fear of god or law of man had a restraining influence." Perhaps most ominous of all, the pestilence did not afflict the Spartans. It reserved its misery for Athens.

The gods were displeased, to say the least, and scapegoats were sought to appease them. At about the same time, a professional soothsayer proposed a law allowing anyone who "did not believe in the gods or who taught theories about celestial phenomena" to be punished for impiety, and the assembly adopted it.[23] The law provided a foundation to move against those whose words had brought such misfortune by offending the gods. Targets included the natural philosophers and Sophists, who had been poking at religious beliefs for some time. They had not been much appreciated before the war, but they had been endured; now, their hectoring, teachings, and writings were viewed as threats to the polis. It was time to clean house, and the juries, which comprised hundreds of citizens, were in no mood to trouble over fine philosophical points. The fate of the city was at stake.

One of the first to be brought to judgment, likely around 430 BCE, was Anaxagoras. The old natural philosopher—best known now for his conclusion that the sun, far from being divine, was a hot hunk of stone—had been operating in Athens without disturbance for about thirty years. Most historians agree that he was targeted, at least in part, to get at his close friend and former student, Pericles, the leader many blamed for the war's calamities. Yet Anaxagoras's ideas certainly qualified as impiety under the new law. He was sentenced to death, a fate he escaped only when Pericles arranged his exile to Asia Minor. For a populace that could still have been walking over bodies on the street, that could not have been far enough.

The Sophist philosopher and rhetorician Protagoras was also tried for impiety. Again, the person charged was an old man who had been teaching in Athens for decades—but now his ideas were recast in a sinister light. It was no surprise, as Protagoras had made a name for himself by arguing that everything is relative to individual experience, judgment, and interpretation. (The aphorism for which he is best known is "Man is the measure of all things.") More galling to the Athenian jury, Protagoras had speculated, both verbally and in his text *On the Gods* as to whether people can even *know* that gods exist. Such epistemological musings may have been interesting to his wealthy students, but they found few takers now. Questioning whether the stricken populace—many of whom now sat in judgment on him—could grasp the existence of the very gods who were decimating them in such numbers was an outrage.

Protagoras was convicted. According to tradition, his writings were collected and set afire in public. If that indeed happened, it was likely the first book burning in Western history. (His personal fate is unclear. Either he was exiled, or, according to another version of events, he fled Athens before the trial and died in a shipwreck.)[24] The destruction, intended to eradicate the texts and ideas they contained, was likely also tied to religious customs. In Athenian cultic practice, as with most cultures at the time, fire played a central role in purification rituals. By using flames to "unwrite" the texts, the polis cleansed itself of polluting ideas that were, most evidently, bringing disaster.

The fate of Athens, and that of the prominent orator, general, and bon vivant Alcibiades, changed forever on a summer morning in 415 BCE. The city's inhabitants discovered to their horror that the oversized erections on the statues of the god Hermes across the city had all been smashed off. The shock was profound. Hermes was, among many other things, a mediator between Olympus and humanity. More importantly, these "herms," which were often located at crossroads, were venerated as signs of the god's divine protection for travelers. Given that the city's military forces were about to embark on a massive high-risk expedition to Sicily, the sight of the desecrated statutes could not have been a worse omen.

The Athenians panicked, and a witch hunt to find the perpetrators commenced. As suspects were apprehended and slaves tortured for information, another sacrilege was revealed: Alcibiades, who had been promoting the Sicily expedition and was to lead it, had, at a symposium, drunkenly revealed the Eleusinian Mysteries, among the city's holiest and most closely guarded secrets. Impersonating the high priest, he had reviled and broken the ancient, unshakable taboos surrounding these secret rites. To call this a profanation would be an understatement. It was earth- and heaven-shaking, and it worsened the city's tenuous relations with the gods and the uncertainty of the Sicilian military campaign. Amid the confusion, Alcibiades's enemies seized the opportunity to have him accused of impiety.

Perhaps confident that he could use his considerable oratorical skills to prove his innocence, Alcibiades demanded an immediate trial, but delays occurred, and he was sent to Sicily anyway. In his absence, he was convicted of impiety as well as attempting to overthrow the government. Upon hearing the verdict and death sentence, he jumped ship and joined the Spartans against Athens. The Athenians were crushed in Sicily, and the war turned decisively against them. By 404 BCE, the entire conflict was lost. Another period of deep political and social upheaval ensued in Athens, including a brief, bloody tyranny.

Such was the setting of the trial of Socrates for impiety in 399 BCE. Much had changed over the forty years during which the old provocateur had been baiting his fellow citizens in the agora. Athens was no longer such a haven for the free exchange of ideas. It had lost the war and its empire, and endured an oligarchic coup. "Fear and loathing [now] kept Athens in their grip," the historian Alexander Rubel writes.[25] Against this background, the philosopher's relentless questioning of everything had become too much to bear. Add to that his friendship with Critias, the most hated of the tyrants, and his past close relationship with Alcibiades, and Athenians could no longer tolerate his presence in the city.

Socrates's accusers charged him with failing to recognize the authority of the city's gods, introducing new divinities, and corrupting Athenian youth with his impious ideas. Given that there are more than seven hundred books dissecting the fine points of the trial and debating the reasons for Socrates's downfall, another lengthy disquisition here cannot add much. In the context of a study of censorship, the trial is notable because his words were seen as a source of pollution for the city, and his death was a collective rite of purification. Nor was he the last of the Greek thinkers to be incriminated. Aristotle, for one, also had to flee Athens in 323 BCE after comparing a political patron to the immortals. The insult to religion was enough to drive him back to Macedonia.

The nature and extent of the Athenian impiety trials are, like so many other aspects of Greek history, the subject of scholarly dispute, so what is presented here is just one incomplete version of the story.[26]

Nevertheless, their cumulative result was the state-imposed sacrifice of intellectual freedom on the altar of conformity—a concept Plato would propel into a comprehensive argument for the near-absolute censorship of personal thought and expression. That he would, in his *Republic*, make this case through the voice of Socrates is one of the signature paradoxes in Western thought. When Plato wrote that book, Socrates had already been put to death for his words; yet Plato has him arguing for aggressive speech limitations on many of the same grounds that were used against him. The Socrates of the *Republic* cultivates a philosophical hemlock brew for nonconforming thinkers, as well as artists of all stripes. (It is only a little less ironic that Plato's own works would be widely censored through the centuries, particularly the same-sex love passages in his *Symposium*.)

Plato laid out a multifaceted mind-control scheme to buttress his ideal state. He detailed a system of restrictions, starting in the nursery, designed to exclude all subversive notions from the consciousness of the republic's future guardians—particularly those emanating from the arts. He maintained that anything in the intellectual and cultural diet that encourages freedom of thought, curiosity, or exploration is to be suppressed. In the perfect republic, art is a tool of state policy; when it diverts from that purpose or ill serves the state, art—and artists—must go.

Plato starts with the notion that art works like a blunt instrument to forge the values and characters of those who consume it, so much so that the untrained cannot be trusted to distinguish truth from fiction, or even figurative from literal representation. To guard against muddled thinking and bad influences, he argued, the republic's future leaders must be shielded from anything that might induce them to behave in less than exemplary ways. This was particularly the case with Homer's epic poetry, which at the time was recited before enormous crowds. The Socrates of the *Republic* cites the exquisite Underworld passage in the *Odyssey* in which the shade of the dead Achilles tells Odysseus that he would rather be an indentured field hand on earth than a warrior-king in the realm of the dead. The beauty and pathos of Achilles's speech only makes more persuasive the "harmful" message that even slavery is preferable to glorious death in battle. Such passages must be stricken out, according to Plato: "The more poetic they are, the less must they be heard."[27]

Tellingly, he quotes at length the offending passages from Homer and other poets whom he condemns as corrosive to the public spirit. As with so much censorship, this attitude betrays a deep arrogance and a double standard. Plato presumes that he and the *Republic*'s highbrow readers are impervious to the weakening influences the texts would have on more impressionable members of society. In other words, what is acceptable for one audience—his own—is harmful to others. In the *Republic*, the main group to be shielded was the youth of the ruling class. In the coming centuries, other groups, primarily women and the poorer classes, would be deemed too mentally weak or politically threatening to consume what the censors and their confederates enjoyed.

Also to be "strictly forbidden" in Plato's ideal republic is poetry that depicts the gods as brutal or immoral—as when Hesiod describes Cronus castrating Uranus and devouring his own children—or portrays them as jealous, vengeful, or treacherous. Rather, the gods must be portrayed as models of virtuous thought and deed, and poetry must be restricted to that which demonstrates that "God is not the author of all things, but of good alone." Moreover, poetry must stress that good mortals meet good ends, and bad ones suffer. Nor may poetry depict men or heroes grieving the deaths of comrades with moaning or wailing, as doing so would lead readers to "lose their sense of shame and their hardihood." Even excessive laughter—a sign of temperamental incontinence—must never be described, as "our guardians ought not to be ready laughers."

Under this regime, little of the Greek literature we know would pass muster, but for Plato that was a fair price to pay to ensure that the leaders of his republic were ready for the job. Any poet refusing to comply "must not be allowed to ply his trade in our city."[28] In his *Laws*, Plato sharpens the point: "I would inflict the heaviest penalties on anyone in the land who should dare to say that there are bad men who lead pleasant lives, or that the profitable and gainful is one thing, and the just another."[29] In other words, poets are to say what the state tells them to say, for the rulers know best. What, then, may be produced and consumed? Not much: Only "hymns to the gods and praises of good men are to be received in our city," he writes in the *Republic*.[30] Like Mao Zedong during China's Cultural Revolution, or the working-class "heroes" of the Soviet Union, the good and great should be constantly extolled as role models of exemplary behavior.

The visual arts fare no better under Plato's saccharine regime. They are inferior media because they are mere imitations of reality, and imitation can imperil even the most resilient souls. Good people and (well-behaved) gods are honest and forthright, but the painter is a deceiver. When he or she depicts, for example, a bed, what is produced is not a bed but a debased version of it, which is itself removed from the essential idea of "bed." No good can come of such a venture, as the viewer of the painting is thrice deceived.[31] As for music, much of it jangles people's souls, which should be composed and dignified. Plato would ban much of it. Theatre, the most mimetic medium of all, is to be rigidly controlled, as it inspires crowds to "lawlessness and boldness," "disobedience to rulers," and "the contempt of oaths and pledges, and no regard at all for the gods." Only by barring "all pandering to the pleasures of the spectators"—that is, by placing theatre under control—can it be allowed to continue.[32] Sophocles, Euripides, Aeschylus, and Aristophanes? They would not last.

Quite a place, this ideal state of Plato's. Remarkably, Plato lived and wrote during a period when Greek culture had reached its sublime apex, when plays were performed before audiences of up to fourteen thousand people. Yet for all the profound flaws in his ideas, he set much of the tone and defined many of the assumptions underlying subsequent Western censorship. Plato saw it as the duty of the ruling class to mold minds for their own good and—of paramount importance—for the state's benefit.

In a later dialog of Plato's, the *Theaetetus*, Socrates states that when we perceive something, we hold it as "wax under the perceptions and thoughts," which is imprinted "just as we make impressions from seal rings." He added that the memory lasts only as long as the impression: "Whatever is rubbed out or cannot be imprinted we forget and do not know."[33] However, memory is nothing like an image impressed on wax. Once something is learned, it remains in the mind—to develop, to be recreated, however imperfectly, and to be transmitted to others, and it cannot readily be rubbed out. That simple truth, which no censor can abide, is demonstrated in the story of Rabbi ben Tradion: his Torah was burned, but the words and the ideas it embodied still soared. That is the message of every work destroyed since then: once transmitted, an idea is not easily extinguished.

The speech restrictions of the Hebrews and the Athenian impiety trials testify to the fear of divine retribution for transgressive words and images. Plato's censorship regime was conceived mainly out of concern for the political effects of the various arts, and to meet his ends he proposed close management of the entire culture, in effect a wide-ranging program of state-sponsored propaganda. Unlike the Athenian juries in the impiety trials, Plato's imagined censors were not protecting their city from the gods; instead, they were demigods themselves.

ANCIENT ROME: TREASONOUS WORDS, ITINERANT ASTROLOGERS, AND MELTED STATUES

Roman authorities rarely hesitated to destroy a text or image to appease the divinities and—often at the same time—protect the prerogatives (and feelings) of the ruling classes. As the Roman republic gave way to empire, the speech liberties of citizens diminished considerably, and censorship evolved from ad hoc responses to a deliberate, if ineffective, tool of state policy. The bonfires of condemned texts increased in size and number, but copies often survived, only to become more coveted as forbidden fruit. As the historian Tacitus wrote in the first century CE:

> One is all the more inclined to laugh at the stupidity of men who suppose that the despotism of the present can actually efface the remembrances of the next generation. On the contrary, the persecution of genius fosters its influence; foreign tyrants, and all who have imitated their oppression, have merely procured infamy for themselves and glory for their victims.[34]

With the founding of the Roman Empire in 27 BCE, the interests of the state and the head of state merged. As the job of emperor was often risky to one's life expectancy, speech causing even the most unjustified imperial fear could be framed as treasonous.

The earliest examples of Roman book burning concerned the writings and handbooks used by itinerant seers, astrologers, and prophets. The public destruction of these texts, like public executions of criminals, was meant to affirm government power and impart blunt political messages. The job of divining the future (by, for example, analyzing the entrails of animals or evaluating bursts of lightning) and other procedures for taking the gods' temperature belonged to state-appointed functionaries. By their very existence, independent soothsayers challenged these augurs and haruspices, and while the freelancers themselves were not often destroyed, their writings were. As with Athens during its conflict with Sparta, the pressures of war often brought matters to a head.

Rome's first large-scale censorship operation took place in 213 BCE, when prodigious wartime losses to Carthage threw the city into upheaval. Hannibal had invaded Italy and handed Rome several cataclysmic military setbacks. The Battle of Cannae three years earlier, which left fifty thousand corpses heaped on an open plain, remains one of the worst defeats in Roman history. As the depth of the calamity sank in, and with much of Italy either going into revolt or defecting to the Carthaginians, many Romans lost their faith in the protections of traditional religious practices. According to the historian Livy, unsanctioned priests and prophets took hold of the people's imaginations and led them to offer sacrifices and prayers according to foreign rites. The longer the war dragged on, the more the population's faith in official religion began to unravel. When people started practicing foreign rites in public, it was time to crack down. Unauthorized practices were barred, and anyone possessing unapproved books of prophecy, prayer, or guides to sacrifices was told to surrender them.[35]

Rome's first recorded instance of outright book burning took place in 181 BCE. Again, the cause was religion. The books in question were said to have belonged to Rome's legendary second king, Numa Pompilius, who had reigned five centuries earlier and was credited with establishing many Roman religious practices. They had been unearthed by peasants from a hill near the city. Half the texts were in

Latin and dealt with pontifical law; the others, the troublesome ones in Greek, appeared to be connected to Pythagorean philosophy. There were questions as to whether the Greek books were forgeries, but they were nevertheless deemed subversive of Roman religion. As the historian Valerius Maximus tells it, the senators did not want to preserve "anything in this state that might take people's minds away from the worship [of] the gods."[36] The Greek writings could have been sequestered along with the Latin texts, but evidently that was not enough. Their link with Numa called contemporary religious practices into question, and for that the Senate decided they had to be destroyed.

In a public ceremony in one of the Roman Forum's most sacred precincts, the books were set alight. The bonfire was presided over by the praetor, a high political magistrate, and prepared by *victimarii*, the slaughterers who performed important animal sacrifices. The involvement of such personnel was significant. The praetor's participation communicated the importance of the destruction to the state, while the use of the *victimarii* stressed the religious dimensions. Observes the historian Daniel Sarefield: "By the use of religious officials to kindle the fire . . . this act of religious censorship became a sacred ceremony, or even a sacrifice." It was "ritualized aggression."[37] As in Athens, fire was the tool of choice for cleansing the state of polluting influences. As Rome rebuilt its institutions after the war with Carthage, the incineration of books also imparted a direct political message: the state was very much in charge of *all* aspects of civic life.

For all his flaws, Julius Caesar accepted criticism with remarkable equanimity. According to the biographer Suetonius, he bore "with good nature the attacks on his reputation" made in several texts about him (except for one that praised his mortal enemy, Pompey; the author was duly exiled).[38] During his consulship, Caesar allowed all the proceedings in the Senate to be published in Europe's first news bulletins, the *Acta Diurna* ("daily public records"), a series of carved stone or metal message boards posted in places such as the Forum. That practice changed with Caesar's touchier successor, Augustus, who barred such news from the *Acta Diurna* and locked down controls on what the public could learn about the machinations of government. Publication of full senatorial proceedings never resumed.

Augustus's responses to direct personal attacks were tentative at first. It was customary, for example, to read the wills of important men in public, in which the deceased often included parting shots at their enemies, including Augustus. A measure was introduced in the Senate to stop this practice, but Augustus interceded to derail it, despite his open displeasure at being derided. But if the dead could speak against him, the living learned otherwise. As anonymous pamphlets assailing him proliferated, circulating even in the Senate, he ruled that those who published anonymous or pseudonymous attacks on *anyone* could be prosecuted. The policy was promptly used against Augustus's antagonists—although fines and exile were the worst punishments, even when the attacks were vicious. At that point, Augustus thought it best to avoid creating political martyrs, while making plain his prerogative to take more aggressive action if he wished. As he counseled his eventual successor, Tiberius, it wasn't necessary to strike with full force at everyone handing out slights. Instead, it was sufficient "if we can stop anyone from doing evil to us."[39]

Augustus waited until 12 BCE, more than a dozen years into his reign, to start burning books, but he made up for lost time. By now he was also pontifex maximus, the empire's highest religious official, and it was in this capacity that he put thousands of books to the flame. Oracular texts were again circulating, in Greek, Latin, and other languages, as were for-hire soothsayers who used the books to predict the fates of their clients, men of power, and the empire itself. These people were known as *vates*, *prophetes*, and *harioli*, and their mysterious books were what the historian David Potter calls a "feature of the literary environment of the Roman empire."[40] In most cases, they offered people some degree of comfort, as fortune-tellers do today. The problem, from Augustus's perspective, was that the books could also be used to predict his own death and succession. That could not be.

He launched a campaign to locate and confiscate all "spurious" writings by what Suetonius called "authors of little repute."[41] Some two thousand texts were rounded up. Suetonius doesn't explain exactly how the books were burned, but we can assume that they were immolated in the Forum in a solemn religious ceremony, presided over by Augustus, as with the burning of the books of King Numa. Of all the prophetic texts, Augustus spared only a series called the Sibylline Books, which, according to tradition, had come to Rome roughly six centuries earlier, during the reign of King Lucius Tarquinius Superbus. The king was said to have bought them from an old woman who claimed they were the writings of the Cumaean Sibyl, a mysterious priestess who received her inspiration from the god Apollo.

It stands to reason that Augustus, as pontifex maximus, maintained the traditions surrounding the Sibylline Books, keeping them locked in a gilded case under the pedestal of a statue of Apollo and allowing only select priests to consult them. What is less apparent is why he made such a public effort to destroy the other soothsaying texts in circulation, and in such a spectacular auto-da-fé. The answer lies more in his role as emperor than as religious official. He likely feared that his enemies were using the texts as part of efforts to engineer his downfall. By eliminating "inauthentic" handbooks of prophecy, Augustus was fulfilling his religious duties as he saw them—but he was also looking after his own hide.

About twenty years later, during the famine of 6–8 CE, Augustus again turned his censorious attention to political speech. Grain prices had skyrocketed, to the point where bread was rationed and partial evacuations from the capital were ordered. Widespread misery sparked revolutionary sentiment, and Rome was soon awash with incendiary pamphlets and messages. In these circumstances, Augustus must have felt he had no choice but to take a hard line. In a move that would be echoed in censorship law until the present day, he expanded the definition of treason to include not only actions against the state but also "libelous writings" and satiric insults.[42] Inevitably, the law's reach was extended to words and writings seen as being unsympathetic to the regime or out of line with state policy.

The restrictions were deployed against educators whose allegiance to the state was less than complete or who were suspected of fostering moral weakness. This was not entirely new. In 155 BCE, a visiting scholar from the Academy in Athens, Carneades the Sceptic, got himself into hot water for a rather-too-cocky display of mental agility. One day, he delivered a lecture on the virtues of Roman justice; on the following day, he gave another lecture refuting everything he had said the day before. This was meant to show that justice was not necessarily tethered to virtue but instead was merely a method for ordering society. To argue the contrasting sides of a question with equal vigor fit the Academy's methods for discovering truth, but such dialectical virtuosity didn't play well in Rome. The Senate found Carneades's methods demoralizing for Rome's youth and sent him packing.

Augustus's Rome had even less patience for a both-sides approach to intellectual discourse, especially when it applied to the emperor's pet initiatives. He had sponsored a series of laws designed to boost the birth rate among the upper ranks by incentivizing the production of legitimate offspring and punishing adultery (though men were still allowed to sate themselves with prostitutes, slaves, and concubines). In about 6 CE, a certain teacher of rhetoric, Corvus, made the mistake of discussing with his students the pros and cons of birth control for married women. He was hauled into court for treasonous harm to the state.[43] We don't know the outcome of the trial, but the case nevertheless marks a direct line from Plato's *Republic*, in which the state only permits lessons that directly buttress its policies. Any messages to the contrary, even for the purposes of discussion, are taken as harmful distractions.

A series of writers and historians were also targeted in high-profile literary treason prosecutions. One of the targeted was an irascible academic, Titus Labienus, known as "Rabienus" ("Rage," from the Latin *rabies*), whom the historian Frederick Cramer identifies as the first Roman to be martyred for intellectual freedom of speech. Labienus had no compunctions about savaging men of rank and missed few opportunities to rail against the Augustan imperial order and the new restrictions on speech. But it was his record of praising Pompey, Julius Caesar's adversary, that did him in. He was charged in the Senate between 6 and 8 CE, and his entire oeuvre was set aflame. Before he committed suicide, Labienus refused his friends' offer to cremate his body, declaring that he would not let the fiery element that had devoured his works touch him.[44]

While Labienus's works were condemned to the flames, his ideas were not so easily dispatched. In a foreshadowing of the novel *Fahrenheit 451*, one Titus Cassius Severus, a lawyer and prominent orator, spoke out in defiance, declaring: "If they really want to destroy the works of Labienus, they must burn me alive. For I have learned them by heart!"[45] Like Labienus, Severus had earned no friends in government with his many barbs aimed at the high and mighty. To his misfortune, his challenge was accepted. The Senate had his books burned in around 8 CE and exiled him to Crete, where, unbowed, he continued to write invectives against the government. More charges were brought, along with the confiscation of his property and his removal to the tiny, uninhabited island of Serifos. There his life ended in misery.

Under the emperor Tiberius, the repressive net was cast wider, the charges grew flimsier, and the punishments became more severe. Witness the unfortunate Aulus Cremutius Cordus, charged in 25 CE with literary treason for his history of the Augustan period. The book, which by that time was more than a decade old, expressed admiration for Julius Caesar's assassins Brutus and Cassius (whom he called "the last Roman") while neglecting to praise Caesar or Augustus.[46] That the text had, years earlier, been recited in front of Augustus himself without objection meant nothing. By writing a history that implied disloyalty—not even to Tiberius, but to the imperial order—Cordus had committed a high crime. His books were confiscated and burned, and it became forbidden to read or own them. The verdict was death; Cordus committed suicide by starving himself.

Cordus delivered a defiant speech at the end of his trial, reputedly telling the senators: "Posterity awards every man the honor he deserves. You may sentence me to death, but then not only Brutus and Cassius will be remembered. I, too, shall not be forgotten."[47] That turned out to be true. His daughter Marcia had secreted away copies of his books, which reentered circulation years later when the emperor Caligula, in an effort to distinguish himself from Tiberius (who had come to be despised for his cruelty), ordered that remaining copies of Cordus's works be located and released.[48] According to the Roman statesman Cassius Dio, the revived works "aroused much greater interest by very reason of Cordus's unhappy fate."[49] His books were eventually included on reading lists for students of rhetoric.

The repressions of Labienus, Severus, and Cordus shocked Rome's intellectual establishment, but there was little they could do besides complain. The reins of censorship never tighten or loosen in response to outcries from targeted writers. Rather, the liberties granted to intellectuals are calibrated to the authorities' sense of security. A book such as Cordus's history must have been irritating to Augustus, but he likely saw no need to take forceful action. Tiberius never acquired such self-assurance, and the expanded treason laws gave him the latitude he needed to move against any implied insults.

There are few records from this period of state responses to speech directly against the government, but those that exist paint a picture of intolerance, even when the dissent was expressed in private. During the reign of Tiberius, a high-ranking *eques* (knight) named Titus Sabinus invited the wrong people to dinner. Knowing Sabinus's hostility to the emperor and his cruel magistrate Lucius Aelius Sejanus (who had imprisoned one of Sabinus's good friends), the guests flattered Sabinus and expressed sympathy for his friend's mistreatment. No doubt spurred by drink, Sabinus burst into tears and unloaded his spleen against Sejanus and Tiberius. But he was mistaken about where his guests' sympathies lay: their plan was to curry favor with Sejanus by delivering a disloyal aristocrat to him. Over the coming days, they elicited further confidences from Sabinus, while arranging for eavesdroppers—senators, no less—to listen through holes in the walls. Sabinus was charged with treason and summarily executed. His corpse was displayed in the Forum and then dragged by hooks into the Tiber River.

The bitter fate of a powerful man such as Sabinus made Rome "distracted and terror-stricken," reports Tacitus. "Meetings, conversations, the ear of friend and stranger were alike shunned; even things mute and lifeless, the very roofs and walls, were eyed with suspicion."[50] This must have been satisfying to Tiberius and Sejanus, as a few high-profile prosecutions are always useful to keep would-be conspirators apprehensive. Those who hoped that this was just another intrigue at society's upper reaches were soon disappointed: the terror ran all the way down to the plebs. For some epigrams he had written that reflected poorly on Tiberius, an insignificant poet, Aelius Saturninus, was executed in the grim tradition reserved for the worst criminals—he was hurled from a steep cliff in the center of Rome known as the Tarpeian Rock.

If the disloyalty of intellectuals and Sabinus disturbed Tiberius, the prognostications of unauthorized astrologers put him in a veritable panic. Tiberius was not the only emperor to believe in astrology, but he embraced it more deeply than his predecessors. He had his own astrologers on staff, and he practiced the art himself, so, in 16 CE, when he learned that enemies had enlisted astrologers, dream readers, and magicians in a plot against him, Tiberius struck hard. The main conspirator, a dissolute aristocrat named Marcus Scribonius Libo Drusus, was brought to trial before the Senate and Tiberius himself; he killed himself before the verdict was entered. The day of his suicide was declared a public holiday, and soon a law was passed banishing all astrologers from Rome—except Tiberius's own.[51]

This was not the first time astrologers were expelled, nor would it be the last, but it was the first time that expulsions were accompanied by executions—and gruesome ones at that. One of the seers was hurled screaming from the Tarpeian Rock; another was led, naked, outside the city and then whipped and beheaded. During this period, "incitement to conspiracy" by oral or written astrological interpretation became a serious type of literary treason as well. Astrology for hire was never a secure profession in Rome, as it was a persistently destabilizing force for authorities. After Tiberius, if an astrologer or soothsayer wished to encourage a client's seditious aims by predicting a sudden change in government, he would have been well advised to be paid in advance, and to be correct.

The crackdowns on astrology were survival measures for the ruling authorities, who meant to suppress rebellious notions among their enemies and also feared that predictions against them would come to pass. For Tiberius, it was better to prevent adverse prognostications than to contend with them once they were made. Speech barred is less risky than speech punished. What neither Tiberius nor anyone else could control, however, was how they would be remembered after they died. For many persons of importance, their destiny after they left this world was to be literally erased.

The Senate decreed that all physical traces of Libo Drusus be eradicated, but this posthumous punishment was mild compared to the fate of Sejanus, Tiberius's hated magistrate. After his downfall, his body was thrown down the Gemonian Stairs—another infamous place of execution—and metal statues depicting Sejanus driving a chariot were torn down and melted to make chamber pots and cookware. Each of these men was subjected to *damnatio memoriae* ("condemnation of memory"), a repertoire of measures used against anyone whose wrongdoing was so egregious that their very memories were intolerable. The practice mainly involved some combination of destroying or mutilating images of the condemned—statues, busts, pictures, even coins and medallions—a ban on using the person's name, and the deletion of the person from public records. It applied to some intellectuals, such as Cremutius Cordus, but was used most pointedly against those at society's apex, from Brutus and Cassius to Mark Antony and even to emperors such as Nero. All of them fell, by greater or lesser degrees, under what Roman law would call an "interdict of silence." That we still know about the likes of Brutus or Nero is not surprising, but the fact that a minor character like Cordus makes an entrance in books such as this one demonstrates what an absurd and futile effort any such interdict is.

All societies recast the past, and as governing authorities change (peacefully or not), some aspects of history are brought to the fore while others are deemphasized. In the ancient world, the past was more than a byproduct of political concerns; it was the means by which cultures defined themselves. The past was present, it was coherent, and it told societies what they were, and why. Such a living presence is not readily altered by decree, and regardless of what is commanded from on high, an individual's memory cannot be erased like a computer file, or rubbed out like a wax tablet. A soldier in Antony's army, for example, would not soon forget his commander; nor can a family un-remember a father, son, or daughter. So when the state commanded its people to expunge all memories of an individual, it required them to engage in a suspension of belief, to commit fraud against their own minds. Yet the Roman practice of *damnatio memoriae* persisted for about eight hundred years, from the fifth century BCE to the sixth century CE.

The destruction or defacing of figurative images was, for the average Roman, the most impressive aspect of *damnatio memoriae*. It was impossible to walk through the capital without being constantly reminded of its history, its heroes and leaders and their deeds. Imperial monuments and statues of the good and great, triumphal arches, and displayed texts and images were clear visual cues defining aspects of Rome's past and present. It must have been rather alarming, therefore, to encounter a familiar statue of an emperor or hero with its eyes, nose, or chin carved out or its head replaced with a likeness of someone else; or an empty space where the statue had once been; or a figure in a relief panel chiseled away; or a wall painting redone to eliminate the person condemned. The anguish of the families of the disgraced, who were required to eliminate all traces of their relatives, was also accompanied by substantial risk. Those found with forbidden pictures or statues were sometimes considered guilty of the same crimes as those they were attempting to honor, and were punished accordingly.[52]

One of the most spectacular examples of *damnatio memoriae* concerns one of the first emperors to whom it was applied: Domitian. As with Sejanus, it was also bitterly ironic, for Domitian had done much to suppress speech. He developed a strong authoritarian streak soon after taking power in 81 CE, appointing himself perpetual censor—a magistrate who, among other things, acted as a guardian of public morals—and moving against anyone whose writings or remarks might reflect poorly on him. He had the historian Hermogenes of Tarsus executed for some derogatory allusions in the latter's *History*. Copies of the book were collected and burned, and the scribes who had copied the book were crucified. But his paranoia was directed mainly at senators, whom he treated with murderous cruelty, subjecting them to constant surveillance and then executing them for transgressions as trivial as making jokey remarks against him.[53] With the lives of the senators also went their writings. According to Tacitus, "The police . . . were given the task of burning in the courtyard of the Forum the memorials of our noblest characters. . . . Even as former generations witnessed the utmost excesses of liberty, so we have the extremes of slavery."[54]

By 96 CE, Domitian's excesses had strained even the loyalties of many of his supporters; he was assassinated as the result of a conspiracy of members of his court and his wife. The Senate reacted with joy and a frenzy of violence. Pliny describes his fellow senators' destruction of the dead emperor's images and statuary:

It was our delight to dash those proud faces to the ground, to smite them with the sword and savage them with the axe, as if blood and agony could follow from every blow. Our transports of joy—so long deferred—were unrestrained; all sought a form of vengeance in beholding those bodies mutilated, limbs hacked in pieces, and finally that baleful, fearsome visage cast into fire, to be melted down, so that from such menacing terror something for man's use and enjoyment should rise out of the flames.[55]

Suetonius also describes the scene in manic terms, adding that the senators, after destroying everything associated with Domitian that they could find, "passed a decree that his inscriptions should everywhere be erased, and all record of him obliterated."[56]

But of course, images, records, and statues of Domitian *do* survive (many statues of him were warehoused, to be recut into other likenesses), as do the identities of the many subsequent emperors subjected to *damnatio memoriae*.[57] In many ways the process had the opposite effect to that intended, as every mutilated statue or now-empty pedestal produced new reminders of the disgraced figures, new prompts to recall the condemned, and new affirmations of memory. When one is told not to mention someone's name, one must, in the words of the historian Charles W. Hedrick, remember to forget: "If one must constantly remember not to mention a person, then one is surely not forgetting that person. . . . The penalty works only so long as those who are condemned remain in the memory."[58] None of this was likely lost on the senators. And when Pliny and Suetonius wrote of the destruction of Domitian's likenesses, they certainly knew that by doing so they were creating new records of his existence.

At best, then, *damnatio memoriae* served only to disgrace a person's memory, not to erase it. Given the violence with which it was enforced, it likely succeeded as a temporary "interdict of silence," but like other acts of thought suppression, it had no chance of lasting. It is noteworthy because it stands as the one of the first examples of state-sponsored efforts to render human beings unknown for political reasons. Like Stalin's erasure of Trotsky from images of early Bolshevik leaders and the Ukrainian government's destruction of thousands

of Lenin statues in the 1990s, such measures usually heighten aware-
ness of the persons disgraced and, in doing so, keep their identities
alive. Yet despite the ineffectiveness of these gestures, the twofold
threat was very real: that felt by the state, and that which the state
imposed on the citizenry. Targeted ideas cannot be eradicated—but for
censoring authorities, it is still worth the effort.

INVIOLATE VIRGINS AND CROSSES OF LIGHT: EARLY CHRISTIANITY TO CONSTANTINE

The early Christians cared little for the past—not when the Messiah
had already come and been crucified and resurrected, and the kingdom of God was at hand. When time and history were about to end,
what use was knowledge accumulated over the past centuries? Many
pagan texts were eliminated as an affirmation of faith and to destroy
the evil laced through their pages. Time and again, especially once the
new religion gained temporal power, the suppression of nonconforming books and ideas became a form of holy violence, to smash dissent,
demonstrate the zeal of the converted, and sanctify the church's authority. Far from learning tolerance from the terrible Roman persecutions against the first generations of Christians, the church embraced
censorship as an article of faith for millennia to come.

It starts with the apostle Paul, who was in Ephesus dazzling the
populace with miracles when some Jewish exorcists, noting his successes, began to use Jesus's name to boost the efficacy of their own
rites. Their effort backfired, particularly when they addressed an
evil spirit that had invaded an unfortunate fellow's body. The spirit
responded by saying, "Jesus I recognize, Paul I know, but who are
you?" The possessed man then attacked the exorcists, causing them to
flee, naked and wounded. The episode set off a mass of conversions
throughout the city, including of several other magicians, who then
publicly burned their books on sorcery.[59]

Other practitioners of the dark arts burned their books as a sign
of their new faith, sometimes for not entirely savory reasons. In the
third century, the sorcerer Cyprian of Antioch reputedly embraced
Christianity after his magic failed to help him seduce a pious Christian

virgin, Justina. As one version of the story goes, Cyprian set his books alight upon learning of the story of Paul and the Ephesian exorcists. Like them, his destruction of his texts was, according to one account, "a visible demonstration of his transformation. . . . He cast out the demons and took God to himself. Oh, such delight!" Christian virgins generally must have been resistant to sorcery, as the demons summoned by two other magicians, Lucianus and Marcianus, failed to trick another such woman into intercourse. The magicians embraced Christ and burned their pagan books in an elaborate public display.[60]

The early Roman repressions of Christianity were horrifying, but they involved attacks on Christians themselves, not the destruction of texts. The inflection point was reached toward the late third century, when the religion, despite the violence against its adherents, had grown from a scattered Jewish offshoot into a network of congregations administered by priestly officials who were often quite educated. By then, a substantial body of Christian Scripture and related literature was being generated and published widely. No suppression of Christianity could hope to be effective without an attack on the books that were pulling Christians away from the Roman gods and traditions.

The "Great Persecution" of Christians commenced in 303, when Emperor Diocletian, after consulting an oracle and concluding that Christianity was a legitimate threat to the state, resolved to suppress it entirely. It began in Nicomedia, in Anatolia, where he and the co-emperor, Galerius, personally presided over the ritualized destruction of Christian scriptures. There, a church was searched and its books and other sacred objects were brought outside and burned, after which the church itself was destroyed. According to one account, "The scene was one of plunder, panic, and confusion." The ceremony was accompanied by edicts, enforced to varying degrees throughout the empire, ordering that churches be razed to the ground and religious texts destroyed by fire.[61]

Of course, the persecution, which lasted for eight years, also involved savage attacks on Christians themselves, about three thousand of them, and the violence was kaleidoscopic in its cruelty. While the torture, killing, and burning did nothing to arrest the religion's spread,

it swelled the ranks of saints and martyrs. Many of them died hero-
ically with their books, such as Saint Euplius of Sicily, who, in 304,
presented himself to the Romans with his Bible and *demanded* martyrdom. The Romans obliged. After gruesome torture, Euplius went
to his death with his Bible hung around his neck.[62] A thick mythology
also emerged of Christian books miraculously restoring themselves
and even retaliating against the Romans. Stories were also told of
burning books leaping to heaven, terrifying spectators and inducing
conversions. As for the edicts themselves, certain Christians lit them
on fire as signs of faith, suffering blessed martyrdom as a result.

The Christian divinity was a threat to Diocletian, but it was just
what Emperor Constantine needed to gain power over the entire empire. In 312, on the day before he was to engage his rival, Maxentius,
in the critical Battle of the Milvian Bridge, he had a vision in which
he beheld a cross of light in the sky bearing the inscription: "In hoc
signo vinces": "In this sign conquer." He did just that, instructing his
soldiers to create a standard with the first two letters of "Christos"
(called the Chi Rho) and to put similar inscriptions on their shields.
Thus fortified, Constantine's army defeated Maxentius, and before too
long, he became the sole ruler of the eastern and western halves of
the empire. (Predictably enough, Maxentius was subjected to *damnatio memoriae*.) Convinced that the Christian God had brought him
victory and that he owed his "whole life" and "every breath" to that
divinity, Constantine became a believer in Christianity (he would not
be baptized until much later), and Rome was on its way to adopting
Christianity as its official religion. Christ, not Jupiter, was becoming
the ruler of the universe.[63]

The momentousness of these events, and their effect on world history, cannot be overstated. Rome's turn toward Christianity ensured
the new faith's dominance in European religion and, later, in much of
the world. Yet Constantine's conversion was motivated less by spiritual yearning than power politics. He allied himself to the Christian
deity in large part because that god had protected him and delivered
a historic victory in battle, thus proving Himself to be more potent
than other gods. Christ's humble life on earth did not seem to interest
Constantine much, and Christ's suffering on the Cross must have been

incomprehensible to him. To Constantine, the Cross was, above all, a symbol of triumph, not humiliation. Yet Constantine's sense of connection with Christianity was genuine, as were his efforts to use the religion and its church to help restore unity to the fractious empire. The problem was that Christianity was rent by its own internal battles. The harsh censorship Constantine used to forge a unified church in service of the Roman state, and the church's own determined adoption of censorship once it gained power, became the model for speech suppression for centuries to come.

2

THE FIRE CURE

Censorship from Late Antiquity to Gutenberg

It must have been head-spinning. For more than a century, Rome had cruelly suppressed Christians, reaching a murderous, book-burning crescendo during the Great Persecution. Now, in 313 CE, the torment ceased suddenly, and Christians were benefitting from official toleration. Their relief was likely matched by confusion on the part of Rome's pagan population, as they came to witness Christian churches—the very places that had just been destroyed as vectors of contamination—being rebuilt with government money. Most shockingly, the god whose adherents had so recently been killed by the thousands was now the deity that Constantine claimed he carried "hidden in my breast" and of whom he declared himself a servant.[1]

If pagans on the streets and in the temples were struggling to understand what was going on, they must have also been confounded by this odd new religion: what *was* Christianity, exactly, and what did Christians believe? One thing was certain, it did not resemble official Roman cults. Rather, it was a far-flung mass of sects with sharply conflicting approaches to their faith, whose adherents seemed to hate each other barely less than the Roman state had so recently reviled them. For the pagan population, this was likely puzzling, but for Constantine it was a political problem. He believed that only a unified institution, subservient to him, with one dogma, would help him bring unity to the empire. His efforts to end Christianity's intractable divisions failed miserably, as Christian sectarian allegiances proved much harder to subdue than any army.

In the ensuing religious conflicts, and as Christianity expanded and solidified its position as the empire's official faith, one constant would be aggressive and often violent censorship. The suppressions of previous centuries would continue, but now they were often in support of Christianity rather than traditional Roman religion—although the state's allegiance to one or another Christian faction was subject to frequent and turbulent change. But regardless of which sect or dogma had the advantage at any point in time, or whether suppressions were orchestrated by the church, the state, or the two in concert, groups that were out of favor could expect to have their texts and beliefs declared illegal—and, too often, their lives threatened.

Constantine was not given to detailed theological speculation, so the question of whether Jesus Christ was of the same essential nature as God the Father was of no burning import to him. But variants on this and other abstruse doctrinal questions were fracturing the religion. For example, a North African priest named Arius gained a large and growing following with the view (*highly* simplified here) that because Christ had been begotten by the Father, there was a time when he did not exist, and thus he could not be of the same eternal essence as God.[2] Arius's opponents attacked this view for undermining the religion's bedrock monotheistic foundation. Debates over such minute issues were not confined to priests and the intelligentsia; rather, they were argued passionately at all levels of society. As recounted by Bishop Gregory of Nysa:

> Everywhere, in the public squares, at crossroads, on the streets and lanes, people would stop you and discourse at random about the Trinity. If you asked something of a moneychanger, he would begin discussing the question of the Begotten and the Unbegotten. If you questioned a baker about the price of bread, he would answer that the Father is greater and the Son is subordinate to Him. If you went to take a bath, the Anomoean bath attendant would tell you that in his opinion the Son simply comes from nothing.[3]

Theology was an urgent matter in the religiously tumultuous fourth century, when Christianity was struggling to define itself. As little as Constantine may have wished to focus on such questions, they had to be settled if the religion was to do him any good.

In 325, he summoned the 1,800 bishops of Christendom to a council in the town of Nicaea, in present-day Turkey, to resolve what became known as the Arian controversy. He was likely irritated by the low turnout—only a few hundred bishops showed up—and the continued sectarianism infuriated him. Many of the bishops had arrived with written denunciations against one another, which Constantine burned without reading—"as if," observes the scholar Dirk Rohmann, "the dissenting petitions had never existed, and the unity of the church had never been challenged."[4] Once this first Council of Nicaea convened, Constantine adopted the position (called the Nicene Creed and, again, simplified here) that God and Jesus were of the same essence. He sent Arius into exile and dispatched authorities to hunt down Arian and other nonconforming texts. Yet Arianism was far from finished. A few years later, Arius demanded that Constantine recognize him or he would form his own separate church. The response: a total ban by Constantine on Arius's works and a decree of death by decapitation for anyone who failed to bring them to authorities for burning.[5]

None of these measures diminished Arius's following; in fact, it continued to increase. In a stunning turn of events, Arianism was adopted after Constantine's death as the dominant faith, and the Nicene Creed was declared heretical for several decades—that is, until Arianism's later defeat. This is, however, a step too far into the dogmatic weeds: the key takeaway from the Arian and similar controversies is that so long as Christianity was decentralized, many Christianities would result. Now, one church would emerge, and its word on doctrine would (at least in theory) be final. Moreover, it would persecute nonconforming Christian groups with the help of imperial Roman muscle. In the two centuries after Constantine, the state burned unsanctioned texts more than a dozen times, and, starting in 385, when the church approved the beheading of a heretical bishop, the lives of dissident Christians were at risk from members of their own faith.[6] Regardless of where the suppression came from, the purposes were the same: to eradicate dissent, vindicate power, and convert heretics and heathens.

The destruction of forbidden texts was a demonstration of belief in the Christian God, as well as a weapon against the demons infesting their words. "If you want to become a Christian," demanded the monk Hypatios of a pagan who wished to convert, "bring me your book."[7] Ecclesiastical canons began to caution Christians to avoid pagan learning, while Saint Augustine, arguably Christianity's most influential thinker, advocated the aggressive suppression of heresy. "There is an unjust persecution which the wicked inflict on the Church of Christ," he wrote, "and there is a just persecution which the Church of Christ inflicts on the wicked." This latter form of persecution was pursued "out of love" and to "save souls." Tolerance was not an option, as it multiplied the curse of forbidden ideas.[8]

Any texts outside the Gospels—in fact, critical learning itself—were condemned by some church fathers, as these fostered an inquisitive outlook that would lead Christians astray. "If we question, it is not faith; for faith sets reasoning at rest," opined John Chrysostom, archbishop of Constantinople (later Saint John Chrysostom), regarding the Greek penchant for research and debate.[9] Because of their tendency to encourage curiosity, the doctrines and methods of pagan philosophy, at least to the extent that they were at odds with Christian doctrine, were often framed as forms of madness to be excluded from the lives of Christians.

As the church and the Roman state fused, the old religions were far from stamped out, and the ongoing suppression of pagan learning became state policy. Urged on by church officials, the state passed laws banning anything that contradicted the biblical view of the universe, including philosophical, scientific, and other texts. Under Theodosius I (r. 379–84), for example, non-Catholic beliefs were declared insane and heretical, and anyone possessing banned texts who did not destroy them immediately was to be executed unless they denounced their authors. During the reign of Justinian I (527–65), pagan learning was banned altogether. By the seventh century, Europe's largest known library, in Seville, contained only a few hundred texts.[10]

The violent use of censorship to suppress non-Christian learning and target political adversaries marked what came to be known as the "magic trials," which began in 369 under Emperors Valens and Valentinian I. In the East, the trials began when Valens became incensed to learn that some diviners in Antioch had presumed to predict his death and identify his successor. His response included widespread executions and torture, including of philosophers, and a direct and thoroughgoing attack on books. While magic and heretical texts were sought in house-to-house searches and burned en masse, pagan works on philosophy, law, and the liberal arts were also targeted. Mere possession of them would constitute evidence of treason and cause for execution—and there were many executions. "Everywhere" reported Ammianus Marcellinus, "the scene was like the slaughtering of cattle."[11]

In the panic, people tried to get rid of their forbidden texts before authorities discovered them. "Throughout the oriental provinces," Ammianus continues, "owners . . . burned their entire libraries; so great was the terror."[12] Other books were thrown into rivers. On one occasion, while the city of Antioch was occupied by soldiers under orders to search for suspicious materials, the young John Chrysostom and a friend were walking by the Orontes River. They pulled what they thought was a piece of linen from the water, only to discover that it was a manuscript on the magic arts—a death warrant if they were caught with it. At that moment, a soldier passed by. "There were we," he later recalled, "congealed with fear. For who would have believed our story that we had picked it up from the river, when all were at that time, even the unsuspected, under strict watch?"[13] They hid the book in John's friend's cloak and threw it back into the water as soon as the soldier had passed.

The violent power of the Roman state was also deployed to fulfill the vindictive prophecies of Saint Simeon Stylites the Younger (521–92), an ascetic miracle healer who passed much of his life perched atop a pillar in Antioch. Evidently, one becomes rather prickly living in such circumstances. Simeon became enraged when pagans destroyed an icon that depicted his likeness, erected after he had cured an artisan's lung ailment. Simeon responded with predictions that a "terrible chief" will come to "flog" the paganism and heresy out of the city's inhabitants and "bring death to many of them through the direst castigation." Three months later, a new imperial administrator arrived, and thousands of cult statues and pagan books including the "gruesome heresies" of science and natural philosophy were publicly set aflame in the city's stadium, where criminals were also executed.

As with the magic trials, Simeon's revenge tale illustrates the overlap of purpose between Christianity's censorious dictates and the Roman state's power politics. The destruction of heretical and pagan texts enforced the church's monopoly on belief, while the state affirmed its own authority through its use of terror and intimidation. Books of magic and prophecy had been outlawed periodically in Rome for centuries, as rulers feared that adverse predictions would either come to pass or at least encourage seditious conspiracies. The ambitions of state censorship expanded significantly when they also started treating books of science and philosophy as dangerous. The Christianization of Rome marks a major step in the West toward using the machinery of a mature state to control thought.

These and other censorship efforts went beyond the suppression of individual books. In the centuries after Justinian, few pre-Christian texts were copied in Europe outside of monasteries, and while such books were reviewed by scholars (mainly to refute their contents), the pressure *not* to teach their contents could be heavy. In 601, Pope Gregory the Great demanded that Christians avoid studies related to classical traditions, even grammar. This sentiment became the law of much of Europe when Charlemagne, in his *Admonitio Generalis* of 789, ruled that "only . . . the words of the holy authors are to be read and expounded" in the Frankish domains.[14]

FROM CHURCH SUPPRESSION OF DRAMA TO DRAMA IN CHURCHES

As the written word was suppressed, so, eventually, were pagan forms of drama. There was little room in Christian thinking for the staged entertainment that had been woven into Roman life.[15] Leaving aside gladiatorial and beast-fighting spectacles, theatrical performances during the early Christian period stressed sex and sensationalism, and often mirrored what went on in brothels. For example, the popular springtime Floralia festival was a kind of sex-trade fair in which prostitutes fought in the arenas as if they were gladiators and performed lewd farces and mime in the theatres. Although they performed while clothed, they never resisted audience demands to strip down for long. If he was insufficiently titillated, Emperor Heliogabalus required actors to have sex onstage.[16] Considering the church's dim view of sex for pleasure, it was inevitable that it would condemn Roman theatre. Unsurprisingly, actors responded in kind by mocking Christianity as part of their performances—especially the rite of baptism.[17]

Despite the strident objections to theatre by church fathers such as Tertullian, Saint Augustine, and Tatian, the spectacles were too enticing for the flock to give up. Even Tertullian's admonishment to Christians to abandon the theatre's earthy fun, turn to the "truth" of church writings, and wait for the Last Judgment for more sensational shows—as alluring as *those* appeals must have been—failed to pull common Christians away.[18] The church was presented with a dilemma: if it overlooked its flock's attachment to the theatre, it would in effect be sanctioning sin. But if it threatened Christians attending theatrical shows with excommunication, it ran the risk of losing many of its adherents.

Instead, the church began gradually to place restrictions on theatre attendance and participation. First, it barred the clergy from entering theatres, while laymen were prohibited from becoming actors or attending performances on Sundays and other church holidays. Actors were later forbidden from dressing as nuns and from being in the company of Christian women and boys. It would take another century or so, and the conquest of the Western Empire by barbarians, who, as the historian John Harris puts it, "favored sword-dances and bagpipes," for drama as it had been known for almost a millennium to diminish substantially, although it never vanished. Despite the church's fulminations, traveling mime and minstrel troupes along with tumblers, jugglers, and stilt walkers continued to perform throughout the Middle Ages. Scripted, secular, and farcical plays were staged as well, earning sporadic condemnation by churchmen. In 679, the Council of Rome also took up the issue of *jocos vel ludos* ("jokes or games"), and ordered English bishops to somehow halt them. About a century later, a church law threatened corporal punishment and exile for any actor who dared to portray a priest. Messages like these seem to have been lost or ignored, however. Minstrel troupes continued to offer their entertainments and "songs of noble deeds," and mimes even amused the Holy Roman emperor Louis I in 835. As late as 1250, it was reported that Oxford students were using masks and engaging in "wrestling and other dishonest plays in cemeteries, theatrical plays and filthy spectacles."[19]

Starting in about the early ninth century, a major change began in the church's stance on theatre: biblical stories were now increasingly depicted dramatically by clerics themselves during church services. The idea was to communicate the mysteries of the Latin Mass to uneducated parishioners who were alienated by a language they did not well understand and in terms they could grasp viscerally. This practice might have begun with the consecration rituals for new churches, during which Christ's descent into hell to free the righteous was acted out. A bishop, assuming the role of Christ, would beat on a church's western doors (representing the gates of hell) while another cleric, playing the devil, cowered behind them. When the doors were finally opened, the devil-cleric would flee into the crowd, symbolizing the purge of evil from the new building. Soon the Passion of Christ itself was depicted, with bishops casting themselves as Jesus and other members of the clergy playing the disciples and other figures, all while making great use of gestures, movement, and accents to convey the story. These weren't exactly plays, but churchmen did much more than recite words in an incomprehensible tongue. In doing so, they invited congregations to embrace the religion's foundational myths on an emotional level. This was the beginning of liturgical drama.

This development, which Harris states had an "electrifying effect . . . on congregations" to "rouse Christianity from the lethargy into which it was sinking," drew predictably fierce objections from some church authorities. They condemned the clergy's mimicry of female voices, sighs, histrionic gestures, and imitations of the agonies of the tortured and dying. But as the popularity and influence of this new movement continued to grow, the church had no choice but to give up its objections. In 1207, Pope Innocent III reversed longstanding ecclesiastical law and ruled that plays and entertainments for devotional purposes were acceptable so long as there was no bawdiness. Eventually, dramatic skills would become helpful for clerical careers: in 1313, the barely literate Walter Reynolds was appointed archbishop of Canterbury because, according to one account, he "excelled in theatrical performances," unlike his otherwise better-qualified competitor.[20]

PICTURES ALIVE AND DEAD IN BYZANTIUM

Early Christianity's dreary attitude toward drama was matched by its view of imagery. For the first two centuries of its existence, the religion categorically rejected visual art and especially the representations of figures, in part to negate idolatrous pagan practices and also in strict obedience to the biblical ban on "graven images."[21] Every likeness—indeed, every form—was an idol, instructed Tertullian, whether crafted of stone or emerging from an arrangement of colors, regardless of what was being depicted.[22] But that arid stance would evaporate: the pull of the figurative image proved overpowering—as a way to address the soul's yearning to conceive the unknowable and as a healing bridge between humanity and the divine. Just as the Jews had struggled to live without graven images, the Christians simply gave in. But they went much further, turning images and forms into objects of feverish devotion.

Starting roughly in the fourth century, two religious props not explicitly barred by the Bible, crosses and relics, were worshipped in and of themselves. Recall that Constantine credited his victory at the Battle of Milvian Bridge to a vision of the Cross; this legend became the major impetus for veneration of the Cross, and images of it proliferated. Fragments of the True Cross, purportedly discovered during Constantine's reign by his mother, Saint Helena, were also sought out and prayed to fervently. At the same time, the bare walls of churches were populated with images of Christ, the Virgin, the apostles, and various saints, whose gazes gave worshippers the solace of believing that their appeals for safety, health, and salvation were being heard, not by an invisible, unknowable god but by recognizable human forms. Before long, some of these images "broke ranks" and were placed in special positions in churches, on doorways, in homes, and on streets, where they were treated with heightened devotion.[23]

At least as early as the sixth century, worshippers started to openly venerate icons. (The word comes from the Greek *eikôn*, meaning "image.") It wasn't long before the icons responded. By the end of the century, stories about iconographic images responding to the faithful's pleas eroded the distinction between images and the figures they depicted. Icons came alive and became active participants in the individual lives of their devotees, the fortunes of cities, and sometimes even the fate of the Byzantine Empire. As devotion to icons during the late sixth and seventh centuries became widespread and increasingly fervid, reports of icon-driven miracles grew more elaborate and, ultimately, became a matter of political and military importance.

Wherever icons were placed in the Byzantine East, believers bowed to them, kissed them, burned lights and incense before them, and begged them for help. Many were thought to be made by holy spirits, and no account of the miracles they worked was too tall for the faithful to embrace. Some icons were said to make demands on the faithful, as in Gregory of Tours's account of an image of the nude crucified Christ that demanded to be covered; others bled, as in the story of a picture of Christ that a Jew had pierced. Icons looked after the pious, as in the case of a devout woman whose dry well filled with water after she lowered an image of Saint Theodore into it, and they cured illness, as experienced by someone whose diseased body was blessed with the melted wax of a seal bearing the image of Saint Artemius.[24]

Icons were also believed to address much more than individual needs. In 544, when the Persians attacked the city of Edessa (now Urfa) in modern-day Turkey, a rectangle of cloth on which an image of Christ had miraculously been imprinted was said to have played a critical role in repelling the invasion. Later versions of the story had the image sending a wind to blow fire at the Persians, immolating them before their final assault could commence. That bit of fabric made Christ tangible and present that day in Edessa, and he rewarded his followers' devotion by saving their lives. As threats increased from the rising Islamic empire to the east, and from the Balkan tribes and Bulgarian Khanate, images of Christ, the Virgin, and other holy personages were carried regularly in processions to invoke their protection—although with diminishing results.[25]

It was the unsuccessful use of holy images against Byzantium's enemies that, in part, motivated two waves of iconoclastic measures, starting around 730, at the hands of Emperor Leo III and some of his successors. The reasons for the repressions have been debated for centuries. The evidence is patchy, and accounts appear to be exaggerated. However, it is irrefutable that as the empire experienced unprecedented pressure from without and severe military reversals, the biblical arguments of critics of icon worship began to resonate: God was allowing the defeat of Byzantium's forces *because* of its idolatrous practices. While the veneration of icons was once thought to bring good fortune, their destruction now served the same purpose. In 727, after a series of victories, the armies of the Umayyad Caliphate reached Nicaea, just miles from Constantinople. The loss of the city would have cleared a path to the capital and, potentially, hastened the end of the empire. During the siege, a Byzantine officer spotted an image of the Virgin on the city's wall, which believers had placed there to invoke her protection. The officer trampled the image until it broke into pieces; before long, the invaders retreated. Opponents of icons duly took note of this message from above.

This and other events, including a terrifying volcanic eruption in the Aegean that Leo was said to interpret as a sign of divine disfavor, likely convinced him that the profligate icon worship of the past two centuries had gone too far. He must have also wished to affirm his own absolute power and superiority over the church, to which end his adoption of the Cross as the sole symbol of the faith—a deliberate nod to Constantine—was an unsubtle message. According to the historian Peter Brown, "To force the Cross to the foreground, so that it should replace all other images, was the sign of a Christian empire stripped for battle and reunited to its triumphant past. . . . Under the Cross alone, and without the help of icons, true Christian emperors would relive the victories of Constantine the Great."[26]

In about 730, an icon of Christ affixed over the gate of the palace in Constantinople was replaced with a cross, and, according to some accounts, throughout the empire, icons (other than images of the Cross and of Leo himself) were destroyed. Those who resisted the measures were persecuted. Leo's son, appropriately named Constantine V, took the throne in 741. He turned back the military advances of both the Umayyad and Abbasid Caliphates and continued his father's iconoclastic sweep, but whereas Leo had proceeded without church sanction, Constantine assembled a council to approve the policy on theological grounds. For good measure, he later had Saint Stephen the Younger, a prominent iconophile, dragged through the streets of Constantinople and clubbed to death (after which various parts of Stephen's body found their way to holy places, where they, ironically enough, were venerated as relics). Hundreds of Stephen's followers were also "imprisoned, tortured, and mutilated."[27]

After Constantine V's death, which was followed by an extended interlude in which religious images were again permitted, the curtain fell once more on images in 811 after Khan Krum of Bulgaria defeated and killed the Byzantine emperor Nicephorus and turned his skull into a drinking cup. The new emperor, Leo V, was shaken by his predecessor's grisly demise and sought to avoid the same fate. He saw the cause of the crisis as "the worship of images and nothing else," and concluded that iconoclastic leaders had a better chance of dying natural deaths than those who venerated religious images. "It is they I intend to imitate," he said. Icons were once more outlawed—that is, until the external pressures on the empire eased.[28]

In 843, icons were again permitted in the Eastern Orthodox church and became, in the words of Robin Cormack, "the sign and symbol of Orthodoxy."[29] The revival of iconographic worship had its champion in the monk John of Damascus, who argued that such images help people, in all their weakness, to perceive otherwise hidden realities, leading them to a heightened perception of the divine. In 867, a mosaic of the Virgin with the Christ child in her lap was laid for the first time in the Hagia Sophia, the massive cathedral erected by Justinian centuries earlier, and churches throughout the Byzantine world were soon crammed with images, mostly mosaics and painted frescoes. The saints returned to the visible court of heaven, again watching over and directly addressing the yearnings of the devout.

The causes and scope of Byzantium's 170-year on-and-off iconoclastic episodes are the subject of intense dispute. Everyone seems to have had a go at explaining them, even Marxist historians and social scientists, who framed the events as a medieval form of class struggle. However, understanding the fine points of these debates is unnecessary for our purpose, which is to show that political regimes, convinced that icon worship represented a danger to their survival—whether from God or the sword—presided over the destruction of Byzantine art. The West would suffer far more violent iconoclastic devastation during the religious dislocations of the Reformation of the sixteenth and seventeenth centuries, and later, during the French Revolution, when religion itself came under attack. In each instance, images were understood as more than mere pictures. They may not have been technically alive, but they still had to be killed.

HOLY BOOKS, CHRIST'S HOROSCOPE, AND REASON

The Roman playwright Terence's proverb "So many men, so many minds" would have found no takers in any corridors of power during the Middle Ages and early Renaissance, because only one mindset at a time was permitted. All dissent was targeted for suppression, not merely because of the ideas expressed but because the very *existence* of intellectual dissonance was feared to undermine secular and church authority. As always, the main imperative for authorities was self-preservation, and unless a line of thinking originated with them, it was ipso facto subversive.

Although they hardly qualified as effective agents of dissent, the most vulnerable targets for suppression were Jews and their holy books. As deniers of Christ the Messiah, Jews were considered the definitive blasphemers, and they suffered nearly continuous degradation, displacement, and violence. Their holy texts fared no better, particularly the massive compendium of legal writings and commentaries, and the centerpiece of Jewish life, known as the Talmud. It bears the bitter distinction of being the only body of text to have been burned for nine straight centuries. Yet Christians were not the Talmud's only antagonists. Some of the earliest advocates of its suppression were Jews themselves. One of the first recorded incidents of the destruction of the Talmud took place after thirteenth-century French rabbis excommunicated a Jewish scholar by the name of Nicolas Donin. The rabbis would come to regret that decision, as Donin soon converted to Catholicism and dedicated himself to taking vengeance.

In 1236, Donin went to Pope Gregory IX and reported that the Talmud contained dozens of blasphemies, including perversions and libels against Jesus and Mary, which, he claimed, caused the Jews to be "obstinate in their perfidy."[30] In response, Gregory ordered authorities in France, England, Castile, Aragon, and Portugal to invade synagogues and confiscate Talmuds and other Jewish writings pending a decision on Donin's accusations. What ensued was a trial of the Talmud itself, which took place in the court of France's King Louis IX and was presided over by church officials—although "trial" is a misnomer, as that term implies some degree of fairness. In this case, the fix was in before the proceedings began.

Donin acted as prosecutor, and four rabbis were appointed as the Talmud's defenders. Donin misrepresented select passages from the six-thousand-page text in a way calculated to inflame passions, while the rabbis—held in separate prison cells and thus unable to communicate with each other—could only argue that the text was indispensable to Jews trying to understand the Bible. The trial and the decision to set the books on fire set in motion a chain of events resulting in the burning of thousands of Talmudic books, primarily in France. Of course, copies survived, and for centuries later the Talmud and other Jewish holy books would be subject to periodic and increasingly violent attacks, which only helped to make Jewish life more precarious. During the Shepherds' Crusade of 1251, almost every Jew in southern France was murdered. As late as 1629, an Italian cardinal would boast of having destroyed ten thousand outlawed Jewish books.

Donin was not the only Jew to push for the censorship of Jewish books. Many Jewish scholars called for the suppression of *The Guide for the Perplexed*, by the towering Jewish philosopher Moses Maimonides. *The Guide*, written in Arabic in about 1190 and soon translated into Hebrew, sought in part to reconcile Judaism with the teachings of Aristotle and the discoveries in the natural sciences. Exploring questions such as the basis of morality, the immortality of the soul, and the concept of God, Maimonides argued that Judaism could be approached rationally as well as spiritually. While he intended to guide Jewish scholars to a deeper understanding of philosophy without compromising their religious commitments, other scholars in the faith saw matters very differently. Theoretical inquiry, they contended, had no place in Jewish thought.

In 1232, in Montpellier, France, the Talmudic scholar Solomon ben Abraham led an attack on *The Guide*. With the support of French rabbis and some important Spanish scholars, the work was banned among Jews on pain of excommunication. The rabbis appealed to heretic-burning Dominican friars for help in ending the study of philosophy among Jews. "You are destroying your heretics," ben Abraham urged them. "Help us to destroy our heretics." The inquisitors did not need persuading and conducted a house-to-house search for Maimonides's writings. All copies of *The Guide* that were found were burned in 1233, in what the scholar William Popper called the first official burning of Hebrew books. A little more than a month later, in Paris, about twelve thousand Jewish volumes were destroyed. Soon Hebrew books were looked upon as the rightful prey not only of the church but of the mob.[31]

Rationalist approaches to the Bible by Christian thinkers also met with hostility. Religious authorities hounded Peter Abelard, a preeminent twelfth-century logician and philosopher (remembered now chiefly for his doomed, turgid love affair with the nun Héloïse d'Argenteuil), in part for his own attempts to reconcile Aristotelian logic with Scripture. Like Maimonides, he had no intention of rejecting faith; rather, he aimed to deepen it through logic, reason, and dialectical analysis. But that ran against the religious dogmas of the day, and in 1122 the Council of Soissons forced him to burn his own books. About twenty years later, Abelard was excommunicated, and Pope Innocent II ordered his books burned "wherever they were found."[32]

In the coming years, as new commentaries and translations of Aristotle spread throughout Europe and fascinated scholars, the church sporadically (and unsuccessfully) banned the study of Aristotelian-based natural philosophy. In 1277, the Bishop of Paris listed 219 "manifest and detestable errors"—that is, ideas—and banned them at the University of Paris on pain of excommunication. Many of these concepts were drawn from Aristotle and natural philosophy, including the propositions that a vacuum is impossible; "nothing more is known through knowing theology"; "the creation [of the world] is not possible"; and, pointedly for university students, "enjoyment of carnal acts does not impede the activity or use of the intellect."[33] Of course, proscription of these ideas only confirmed that they were already well in circulation, and if the church thought it could end rationalist inquiry (or erotic assignations) simply by commanding them to end, it was mistaken.

The study of Aristotle and his commentators continued apace . . . as did sex among students.

At about the same time, both church and state entered the Bible-suppression business, focusing on Scripture translated into vernacular languages. While such books were considered as poisonous heresies, the key motive behind the censorship was to safeguard the church's exclusive control of the instruments and channels of faith, of which the Bible was obviously the most important. King James I of Aragon, a man "of the severest character," in the words of the historian Henry Lea, was one of the first rulers to ban vernacular Bibles. In 1234, he demanded that anyone possessing New or Old Testaments "in Romancio" deliver them to their bishops to be burned, or else suffer accusations of heresy.[34] Even advocating such translations was heretical.

The proto-Protestant fourteenth-century theologian John Wycliffe, of Oxford, maintained that Scripture, not the church, was the supreme authority on faith and advocated strongly for a vernacular Bible. He oversaw its translation into Middle English, arguing that ordinary people should be able to know it without church intervention. For that, and for his many other challenges to ecclesiastical authority, he was condemned repeatedly by the Vatican. His works were banned and destroyed, and it was ordered that any unauthorized Bible translations would be barred. It is remarkable that Wycliffe was able to live out his life in safety, but his body would know no peace: in 1415, forty years after his death, his bones were exhumed and burned, and the ashes were thrown in a river.[35] The travails of Wycliffe and the persecution of his followers, known as the Lollards, illustrate just how jealously the church guarded its exclusive control of Scripture.

Challenges to papal political power were also met with censorious intolerance, as occurred in connection with the Florentine poet Dante Alighieri's work *On Monarchy*, published around 1310 and condemned by the church in 1329. Although he was a devout Catholic, Dante had long been jousting with the church when he wrote the book. (Pope Boniface VIII, who had banished Dante from Florence, would be consigned to the eighth circle of hell in Dante's *Inferno*.) *On Monarchy* launched a direct attack on papal power, particularly the Vatican's self-serving claim that political leaders derived their authority from the pope. Dante's argument that Scripture accords no power to the church over nonreligious matters pulled at a sensitive nerve in Rome. The book was burned at the pope's behest and would remain banned to Catholics for six hundred years.

Dante's book was, perhaps, reasonably feared to exacerbate the ongoing battles between the Vatican and temporal leaders. However, the predictions of the physician and astrologer Francesco degli Stabili, known as Cecco d'Ascoli, posed no such threat. He was in constant trouble with authorities for his prognostications, but the crime that cost him his life was his horoscope of Jesus Christ, which identified a rising Libra on the day of Christ's birth—evidently suggesting that the Crucifixion had been inevitable.[36] Both d'Ascoli and his offending writings were burned, and anyone who read them was threatened with excommunication. As the fire was lit, the multitude watched to see whether evil spirits would rescue him. If that did indeed occur, then only his invisible soul was saved: his body, books, and the horoscope went up in flames.

The apogee of Florentine censorship during this period was reached with the turbulent life and violent end of Girolamo Savonarola, the charismatic holy roller, false prophet, and, by all signs, madman. The Dominican friar's brand of Christianity was austere and hateful. Everything disgusted him: reason, poetry, wealth, the grandees ruling Florence . . . and the Vatican. According to Savonarola, the world was in desperate need of spiritual housecleaning, and he believed he had been appointed by God to lead it. As the crowds attending his increasingly crazed sermons grew, so did his sense of holy mission. A series of visions led him to prophesy everything from the French invasion of Italy to the appearance of a cross of gold above Jerusalem, and, critically, Christ's return in a chariot, his wake strewn with heretics whose books had been burned and images smashed. Many of his predictions and fulminations ended up in his *Compendium Revelationum* (1495), which added that God had sent him to Florence "to cleanse his Church with a mighty scourge."

For several years up to 1497, Savonarola orchestrated his infamous "bonfires of the vanities" in the city's main square, the Piazza della Signoria, which were fueled by the books of Plato, Ovid,

Dante, and Boccaccio, as well as chessboards, dice, harps, wigs, and less-than-decent images of the Virgin Mary. All were immolated as trumpets blared and children sang. Savonarola's followers broke into houses to confiscate many of these "vanities," but others were tossed onto the fires by their owners and creators, most tragically by the painter Sandro Botticelli. According to the biographer Giorgio Vasari, Botticelli was "so zealous a partisan" of Savonarola that he abandoned painting altogether. Botticelli's masterpieces *Primavera* and *The Birth of Venus* were saved from destruction only because they were held at a Medici residence outside the city, beyond the reach of Savonarola's followers and Botticelli himself.[37]

It would not be long before Savonarola joined the vanities on the pyre. By 1498, the citizenry had grown tired of his relentless hectoring and demands for asceticism. When Savonarola claimed that the pope was neither a true Christian nor a true pope, the church, which had barely tolerated his harangues, ran out of patience. Under papal orders, he was arrested for heresy and schism, forced to confess under torture, and hanged. His corpse was set aflame along with his own books, in the same spot in Florence's Piazza della Signoria where his bonfires had so recently taken place. His ashes were tossed in the Arno River. A century later, his writings would be placed on the Vatican's *Index of Forbidden Books*.[38]

TURF WARS AND TREASON IN ENGLAND

While the Magna Carta of 1215 does not touch on freedom of expression, its mild curbs on royal control of lands allowed the lower orders to begin to imagine commandeering public spaces to make their grievances known. This document, and the 1217 Charter of the Forest, safeguarded some common rights to forests and pasturelands, which was critical to the mass of people who depended on the lands for their subsistence. But these small steps did not come close to resolving the full measure of the commoners' discontents. The deprivations caused by the Black Death of the 1340s, draconian taxes and wage controls, and daily displays of upper-class arrogance brought matters to a full boil in the Peasants' Revolt of 1381. During this first great popular uprising in English history, the rebels invaded government-controlled marketplaces, thus usurping elite control, if only for a flash of time, over the realm's newest and most effective communications hubs.

During the thirteenth and fourteenth centuries, English marketplaces proliferated, becoming vibrant social institutions. Much more than merely places to buy and sell, they were where peasants, artisans, merchants, clerics, and others mixed, news and gossip were exchanged, and authority made its presence known. Markets had existed before this time, of course, but they were few, and their reach had not extended into the countryside, where most people lived. The state took propagandistic advantage of the gatherings by having bailiffs and criers make formalized proclamations about goings-on in government and the realm. While some announcements were mundane (such as the adoption of a new royal seal), and others momentous (news about wars, for example), they were all meant to emphasize royal authority and the king's indispensable role as guarantor of security.

English royalty had earlier seen little reason to communicate directly with commoners, but the state was becoming more complex. Certain government initiatives, such as summonses to court or demands for information, were starting to require broad participation. "The enterprise of tapping into the loyalties and resources of the base of society lay at the heart of state formation in the period," explains the historian James Masschaele. "For the first time . . . peasants and burgesses were being invited into networks of knowledge and communication that previously had extended only to the gentry and the nobility."[39] But there were no fact-checkers back then, and marketplace communiqués frequently twisted the news to serve the ends of the state. For example, in 1310, after being forced to adopt limits on how he could govern, King Edward II had marketplace proclamations issued asserting that the changes were his own doing and were adopted not as a concession, but affirmatively, for the well-being of the realm.

Marketplaces also became theatres for punishment and humiliation. Most were equipped with pillories that either were occupied or awaited the next thief, pox-spreading prostitute, or seller of bad fish. When pillories were not used, stocks (wooden leg restraints), threws (neck rings attached to posts), tumbrels (manure carts), and other instruments of disgrace were deployed. These devices were not especially harmful, but by disabling miscreants in crowded marketplaces, authorities permitted passersby to do violence to them, which seems to have happened with some frequency. Church-imposed penances were also imposed in marketplaces. It was common to see sinners dressed in sheets and walking barefoot while being whipped by clerics, or reciting confessions of their sins as bystanders insulted them. Whatever the forms of confinement or disgrace, the authorities' main aims—to shame offenders, warn the citizenry, and display power—were achieved because they were imposed in public.

Not surprisingly, the state exerted tight control over marketplaces. Markets could not operate without a royal charter, and once one was issued, everything that went on there was carefully regulated. Yet once assumed, authority must be constantly vindicated. By actively asserting its dominance over such places and turning them into channels for propaganda and punishment, the state created a new point of vulnerability for itself. Any unauthorized incursion into its zone of control or use of such places for antigovernment communication was perforce a loss of power. The peasants grasped, at least implicitly, the political dimensions of marketplaces. During the Peasants' Revolt, they took steps toward transforming them into their own conduits for speech, propaganda, and revenge. In the town of St. Albans, rebelling peasants and artisans returned to the marketplace to express, with violence, their hatred for their monastic overlord. Early in the revolt, they demanded access to neighboring forests, which they punctuated by nailing an unfortunate rabbit to the marketplace pillory. Later, they forced the abbot to release prisoners from jail, one of whom they promptly beheaded. The severed head was brought to the same pillory, where, according to one account, "it would appear openly to all that [the peasants] were able to enjoy new laws."[40] The use of the animal to symbolize the demand for hunting rights and the liberation of the prisoners sent clear enough messages, but affixing the creature and the head to the pillory communicated another critical point: that the marketplace and its instruments of punishment were now in the rebels' hands.

On the same day, in the village of Lakenheath, rebels captured prey of a much higher status: Sir John Cavendish, the chief justice of the Court of King's Bench, who personified the injustice emanating from high places. Cavendish was attacked by a mob and beheaded.

This strike against such a prominent figure was amplified when they carried his head fifteen miles to the marketplace of Bury St. Edmunds and attached it to the pillory for public viewing and derision. There was a vicious irony in this display: the rough justice that had routinely been meted out to the lower classes had been turned on the oppressors. But, as in St. Albans, the choice of venue to spread the news made the additional statement that authorities had lost control of the marketplace. Messages were now being transmitted to the regime from below, rather than to the peasantry from above, and in the king's own venue.[41]

Cavendish's head was removed eight days later, and the rebellion was crushed, but a key first stage in the development of free speech in England had nevertheless been reached. Marketplaces were not the only public spaces in which peasants could gather during the late Middle Ages—streets, village greens, and other places were also available—but they had become unique, state-controlled communications centers. Displaying the bloody emblems of revolt there demonstrated the rebels' understanding that taking over the marketplaces was itself a form of seditious speech. By briefly hijacking some market squares and, albeit in a crude manner, converting them into conduits for expression, the rebels of the Peasants' Revolt did more than convey grievances; they also struck at an important tool of power itself. The control of public spaces would continue as a flashpoint in free-speech battles well into the present day, where the struggle continues both on- and offline.

Meanwhile, laws against treason were developing in a way that would have profound effects on freedom of speech in England and, eventually, the United States. We have already seen how some Roman emperors equated their own psychological well-being with the state's welfare, and how they expanded the scope of treason to include insults against them. Starting in the fourteenth century and continuing for more than four centuries, the same dynamic applied in England, as the state repeatedly broadened the high crime of treason to encompass mere "imaginings" against the king—and then narrowed it again once the inevitable abuses occurred.

The punishments for treason were extreme. Offenders were torn into four pieces and their remains, along with their heads, were displayed in different places around London. The unwritten law also allowed the Crown to confiscate the property of the convicted, motivating some arbitrary prosecutions—such as for unauthorized hunting in the king's forest—and causing, in the marvelous understatement of Sir Matthew Hale, "great inconvenience and uncertainty."[42] In 1351, Parliament attempted to fix the situation with the first written Statute of Treasons, which confined the offense to direct action against the government but also targeted those who "compass or imagine the Death of our Lord the King" and his family.[43] While that phrase was meant to cover treasonous imaginings when accompanied by overt action against the monarch, later kings chafed at the limitation.

Richard II, whose reign was marked in its early years by the terror of the Peasants' Revolt, had the law amended in 1397 to eliminate the overt-act requirement. This new rule—in essence, a thought-crime— was adopted as Richard was combating intrigues, denuding Parliament of power, and violently settling old scores with several of his longstanding antagonists. In this anxious atmosphere, the prospect of death and dismemberment for errant speech or intention was deadly real. According to the historian James Stephen, "It is difficult to understand the object of this statute unless it was to convert treason into words, or indeed anything whatever which could be considered to indicate in any way hostility to the king."[44] Richard even made it treasonous to attempt to repeal the new treason law.

Whatever Richard II really intended (his mental health at this time is much debated), the new law failed to protect him. He was deposed in 1399 and died, likely by murder, the following year. His successor, Henry IV, reinstated the overt-act requirement for treason because, according to Hale, under Richard's regime "no man knew how he ought to behave himself, to do, to speak, or say for doubt of such pains of treason."[45] Richard's experiment with imagining-as-treason lasted barely two years, but it would periodically reappear in the English government's censorship toolkit in the centuries to come. Some later monarchs, particularly Henry VIII and George III, simply could not resist the urge to punish those who envisioned their downfall, affronted their dignity, or even agitated for the right to vote. The amorphous phrase "imagining the death of the King" gave them the latitude they needed to strike.

Two hundred years after the death of Richard II, the very memory of his defeat and demise spurred its own paranoid reactions. Early editions of Shakespeare's *The Life and Death of King Richard the Second* omitted the scene in which the "tired majesty" was deposed—a measure, some say, that was taken in deference to Queen Elizabeth, who saw uncomfortable parallels between Richard and herself. It seems that that bit of censorship was a prudent act of self-preservation by the printer rather than an act of government, but there was no ambiguity about the fate of the historian John Hayward. In 1599, after writing a pamphlet that described Richard's downfall and death, Elizabeth herself ordered him and his printer confined to the Tower of London.[46]

But before all that took place, the harried and debt-ridden Johannes Gutenberg would pull the first printed page from the first moveable-type press. This happened around 1450—he didn't bother to record the exact date—and with it, a process that had begun thousands of years earlier with the use of carved cylindrical seals on clay tablets was fulfilled. The modern world arguably began then, and censorship entered a new phase.

3

THE PRINTQUAKES OF THE SIXTEENTH
AND SEVENTEENTH CENTURIES

"Perhaps your fear in passing judgment on me is greater than my fear in receiving it." With those words to his judges, Giordano Bruno, one of the Italian Renaissance's foremost philosophers, was led to Rome's Campo de Fiori and burned alive with his books. His execution by the Roman Catholic Church in 1600 put an early end to a life that embodied an era in which all beliefs about the nature of the universe, the authority of states, and the role of the church in dictating faith were put under review. With the advent of the printing press, the circulation of ideas accelerated to what must have seemed like warp speed, leaving authorities to chase unorthodox ideas with increasingly futile—if brutal—measures. While Bruno posed no direct threat to the church, his widely read publications questioning its doctrines undermined the facade of infallibility on which church authority depended. Bruno's life and copies of his books were easily dispatched, but his judges' fears remained.

Bruno lived a peripatetic existence in a turbulent age. A lapsed Dominican priest, excommunicated Calvinist, and devotee of Copernicus, he wandered Protestant and Catholic Europe. He dodged censors, gave lessons, and published his theories about a centerless cosmos with endless celestial worlds in which God was manifest in a grain of sand, in all of life, and in the limitless stars. In his conception, there was neither absolute truth nor a limit to knowledge, and those who maintained otherwise were deluded. The Bible? Its moral teaching was worthwhile, but not much else. When asked during his trial about the Trinity, he said he doubted it. And when he was invited to recant his positions—after being held in a dungeon for seven years and facing death—he refused. To Bruno, retracting beliefs he had obtained through reasoned inquiry was impossible, particularly when the alternative was plainly absurd dogma.[1]

A spirit like Bruno's was the product of an era in which, to borrow from Yeats, the center of European society had failed to hold. By the time of Bruno's death, Europe was experiencing the convulsions of the Protestant Reformation, the Catholic Counter-Reformation, and ongoing wars realigning its power structures. The investigations of Copernicus had unmoored the fixed coordinates of the cosmos, while new voyages of discovery had invalidated maps and opened new frontiers of conflict. The old verities were disappearing, and a fresh intellectual climate was starting to take shape—one that accepted nothing on faith alone and encouraged discussion and reasoned inquiry. And despite mounting restrictions, books and pamphlets were spreading new ideas and driving debates everywhere. With every circumvented censorship decree, authorities were reminded of the limitations of their power. The Inquisition destroyed all the texts by Bruno that it could find, but copies survived. His works would influence thinkers such as Spinoza and Leibniz in the years to come and can be found online today.

MATH PRIMERS, MARTIN LUTHER, AND THE FIRST LOCKDOWNS

Most of the early printed books had nothing to do with the cosmos or new thinking. They were Greek and Roman classics, arithmetic and Latin guides, and even letter-writing manuals. Their circulation facilitated an informal teach-in of basic skills that fueled demand for more works on a broader range of subjects. As of 1500, at least thirty thousand editions had been printed across Europe, and a vibrant international distribution network was taking shape. Hundreds of presses churned out editions of a thousand or more books, often in vernacular languages and with multiple reprints of popular titles. Before printing, few people had owned more than a handful of books, but now vast libraries were being amassed. By 1539, for example, Christopher Columbus's son owned some fifteen thousand titles. As volume grew and prices dropped, even shopkeepers and artisans could afford to own a dozen or two vernacular books, which would have been inconceivable a generation earlier.[2]

The quantity of printed matter resulted in an astounding diffusion of knowledge, but equally significant was how it affected intellectual exchange. Before printing presses allowed people to publish their opinions, debates were conducted largely through letters or in person. It took a lot of time for ideas and opposing views to spread. Printing thrust opinions onto mass audiences and allowed anyone to respond, or simply to monitor debates and, if they wished, jump in with their own contributions—sometimes in a matter of weeks. Just as the Internet has metastasized controversies in our own day, so did the rapid circulation of printed material during this period. "Renaissance men may not have been more argumentative than their predecessors," observed the scholar Paul Grendler, "but the press amplified their words enormously."[3]

Print's disruptive potential was not lost on secular or religious establishments. As early as 1501, Pope Alexander VI declared that print could "widen the influence of pernicious works," and concluded that "full control over the printers" was necessary. Governments, meanwhile, began to pass restrictive laws. Vague censorship standards were set, such as Antwerp's 1529 ban on "evil doctrines or theological error," France's 1531 edict against "false doctrine," and the Swiss canton of Zurich's peculiar concern with "sneering at matrimony."[4] But these measures were mild next to the backlash against Martin Luther, the cantankerous monk whose stream of incisive attacks on the church and translation of the Bible into German assaulted the church's hegemony on faith, catalyzed the Protestant Reformation, and turned Europe's religious and political structures upside down. Authorities had their hands full. Luther and the press were made for each other; he used plain, emotional language and turned out pamphlets at a blistering clip. No sooner would one of Luther's targets respond to his printed diatribes than he would discover that the market was flooded with more provocative ones. There would have been no Reformation without Luther, and Luther—the first media star—was nothing without the printing press.

In 1520, soon after Luther is said to have nailed his Ninety-Five Theses against the door of Wittenberg's cathedral, Pope Leo X issued a bull ordering all the monk's books—which he likened to a "plague," a "wild boar," and a "cancerous disease"—burned. Luther's followers responded by burning the bull and other Catholic writings, as well as an effigy of the "antichrist" pope. Luther was excommunicated in 1521. This was followed the same year by the Hapsburg emperor Charles V's Edict of Worms, which contained a "law of printing" that prohibited Luther's works as well as any publications attacking the church, princes, or "honest people."[5] As the Reformation spread, Catholics and Protestants hardened their positions. Europe came apart, and censorship laws proliferated. The pages of vernacular Bibles were stuffed into the mouths and wounds of slaughtered Protestants, and the Inquisition and Catholic princes kept the bonfires lit with Protestant literature. Protestant authorities were no less censorious. They targeted the texts of Catholics, Jews, and—as rival Protestant sects multiplied—one another.

After a half century of chaos, authorities systematized their censorship efforts, issuing catalogs of offending books, licensing schemes to pre-clear or refuse texts, and imposing import restrictions. The most important catalog was the Vatican's *Index of Forbidden Books* (*Index Librorum Prohibitorum* (1559), which was intended to "expunge from human memory" the names of heretics, blacklisted printers, purveyors of certain sexual works, and other offending matter such as vernacular Bibles.[6] This wasn't the first such list; Pope Gelasius I had catalogued sixty "bad" books way back in 496.[7] It was the most extreme, however, banning the work of about 550 authors, including Luther, Calvin, Machiavelli, and Rabelais. Protestant scientists were also banned, not necessarily for their heretical opinions but because their faith was seen to contaminate all their work.

This first *Index* proved too draconian even for the church, and after several cities refused to enforce it, it was modified in 1564. The new *Index*, a work in progress until its abolition in 1966, incorporated most of the bans of its predecessor and included elaborate prepublication and enforcement rules, but it also allowed some previously forbidden books to squeak through. If a book's "chief matter" was "good," even though it contained some errors, the church would tolerate it if offending passages were expurgated. This policy made allowances for some scientific books by Protestant authors, but it also led to some peculiar results, particularly in the case of the Talmud. The new *Index* allowed the Talmud, as long as its "calumnies and insults to the Christian religion" were excised. In practice, this meant that all references to Jesus or his works were to be cut out (to the extent they existed), as well as mentions of Rome, the Jewish conception of the Messiah, and, oddly, the word "evil" — deletions that, taken together, made the text unintelligible in some instances. Talmudic scholars found ways to circumvent the expurgations. Censored sections were handwritten back into the margins of the texts, and the ink used to blot out passages was sometimes simply washed away—that is, until later popes and ecclesiastical authorities once again ordered that the entire text be burned.[8]

In the fractious Europe of the sixteenth and seventeenth centuries, where boundaries were being drawn and redrawn by the era's religious and other wars, it was not difficult to avoid censorship decrees and ignore the *Index*. Elaborate clandestine networks materialized to satisfy demand for banned books, which tended to become more popular because they were prohibited. When Galileo's *Dialogue on Two World Systems* went on the *Index* in the early seventeenth century, even Catholic monks rushed to get it, helping to push the black-market price to ten times the original. One canny German publisher told its authors to "write anything . . . that will be forbidden."[9] If authors ran into restrictions in one location, they could move elsewhere; a false title page or well-placed bribe was usually sufficient to move contraband across frontiers. And despite the harsh laws, scholars collected each other's works. When Gian Vincenzo Pinelli, whose personal lending library was perhaps the largest in Italy, wrote to a friend in Paris in 1574 to ask that books be shipped to him via Frankfurt into Venetian territory "because here in Venice I have the father inquisitor who is my friend," he did what others did every day: use petty corruption to keep ideas in circulation.[10]

The travails of William Tyndale, the first translator of the Bible into anything close to modern English, illustrate the savagery of censorship during this period as well as its futility, and the way it shapeshifted with the political tides. In 1522, Tyndale, an Oxford- and Cambridge-educated priest of extraordinary intellectual gifts, read Luther's illegal translation into German of the New Testament and resolved to do the same in his own language. He sought permission for the project from Cuthbert Tunstall, the bishop of London, but the bishop, following Catholic doctrine, declared the proposal heretical, so Tyndale went to the Continent to undertake the work. His first translation of the New Testament was published in Germany in 1526, and thousands of copies were smuggled into England. Those that were discovered were promptly set ablaze, and at least one printer was executed for selling them. Others were tortured and killed for reading them. Yet the smuggling continued, and Tunstall resorted to buying copies in bulk in order to destroy them. Tyndale himself reportedly sold copies to the bishop's agents to finance his work, which resulted in more of his Bibles being smuggled. Finally, Tyndale was betrayed to the church, excommunicated, and burned alive in 1536 near Brussels, along with copies of his works. His final words were "Lord, Open the King of England's eyes!" At the time of his execution, about fifty thousand copies of the Tyndale Bible were circulating in England.[11]

Tyndale's dying wish did not sway Henry VIII, but where he failed, English politics and the king's desire to divorce Catherine of Aragon succeeded. Tyndale was arrested just after Henry broke with the Vatican, which would not grant him his divorce, and established the Church of England under his supreme authority. Once Henry became an adversary of the Catholic Church, he no longer objected to Tyndale's translation, which was incorporated in large part into both the Great Bible authorized by Henry in 1538 and, nearly one hundred years later, the King James Bible.[12] Tyndale is now remembered as a martyr of the Reformation and, with Shakespeare, one of the architects of the modern English language. (The number of now-common phrases he coined—including "fall flat on his face," "pour out one's heart," "the apple of his eye," "fleshpots," and "go the extra mile"— is mind-boggling.) But he was a victim of bad timing: Had he translated the Bible a few years later, he might have been welcomed back to England. Instead, he paid with his life for violating censorship laws that would soon change in favor of his life's work. In 1994, the British Library paid more than one million pounds for one of Tyndale's original illustrated New Testaments, which it called "the most important printed book in the English language."[13]

WOODCUTS, BROKEN GLASS, AND MANGLED ORGANS: IMAGES AND ICONOCLASM

Printed images were also aggressively censored during the Reformation. Because European society was still largely illiterate, pictures delivered messages to a much wider audience than text, and often with a stronger impact—which Lutheran reformers grasped instinctively. In mass-produced woodcuts, the pope and the Catholic clergy were depicted as debauched demons, wallowing in ill-gotten luxury. Luther supervised the production of the *Passional Christi und Antichristi* (1521), a broadsheet illustrated by Lucas Cranach's woodcuts that juxtaposed the exemplary Jesus with the pope, who is depicted as the Antichrist. In another broadsheet, Luther is shown humbly studying Scripture while the pope gorges himself on food and drink and monks vomit around him from overindulgence. As Lutheranism spread, Luther's own image proliferated. He was often depicted with the rays of a halo emanating from his head, which his followers were said to kiss in reverence.[14] It was for these reasons that Charles V's Edict of Worms subjected "both printed and illustrated" materials to censorship, while other Catholic jurisdictions tried time and again to suppress unauthorized images.

Lutheranism did not object to sacred art in churches, but leaders of other Protestant sects, such as John Calvin and Huldrych Zwingli, felt very differently. Manic iconoclastic riots exploded throughout Protestant Europe and involved the destruction of religious images as well as organs, candlesticks, stained-glass windows, chalices, and other objects associated with Catholicism. Such things were said to violate the second commandment, against graven images, and had no place where the infinite and holy were concerned. Rather, they were seen as emblems of the wealth of the hated Catholic Church, its turn toward idolatry, and its insistence that only it could be the mediator between human beings and the divine. For the iconoclasts, the smashing of images and objects was a defining act of faith. Just as the burning of pagan books in late antiquity was an element of Christian conversions, so the wrecking of images was intended to vanquish the demons the church had planted in the spirit.

The August 1566 riots in Antwerp exemplify the vehement frenzy typical of the *Beeldenstorm*—"image storm"—in the Low Countries. Sparked in part by Calvinist ministers preaching to crowds in open-air meetings, the destruction soon gained its own momentum. In one night, according to a Protestant Welshman's account, "all the churches, chapels and houses of religion were utterly defaced, and no kind of thing left whole within them, but broken and utterly destroyed."[15] A horrified Catholic Englishman recounted the destruction of much of the Cathedral of Our Lady of Antwerp:

> These fresh followers of this new preaching threw down the graven and defaced the painted images, not only of our Lady but of all others in the town. They tore the curtains, dashed in pieces the carved work of brass and stone, brake the altars, spoiled the clothes and corporesses, wrested the irons, conveyed away or brake the chalices, pulled up the brass of the gravestones, not sparing the glass windows. . . .
>
> What shall I speak of the Blessed Sacrament of the altar, which they trod under their feet and (horrible it is to say!) shed also their stinking piss upon it.[16]

This was just one night, in one location, during a hot summer of devastation. There was a complex matrix of economic and political intrigue behind the plunder—including Protestant nobles fanning anti-Catholic and anti-Spanish sentiment for their own ends—but it was primarily motivated by religious zeal. One does not normally "shed . . . stinking piss" on sacramental bread and wine merely to advance another person's material objectives. By battering a cross or statue into fragments or smashing a stained-glass window, the iconoclasts meant to eliminate religious traditions that, in their view, had become idolatrous. Only by revealing such objects as so much worthless wood, stone, metal, or glass could they liberate the holiness from the materials in which it had been imprisoned.[17]

Bouts of iconoclasm began in England soon after Henry VIII broke with Rome in 1536 and went into high gear in 1547, when his ten-year-old son, Edward VI, took the crown. That year, the archbishop of Canterbury, Thomas Cranmer, oversaw a series of iconoclastic injunctions, starting with one to "see the suppression of idolatry and superstition" and ordering the clergy to forthwith "take away, utterly extinct, and destroy" a range of images and objects, including "shrines, all tables, candlesticks, trindles or rolls of wax, pictures, paintings, and all other monuments of . . . idolatry, and superstition: so that there remain no memory of the same in walls, glass-windows, or elsewhere."[18] Images in St. Paul's Cathedral and many London churches were destroyed. The process continued under Elizabeth I and, most horrifyingly, during the English Civil War of 1642–51 when, to choose one of countless examples, one thousand stained-glass images at Clare Church in Suffolk were wrecked in a single day.[19]

The gargantuan scale of iconoclastic destruction during the Reformation leaves one numb, as does the deeply troubling sight of a medieval statue of the crucified Christ with its feet, arms, and hands pounded off by sixteenth-century English reformers. When the Romans practiced *damnatio memoriae*, the aim was to obliterate the memory of the person depicted. When the Taliban shelled the giant Buddhas of Bamyan in Afghanistan in 2001, they meant to accomplish many things, but honoring Buddhism was not one of them. In this context, the batterers of Christ's statue meant, perhaps, to *protect* their savior by destroying his image, effectively crucifying him again.

MORE TREASONOUS IMAGININGS

Henry VIII suppressed dissent by any means necessary, without fussing over the details. He issued his own list of prohibited texts in 1529, set up England's first controls over the printing trade, with the aim of stamping out, among other things, "seditious opinions," and imposed fearsome penalties for anyone who dared disobey or disrespect him. It did not matter whether the targeted speech was religious or political. With the submission of the clergy to his authority, there was no longer a meaningful distinction between the two: Henry *was* the church and the state of England, and he guarded his top-dog status in both realms with acute and violent paranoia.

In this vein, the king took a page from Richard II and had laws passed that made it treason to express any words that offended his swollen self-regard. One could be disemboweled and quartered not just for rebellious actions but also for spoken or written words that "imagine[d]" or expressed a "wish, will, or desire" for harm against him; that declared him a heretic, usurper, tyrant, or schismatic; or that deprived the king of his "dignity." The situation at court became so uncertain that Henry's doctors were terrified to declare him ill, lest that lead them to the executioner.[20] As Henry's failed marriages multiplied and his wives met unpleasant ends, additional treason laws accumulated to keep the populace in line with his mercurial affections. After he divorced Catherine of Aragon and married Anne Boleyn, one could be executed for treason for questioning the validity of his new marriage. And once Anne was parted from her head, it became treason for anyone to express belief that Henry's marriages with either Anne or Catherine were lawful, or that the offspring from those unions were legitimate. Anyone refusing to take an oath to this effect would also be guilty of high treason.[21]

These pathological treason laws were repealed after Henry died, and England returned to the original "compassing or imagining the death of the King" statute from 1351. But even brief lapses in important rights scar the law: the forces of repression are often left stronger and the law's protections diminished. Richard II's short-lived expansion of the definition of treason in the fourteenth century to encompass mere words or wishes gave Henry a precedent with which to do the same more than a century later. After Henry VIII, there were few such prosecutions until the late eighteenth century, but those that were brought, as the historian Fredrick Siebert put it, "served to remind printers and publishers of the fate which awaited those who violated the law."[22] An overt action would again be necessary for a treason charge to stick but barely: That requirement could now be met merely by writing or printing materials that spoke of revolt. Regardless of whether the writings in fact caused an insurrection, their support for the idea was enough to bring an author or printer to a gruesome end.

This was the wretched fate that befell John Twyn, who printed an anonymously written pamphlet, *A Treatise of the Execution of Justice*, which argued for King Charles II's accountability to his subjects and the people's right to revolt if he refuses. Twyn's trial, conducted in 1664 in London's Old Bailey, was a pathetic affair. Twyn seemed confused by what was going on around him and befuddled by the idea that his life was hanging by a thread. Claiming that he was a "very poor man" and had not read the offending pamphlet, he begged to be judged "in the presence of God," and for a lawyer to help him. The chief judge assured him that God was in the courtroom and, as Twyn had no one to represent him, the judges "are to be of counsel with you." Little good they did him. The chief judge announced to the jury that the book's title was enough to establish treason, and each sentence of its text "is as absolute high treason as ever I yet heard of. . . . What a horrid thing this is!"

The judgment was as much as preordained. Merely for printing the pamphlet, and with no evidence that it had incited revolt, Twyn was sentenced to die. The book itself was regarded as a declaration of war against the king. It was, argued the prosecutor, "as if [Twyn] had raised an army to do this." After Twyn was convicted, the prison chaplain told him that he might be allowed to live if he exposed the pamphlet's author. In one of history's quiet acts of breathtaking honor, Twyn refused, stating that it was "better one suffer than many." Protesting his ignorance and innocence to the end, Twyn was beheaded and his body cut into four pieces. His head was placed on a spike over Ludgate, the westernmost gate in London Wall, and his quartered body was displayed at other gates.[23]

Also beheaded was Algernon Sidney, for what can best be termed treasonous thoughts. Unlike the hapless Twyn, Sidney had quite the résumé: a member of Parliament, he fought on the side of Oliver Cromwell and his Roundheads during the English Civil War. Later, when the monarchy had been restored, he became an active critic of Charles II. Upon his arrest in 1683 for plotting against Charles, his house was searched and an unpublished manuscript, *Discourses Concerning Government*, was discovered. That document, which argued eloquently for the people's right to choose their own form of government and to revolt when their trust was violated, became the main basis for prosecution, as there was little other evidence. Sidney objected at trial to his private musings being used against him: "Tis a right of mankind," he argued, "to write in their own closets what they please for their own memory" and from which no harm results "unless they publish it." The judge's response: "Curse not the King, not in thy thoughts, not in thy bedchamber, or the birds of the air will carry it."[24] Sidney was executed, but the birds flew far. The Founding Fathers of the United States read the *Discourses* avidly, and the work would later be described as a "textbook of revolution" in America.[25]

OTHER ENGLISH SPEECH RESTRICTIONS: SLIT NOSES, SEDITIOUS LIBEL, AND THE RISK OF TRUTH

The executions of Twyn and Sidney must have been quite the sights: heads rolling and bodies disemboweled, all because of words and thoughts. Yet in the charged political atmosphere of the times, such gory spectacles risked causing rebellion, rather than suppressing it. And given the profusion of seditious materials in circulation, it was impractical to use the cumbersome legal machinery of treason against every troublemaker. So the Crown and Parliament used less heavy-handed methods of silencing critics and terrorizing the populace. If beheading and quartering people were too provocative, controlling the printing trade and jailing and mutilating pamphleteers seemed appropriate, especially when they spoke the truth.

First, the government monopolized the printing trade through the Stationers' Company. During the reign of Elizabeth I and well into the seventeenth century, nothing could be printed, nor could a printer operate, without the guild's approval. The Stationers' Company had nearly unchecked power to seek out and destroy materials either printed without a license or deemed dangerous to religious or civil authority, and to arrest violators and destroy their presses. Stationers' Company officers showed up unannounced regularly at London printing houses to see what was being produced, which was hazardous work: printers often attacked the company's officers, and the guild was compelled to pay for court cases against the assailants.

Offending materials were taken to the Stationers' Hall and burned, but forbidden texts often squeaked through the inspections—as occurred with a 1579 publication that infuriated Queen Elizabeth, bearing the snappy title *The Discovery of a Gaping Gulf whereunto England is like to be swallowed by another French Marriage, if the Lord forbid not the banns, by letting her Majesty see the sin and punishment thereof.* The pamphlet, written and published anonymously by the lawyer John Stubbs, was a cri de coeur against the queen's possible marriage to the brother of the king of France, the Duke of Anjou. Elizabeth had, most likely, not been serious about the union—betting men in London gave the marriage one-to-three odds—but the possibility of her marrying a Catholic, and a French one, no less, was enough to drive Protestants such as Stubbs to near apoplexy.[26]

Gaping Gulf argued that the marriage would obliterate the gains made by the Reformation and work to England's disadvantage, but Stubbs also railed against the "hissing and lisping" duke, spoke of "Our Dear Queen Elizabeth . . . led blindfold as a poor lamb to the slaughter," and compared the union to "the uneven yoking of a clean ox to an unclean ass." As if these intemperate comments were not enough to put Elizabeth into a rage, Stubbs also had the temerity to discuss the forty-six-year-old monarch's ability to conceive. It wasn't just the substance of these comments that riled the queen; she appears to have been even more incensed by a mere subject's impudence in presuming to criticize her decisions. She issued a lengthy, violent proclamation against the pamphlet, accusing it of "seditiously and rebelliously stirring up . . . Her Majesty's subjects to fear their own utter ruin." Elizabeth ordered the Stationers' Company to discover who had printed it and to destroy all available copies. Stubbs was soon apprehended and, in a fast-tracked trial, sentenced to lose his right hand. Before that was done, he apologized to Elizabeth, saying he felt worse about displeasing her than about being mutilated. Immediately after his hand was severed, he doffed his hat with his remaining one and cried, "God save the Queen!"

Stubbs was punished under a law against "authors and sowers of seditious writings."[27] Had he published his tract a few decades later, he could have been convicted of seditious libel, one of England's, and later (in various forms), the United States' most effective censorship tools. Born in the swamp of the Star Chamber in 1606, it allowed whipping, branding, mutilation, and indefinite imprisonment for speech that evinced disrespect for the government or church, even—or especially—when it was true. The idea was that authorities were infallible: they existed for the people's own good, and anything that diminished their majesty had to be suppressed.[28] As explained in 1704 by John Holt, lord chief justice, in a case involving accusations of government corruption, "No government can subsist" when "the people [have] an ill opinion" of it.[29] Since factual statements were more likely to invite derision against authority than false ones, that was all the more reason to condemn them. While seditious libel convictions spared the lives of critics, their slit noses, brands, or severed ears were loud and lasting testaments to the risks of criticizing arbitrary power.

Among the best-known seditious libel cases during this period are those brought against the Puritan lawyer and tireless killjoy William Prynne, whose attacks on contemporary church decorations and mores put him into repeated conflict with ecclesiastical and temporal authorities. His thousand-page *Histriomastix* (often translated as *The Player's Scourge*, 1632)—a hysterical assault on stage plays and other "intolerable mischiefs" such as hunting, Christmas-keeping, and dancing—was interpreted as an attack on King Charles I and his queen, who had participated in a play just as the book was published. Prynne was brought before the Star Chamber, railroaded to conviction, and then pilloried, fined, imprisoned, and deprived of his ears. The court would have done better to remove his fingers, for he continued to write and publish denunciations of what he believed were the excesses of the Church of England and the archbishop of Canterbury, William Laud, among other prelates. For this he was tried again for seditious libel; his ear stumps were cut off; his cheeks branded with the letters "SL," for "seditious libeler"; and he was sentenced to prison for life.[30] His first punishment had been barely noticed; during the second, a large crowd watched in horror, to the surprise of authorities. Prynne's resilience in the face of such cruel treatment helped to galvanize support for the Puritans and antagonism against Laud and the bishops.

The final engine for speech suppression in sixteenth- and seventeenth-century England was Parliament itself, which was aggressive in stifling public knowledge about its own proceedings and punishing slights against itself and its members. Ironically, these repressions grew from Parliament's own appeals for freedom of speech within its own halls and in its interactions with the Crown. Starting in about the fourteenth century, the speaker of the House of Commons, fearful of the king's wrath, opened each session with a request to the king for forgiveness for anything he would say that was displeasing.[31] By the reign of Henry VIII, that plea had evolved into a petition for free discussion within Parliament, which was not recognized until 1689, when the English Bill of Rights guaranteed that "the Freedom of speech and debates in Parliament ought not to be impeached or questioned in any court or place out of Parliament."

Notably, that guarantee did not extend to the citizenry or to the press, and as Parliament's power grew, it became a dedicated enforcer of speech repression. Even though, technically, it represented the populace, Parliament rejected the notion that it was *accountable* to them, which helps to explain why it so actively suppressed reporting on its own proceedings. The House of Lords shut down all reports of its voting or deliberations. The House of Commons even barred the speaker from publishing his own speeches without permission, but in 1681 it allowed official reports of its voting, as censored by the speaker. Yet despite these prohibitions, leaks happened repeatedly as rival parliamentary factions strove to gain popular support for their positions—which were often published in coffeehouse newsletters.[32] At one point, a newsletter publisher was beaten up by a member of the House of Lords who was unhappy about being mentioned (no doubt unfavorably) in one of the issues. And in 1667, the Lords charged one William Carr for publishing something "libelous and scandalous" in a newsletter that offended Lord Gerard of Brandon. The newsletter was ordered burned, while Carr was fined, sentenced to stand in the pillory, and imprisoned indefinitely.[33]

The English licensing laws would come and go, finally to lapse forever in 1694, and treason would rarely be charged against mere dissent until its revival under George III, at the end of the eighteenth century. Yet hardly a year would pass without at least a few unfortunate writers, speakers, or publishers facing a seditious libel charge. By the late 1760s, when William Blackstone's seminal *Commentaries on the Laws of England* was published, the doctrine had hardened: there would be no prior restraints against speech, but should the speech, once published, be deemed seditious, then criminal proceedings could proceed. In that case, Blackstone wrote, "The liberty of the press, properly understood, is by no means infringed or violated."[34]

THE TENTATIVE EMERGENCE OF REASONED ARGUMENTS FOR FREEDOM OF SPEECH

The chaos that plagued seventeenth-century Britain—religious strife, a king beheaded for treason, and a civil war, among other things— quickened reflections on the nature and purpose of speech and how it should be governed. The idea began to emerge that liberty of expression and thought were rights in themselves, and the role of government was to protect those rights, not to curtail them arbitrarily. The advocates for such rights were chiefly interested in their own safety and in that of their confederates, but they started to craft their arguments in terms that spoke of the universal values of free speech—for individual development and as elements of a just society. While these ideals would have to wait until the next century to find their way into any state's governing documents—and even the most committed libertarians at the time remained uncomfortable with speech made directly against the state—those who resisted censorship were given a new and compelling lexicon to use in their struggles.

The Puritan Revolution and the English Civil War led to an unprecedented, if quite brief and chaotic, collapse of authority over the press in England. "Quite simply," explains the historian Margaret Jacob, "the mechanism of censorship (as of much else) broke down under the impact of civil war."[35] The abolition of the Star Chamber in 1641 freed the printing trade of one royal master, while the Stationers' Company was beset by confusion. Into the breach (and until Parliament soon issued new controls) poured a wave of unlicensed proto-newspapers called "newsbooks," whose number rose from 4 in 1641 to 722 in 1645. Pamphlets, too, proliferated, with many of their authors addressing questions of whether and how speech should be regulated.[36]

Some of the most important of these authors came from the ranks of radical dissidents called the Levellers, who spoke forcefully against censorship and licensing and in favor of freedom of religion and popular sovereignty. Many of their tracts—the scholar Margaret Atwood Judson called them "the first great outburst of democratic thought in history"—argued for "the least restraint upon the Press," and held that people could not enjoy liberty without "speaking, writing, printing, and publishing their minds freely."[37] But even William Walwyn, one of the more consistently radical Leveller thinkers, could not bring himself to embrace a system in which *all* speech was allowed. In *The Compassionate Samaritane* (1644) he argued against the state-sanctioned licensing system, which had returned the year before, and for liberty of conscience and freedom of expression, yet he was still not prepared to embrace complete freedom. Materials "dangerous or scandalous to the state," he emphasized, are "justly and on good grounds prohibited."[38]

Also published in 1644 was the Puritan poet John Milton's *Areopagitica*, perhaps the most important of this period's polemics against censorship. The tract, written after he had gotten into trouble with the Stationers' Company and Parliament over his unlicensed pamphlets defending divorce (his wife had deserted him) was mainly an argument for "the liberty of unlicenc'd printing," but it was also a brilliant disquisition on freedom of mind, the unhindered pursuit of truth through the clash of opinions, and the tyranny of authorities that insist on uniform beliefs. Drawing on precedents reaching back to ancient Greece (the title derives from a speech by the Greek orator Isocrates), he argued, "He who destroys a good book kills reason itself, kills the image of God, as it were in the eye." As for Milton himself, he demanded freedom of expression, writing: "Give *me* the liberty to know, to utter, and to argue freely, according to conscience, above all liberties." (Italics added.)

Impressive, but there were important catches, and they start with the personal pronoun "me." Milton's pleas for tolerance extended only to ideas emerging from the minds and mouths of Protestants. "No law," he wrote, "can possibly permit" the ideas of Catholics, atheists, or non-Christians—that is, most of humanity—to circulate freely. Rather, they should be "extirpat[ed]." And while he was firmly against the prepublication licensing of books, he readily agreed that "mischievous and libelous" materials should be destroyed, finding "the fire and the executioner will be the most effectuall remedy that mans prevention can use." It also appears that Milton intended the freedoms he advocated to cover only serious and scholarly books and not the budding partisan press. In 1651, he briefly took on the post of official censor of at least two newsbooks.[39]

Before we judge Milton or Walwyn harshly, we should bear in mind that there was no tradition in the seventeenth century of supporting total freedom of expression. In the face of centuries of aggressive censorship, their pleas for toleration of even some forms of unauthorized or dissenting speech were groundbreaking, both in their audacity and in their rationales. Merely to appeal for liberty of expression and thought as rights in themselves was profoundly radical and unprecedented, and it carried real personal risk.

Perhaps the most unqualified polemic for freedom of individual thought came out of Amsterdam. In his *Tractatus Theologico-Politicus* (1670), the philosopher Baruch Spinoza argued that in a free state everyone should be "allowed to think what he will and to say what he thinks," as "everyone is by absolute natural right the master of his own thoughts." He concluded that "it is impossible for the mind to be completely under another's control," and therefore it is useless for governments to try: "The greater the effort to deprive them of freedom of speech, the more obstinately do they resist." As such "freedom can be granted without detriment to public peace, to piety, and to the right of the sovereign . . . it must be granted if these are to be preserved."[40]

Yet Spinoza still would not protect calls to overthrow the government or disobey laws, or speech that could "stir up popular hatred" against authorities. People should be free to argue for change, but it must be done through rational argument. If that is unsuccessful, then that should be the end of the matter. Even with these caveats, Spinoza's book was greeted with alarm. The Catholic Church denounced it as "a book forged in hell by a renegade Jew and the devil," and the book, along with other of Spinoza's works, was banned at least fifty times.[41] Nor was this the first time Spinoza had suffered opprobrium for his unorthodox ideas. Some fourteen years before his *Tractatus*, he had been excommunicated by his own Portuguese-Jewish community in Amsterdam.

Meanwhile, across the pond, the American colonies adopted English speech restrictions wholesale. "The American people," observed the historian Leonard Levy, "simply did not understand that freedom of thought and expression means equal freedom of thought and expression for the other fellow, especially the one with hated ideas."[42] One of the first book burnings took place in Boston in 1650, when William Pynchon's "erroneous," "unsound," and "heretical" *The Meritorious Price of Our Redemption* was torched by the public executioner. Pynchon, a prosperous fur trader (and ancestor of the novelist Thomas Pynchon), had been butting heads with the Puritans running the Massachusetts Bay Colony for some time, and his dense little book did not help matters. Not only did it question many precepts of Puritan theology, but, worse, it challenged the local clergy's monopoly on biblical interpretation and implicitly argued for religious tolerance, which the Puritans took as a direct threat. Before Pynchon's personal situation became too precarious, he absconded to England.[43]

The colonies' first multipage newspaper, *Publick Occurrences both Foreign and Domestic*, was shuttered in 1690 after one issue. The reason given was that it had been printed without a license, but the Massachusetts governor was likely more incensed at the content of the paper's articles, including one that accused the French king of having slept with his own daughter-in-law—something Puritan clergymen thought unsuitable for their parishioners' delicate sensibilities.[44] No other newspaper would be printed in Boston for ten years. The publisher, Benjamin Harris, had been running into legal headwinds on account of his stories for years, and this was not his last. Prior to his arrival in Massachusetts he had been pilloried and imprisoned in England for publishing a piece advocating the dissolution of Parliament. When he returned to England in 1695, he continued publishing provocative political opinions and getting arrested.

Nothing strained the social fabric of the Massachusetts colony more than the witch trials of 1692–93, when hundreds of people were accused of witchcraft, and twenty were executed. Few publicly criticized the colony's murderous hysteria more pointedly than Thomas Maule, a Quaker who became America's first victor for freedom of the press. Two years after the trials ended, Maule wrote *Truth Held Forth and Maintained according to the Testimony of the Holy Prophets*

Christ and his Apostles recorded in the Holy Scriptures, which caustically, and, as the title suggests, tediously, criticized the grandees who had led the witch hunts and let the trials get so out of hand. In good time, he wrote, God would exact His own vengeance. Maule was promptly arrested. The book was burned, and Maule was jailed for a year. At the trial, the judges instructed the jury to convict, but the jurors refused and entered a verdict of not guilty. When asked to explain the verdict, the foreman said the case should have been decided by "divines," rather that civil judges and jurors.[45]

No one discussed freedom of the press at Maule's trial, which seems to have been decided more as a matter of the jury's religious conscience, and in response to Maule's passionate courtroom theatrics, than anything else. Again, neither the vocabulary nor the mindset of free speech was in place at that time, and there is no indication that Maule, who in fact believed in witches, had the liberties of anyone other than himself and perhaps other Quakers in mind. But the verdict, and the jury's readiness to ignore the judges' direct instructions, kindled a faint spark of light illuminating a very long path toward free expression in America.

4

REVOLUTION AND CONTROL
IN THE EIGHTEENTH CENTURY

The eighteenth century tried on the idea of free expression, and didn't like the way it fit. Throughout this period, there were increasingly muscular pushes to open unrestrained debate, often led by groups seeking power, only to see those same parties often slam the door shut once their political objectives were realized. We have the eighteenth century to thank for such milestones as the First Amendment and the French Declaration of the Rights of Man and of the Citizen, but the broad ideals expressed by these documents would not come close to being made a practical reality for quite some time.

Society was changing fundamentally, beyond the powers of any individual malcontents to influence much. The uneven spread of prosperity and literacy, the start of the great migration from the countryside to the cities as the Industrial Revolution started to get under way, and the rush of information across borders and among classes rattled institutions at their foundations. Each transformation diminished old rationales for state authority. Soon, revolution was in the air and on the barricades, triggering more demands for reform. In response, Britain and the new French and American regimes frantically tried to maintain control by restricting the press and individual expression.

While speech never had more than fleeting and incomplete protection from the law, *freedom of speech* emerged as a rallying cry, and a host of advocates—from the highbrow to the lowly pamphleteer—propelled their demands for political change with the first full-throated arguments for liberty of expression.

"Only the wicked Governors of Men dread what is said of them," wrote the influential English pamphleteers known together as Cato.[1] There was plenty of dread to go around. The notions that governments derive their power from the governed and are answerable to the people alone constituted a direct threat to established authority. The motors of repression fired on all cylinders to stop the spread of such ideas. In 1775, for example, debates in Parliament over the American colonies' rebellion were closed to reporters, while Spain, Russia, Bavaria, and Austria banned writings favorable to the French Revolution. In some cases, all books from France were banned.[2] The events in France so rattled the British government that it jailed a printer for publishing the lyrics to a popular song celebrating the fall of the Bastille, and charged a lunatic with treason for prophesying the fall of the British Empire.

Yet there were more similarities between the pre- and post-revolutionary orders than anyone would have admitted. In 1792, three years after freedom of speech and the press was guaranteed in France, censorship returned with deadly force: books were burned, and writers out of step with the regime were persecuted and killed. In the United States, in 1798—just a few years after the First Amendment was ratified—Congress passed a sedition law criminalizing most political dissent. When that law expired, President Thomas Jefferson pardoned those who had been targeted under it, while advocating privately for the prosecution of his own critics.

There is a wide gulf between arguing for free expression and adopting it as government policy, and those fighting for power often forget that the speech of their adversaries is no less worthy of protection than their own. "Freedom of Speech is the great Bulwark of Liberty; they prosper and die together," wrote Cato in 1721. The eighteenth century saw the ideals of toleration prosper, while also witnessing the demise of many for writing or speaking their minds.

SUPPRESSING THE MIND'S "NATURAL DICTATES" IN BRITAIN

British censorship controversies turned on sharply conflicting notions about the nature of government authority and human rights. On one side of the debate, there were popular agitators such as Cato, who drew on the ideas of the philosopher John Locke and others to assert that everyone is born with natural, inalienable liberties, which government may restrain only in extraordinary circumstances. These include the rights to "pursue the natural . . . Dictates of [one's] own Mind; to think what he will, and act as he thinks," and the right of citizens to check tyranny by speaking out against government abuses.[3] Pamphlets advancing these ideas were strewn on tables in pubs and coffee houses, and were joined toward the century's end by the immensely popular works of Thomas Paine (1737–1809), which spoke of revolution. The ideas of Cato, Paine, and their fellow travelers were as galvanizing to a restive population as they were menacing to the Crown and Parliament.

On the debate's other side, representing the traditional order, were figures such as the influential jurist William Blackstone. He agreed that the law should protect basic immutable rights but also wrote that natural liberty was a "wild and savage" condition, infinitely less desirable than "legal obedience and conformity." A well-governed society requires "due subordination of rank; that the people may know . . . such as are set over them, in order to yield them their due respect and obedience."[4] Put another way, society's stability depends on the lower ranks knowing their place and staying there. Given this view, it followed that "blasphemous, immoral . . . or seditious libels" reflected not liberty but licentiousness, which should (after trial) be punished "for the preservation of peace and good order, of government and religion."[5] People must be free to speak without first obtaining government permission, but if what they said undermined respect for authority, that could be criminalized.

The end of prepublication licensing in 1694 launched a spate of newspapers and other publications, particularly from Grub Street, the tawdry London lane where hack writers, printers, and publishers operated. The free-for-all didn't last long. Decrying the "evil" of "false and scandalous Libels such as are a reproach to any government," Queen

Anne urged Parliament in 1712 to shut down the news trade, which it tried to do with taxes, in a series of Stamp Acts. Expressing alarm at the new laws, Jonathan Swift, one of Grub Street's better-known denizens, wrote to a friend: "Did you hear that Grub Street is dead and gone last week? . . . I know not how long it will hold."[6] As it turned out, quite long indeed. While the taxes were burdensome—and made hacks-for-hire such as Swift, Daniel Defoe, and Henry Fielding even more susceptible to bribes than they already were—publishers ingeniously exploited the laws' many loopholes, and the press pressed on. "Grub Street" soon went from a geographical designation to a shorthand term for all manner of lower-end publishing.

The British government also deployed seditious libel and prosecutions by Parliament against troublesome speech, exposing writers and publishers to imprisonment, fines, and other indignities. It was here that the rubber of Blackstone's "due subordination of rank" and "good order of government and religion" arguments met the road. Laced through these ideas was the notion that the king—indeed, the entire government—was due not just obedience but outright reverence: criticism violated God's plan for a well-ordered society. The quasi-religious overtones of seditious libel were revealed in a famous 1735 New York colony case (applying English law), whereby the newspaperman John Peter Zenger was charged with denigrating the colonial governor. The jury was told that words disparaging an official, even if true, were *worse* than those against a private person because they injured the government. The prosecutor invoked Saint Paul's teaching that speaking out against the state was an offense against God, "for it is written, thou shalt not speak evil of the ruler of the People."[7]

The principle that the king and his government were above reproach, and could jail anyone who exposed them to contempt, drove continuous seditious libel prosecutions—often accompanied, for maximum intimidation, by raids, searches, and pretrial imprisonment. The fact that juries were only allowed to determine whether the publication had occurred and that judges (members of government, after all) decided whether the writings were illegal resulted in many convictions, but juries were sometimes too outraged to play along. This occurred in the famous Junius trials of 1769–70, named for the pseudonymous author of a bitingly critical open letter to King George III, which warned the king of revolution. It was published in Henry Woodfall's newspaper, the *Public Advertiser*; the edition sold out within hours, following which it was reprinted in five more papers. The government never found "Junius," so it channeled its fury at the six publishers, along with an unfortunate Piccadilly bookseller who had sold a copy to a government agent. They were all charged with seditious libel.

The book merchant was quickly convicted. The next trial, against Woodfall, should have been another cakewalk for the prosecution, but the new, less cooperative jury threw egg on its face instead. Defying the judge's instructions, the jury found Woodfall guilty of "printing and publishing only," which sent the proceedings into chaos and ultimately saved him from prison. A retrial was prevented after a juror walked off with the government's only copy of Woodfall's newspaper. The trials that followed, against two of the other publishers, produced explicit not-guilty jury verdicts. The government wisely decided to cut its losses and did not bring the other publishers to trial.[8]

The juries' defiant refusals to jail their countrymen was reported by the popular press on a minute-by-minute basis. The coverage amplified the populace's shifting mood and highlighted that seditious libel had become a less-than-surefire weapon against antigovernment speech. That is not to say, however, that it was dead. Prosecutions and convictions continued throughout the century, and the prospect of jail, the pillory, and fines for speaking out against the government, or even publishing a disloyal verse, surely led to broad self-censorship. Imagine the impression made when James Montgomery, a Scottish poet and newspaper publisher, was hauled into court for printing the lyrics to a ditty titled "A Patriotic Song by a Clergyman of Belfast," which celebrated the start of the French Revolution. Montgomery printed it in 1794, two years after it was first published and, critically, one year after England had gone to war with France. The judge told the jury that the song might have been innocent when it was first published (i.e., while England and France were at relative peace), but changing conditions could make it "grossly seditious." If the song could now be construed as advocating England's defeat, it was illegal. Undoubtedly roused by war fervor, the jury agreed, and Montgomery went to prison.[9]

One of the most colorful targets of seditious libel actions was the radical MP and charismatic scallywag John Wilkes (1725–97), whose provocations and mistreatment by the government of George III made him a transatlantic hero in the cause of freedom of the press. Brilliant and flamboyant, he managed to turn his trials into entertaining spectacles. After meeting Wilkes, the historian Edward Gibbon echoed others in describing him as "stained with every vice," "full of blasphemy and bawdy," and resolved to exploit "this time of dissension" to "make his fortune." Still, even the gentleman scholar conceded that Wilkes had "infinite wit and humor," and he "scarce . . . met with a better companion."[10] Major players in the cause of civil rights are rarely exemplary characters, but those who pass their lives in quiet obedience to the rules are rarely willing to take risks to bring about change. Wilkes was no model of rectitude, but his magnetic mix of theatricality and opportunism pounded new cracks into the government's façade of infallibility.

Looking to make some money and increase his profile after being elected to Parliament, Wilkes started the *North Briton* in 1762. The first issue lifted from Cato to declare: "The liberty of the press is the birthright of a BRITON, and is justly esteemed the firmest bulwark of the liberties of this country. It has been the terror of all bad ministers." Wilkes's sharp rhetoric and relentless barbs against his enemies in government resonated, and soon he was publishing the *North Briton* in large weekly runs. When asked how far the liberty of the press extended in England, he responded, "I cannot tell, but I am trying to know."[11] He found out in 1763 with the *North Briton*'s forty-fifth issue, in which he castigated the king and certain ministers for their incompetence in managing the conclusion of the Seven Years' War. His arrest, along with dozens of others who printed and sold the paper, set off a series of high-profile jousts in Parliament and the courts, every stage of which he played for maximum public-relations effect. When, for example, he managed to extricate himself from the Tower of London on a technicality after his arrest, ten thousand supporters escorted him home, shouting, "Wilkes and liberty!" Yet there was never any doubt about the ultimate outcome of the case. "No. 45" was, after a series of machinations, found to constitute seditious libel, and was ordered burned.

Wilkes's fortunes weren't helped when "An Essay on Woman," an unpublished bawdy parody of Alexander Pope's *An Essay on Man*, which Wilkes had cowritten, came into Parliament's possession. (A sample of its unadorned content: "Let us [have sex] since life can little more supply / Than a few good Fucks, and then we die.") Nor were Parliament and the king amused that the book's cover featured a large phallus, which the preface said belonged to a bishop. The work was, curiously, read in its entirety before the House of Lords, and Wilkes was charged with blasphemy. He skipped the country to France and was convicted in absentia. Broke and hungry for attention, he returned to England in 1768, where he was again elected to Parliament and jailed for his earlier offenses. From prison, he continued to poke his enemies with his pen and his incarceration sparked what became known as the St. George's Field riots. Wilkes was again expelled from Parliament but later was back in the Commons as one of its most popular members—that is, until he was ousted again. Turning to London city politics, he became an alderman and enlisted a mob of supporters to back a successful effort to secure de facto permission for newspapers to report on the proceedings in the Commons.

The vicissitudes of Wilkes's life were far from over, but the details matter less than how he was perceived. Many of his enemies viewed him—not unfairly—as a contemptible rabble-rouser, but for advocates of free speech and those critical of abuses of power, he was a fearless provocateur willing to throw himself against the machine of a hidebound government bent on guarding its privileges and imprisoning critics. Along with "Junius," "Wilkes" became a byword for bold action among the leaders of the American Revolution, and his defiance of the Crown and Parliament inspired Colonial resistance against the mother country.

England's most fervent supporter of the American Revolution, and its most influential and incendiary pamphleteer by far, was Thomas Paine. His immensely popular *Common Sense*, written in the American Colonies in 1776, was a plainspoken denunciation of monarchy and a defense of American independence from British rule, which had been fully metabolized by Thomas Jefferson when he wrote the Declaration of Independence later that year. Returning to England and throwing his support behind the French Revolution, Paine unleashed *Rights of Man* in 1791–92, which celebrated the French National Assembly's recognition of the right to "speak, write, and publish freely" and affirmed that "speech is . . . one of the natural rights of man always retained." Paine's revolutionary program went much further, proposing reforms to raise taxes on the wealthy and reduce the burden on the artisan and working classes. He also advocated free education, old-age and veterans' pensions, free meals for the hungry, and much more. In his proposals, one can see the germ of a new idea: government should look after the well-being of its citizens, particularly the disadvantaged.

The perfect text for its time, *Rights of Man* sold explosively, inspiring the formation of political societies and becoming one of the foundation texts of the English working-class movement.[12] According to Leonard Levy, "If the hod carrier, prostitute, and common soldier could read, Paine was their favorite, and if they could not read, they could understand what Paine meant if someone read him aloud."[13] Neither the sales figures nor the text's resonance with the revolutionary rhetoric prevalent in France was lost on the British government, which responded with characteristic force. Propaganda against "mad Tom" poured from official channels, booksellers carrying the work were harassed, and Prime Minister William Pitt declared that it advocated "the destruction of monarchy and religion and the total subversion of the established form of government."[14]

After Paine's publisher pleaded guilty to seditious libel, Paine left England for—where else?—France and was tried in absentia on the same charge. The prosecutor argued that the book was seditious not only for its content but because it was addressed to those "whose minds cannot be supposed to be conversant with subjects of this sort" and because it was sold on the cheap. In other words, *Rights of Man* spoke directly to those whose lot its author intended to improve. Despite a brilliant, theatrical defense by Paine's attorney, Thomas Erskine—who fainted during his four-hour-long closing argument—the result was a foregone conclusion: Paine was convicted. From that point forward, every bookseller hawking *Rights of Man* risked being prosecuted, and many were. Paine received French citizenship and was elected to the new republic's National Convention, but soon fell out of favor due to, among other things, his vocal objection to the beheading of King Louis XVI. With the help of pressure by friendly Americans, he barely escaped the guillotine.

Political speech could indeed be dangerous business in the century's closing years, and while the British government was officially appalled at developments in revolutionary France, it often appeared to emulate the Revolution's murderous elimination of dissenters. In 1794, the Crown sought death for treason of twelve leaders of the fast-growing movement for parliamentary reform and universal male suffrage. The immediate circumstances were the beheading of Louis XVI, the war with France, and the not unreasonable fear of plots by French agents against George III. Equally significant, however, was the entry of the artisan and working classes onto the British political scene. Previous parliamentary reform movements (none of which demanded the popular vote) had been the province of what Lord Lansdowne called "a few men of superior sense" and not, as the Earl of Lauderdale put it, the "refuse of the people," who had been egged on by the likes of Paine. The former were salutary; the latter, seditious.[15] The government began arresting the new reform movement's leaders, ransacking their homes, and throwing them into the Tower of London. Determined to make a lasting impression on the rabble, it dusted off the fourteenth-century Statute of Treasons and charged the reformers with the capital crime of imagining the king's death. No evidence was produced that the defendants harbored, much less acted on, murderous intent toward the king, because there was none. Rather, the idea was that the reform movement's challenges to the political status quo were treasonous because they amounted to a threat on George's "political body." The prosecutors argued that those who seek revisions to the political order, especially when they spoke to the lower classes, deserve the state's most severe punishment, regardless of whether they had tangible designs on the king's life.

None of the juries bought this brand of metaphysics. In the first trial, the Crown deployed eight lawyers against the cobbler-cum-political-organizer Thomas Hardy, but for all their bluster, the case fell apart. They could only muster a grab bag of weak evidence, including the adoption by Hardy and his confederates of Paine's theories, their vision of a government without a king or House of Lords, and the unsupported accusation that they intended to violently depose the monarch and establish a republic.[16] To these ends, they presented the jury with . . . a song. With great fanfare, they brandished a sheet found in Hardy's house containing the lyrics to "The Vicar of Bray," which opens thus:

> *Why vainly do we waste our prime*
> > *Repeating our oppressions?*
> *Come, rouze to arms, 'tis now the time*
> > *To punish past transgressions.*
> *'Tis said that Kings can do no wrong;*
> > *Their murderous deeds deny it:*
> *And since from us their power has sprung*
> > *We have the right to try it.*[17]

Hardy's barrister, Thomas Erskine, who had represented Paine, had little trouble demolishing the Crown's case and, in fact, accused the prosecution of itself "imagining" the king's death merely by pursuing the treason charge. "I hope," Erskine added, "never to hear it repeated . . . that peacefully to convene the people on the subject of their own privileges, can lead to the destruction of the king: they are the king's worse enemies who hold this language."[18] Hardy was acquitted, and far from being executed as a traitor, he was carried through London by a jubilant crowd. Two more acquittals, of John Horne Tooke and John Thelwall, followed close upon Hardy's, after which the government quietly dropped the other cases.

Yet the Crown could not let go of speech-as-treason, and having lost against genuine reformers, it sought an easier win against a deranged religious fanatic. In 1795, Richard Brothers, a self-proclaimed "Prince of the Hebrews" and "Nephew of God," was charged with imagining the king's death. His briskly selling book, *A Revealed Knowledge of the Prophesies & Times . . . Wrote under the Direction of the Lord God, and Published by his Sacred Command*, reported that he had interceded with God to save London ("Spiritual Babylon") from divine destruction; but before Brothers would again come to the rescue, Londoners must turn from their corrupt ways and England must withdraw from the sinful war with France. In the book's 1795 edition, Brothers issued this demand to the king:

The Lord God commands me to say to you, George the Third . . . that immediately upon my being revealed, in London, to the Hebrews as their Prince . . . your crown must be delivered up to me, that all your power and authority may instantly cease. . . . It is for your contempt to me that your country is ordered to be invaded, and your power to be destroyed.[19]

Unpersuaded of Brothers's divine authority, government officers arrested him soon after this edition was published. *The Times* praised the arrest, calling him a "tool of faction, employed to seduce the people, and to spread fear and alarms," while royalists declared him a front man for an elaborate conspiracy, "all the more insidious," according to the historian John Barrell, "because no clear evidence could be found of its existence."[20] Despite Brothers's explicit, if unmoored, imagining of the king's death, this case also ended with a whimper: Brothers was declared a long-term lunatic and thus could not be held liable for treason. He was still subject to extended detention, however, and was put away for eleven years. His book continued to sell.

The treason trials further galvanized the reform movement, as well as popular hostility toward the king. On October 26, 1795, reformers held a meeting in London with hundreds of thousands in attendance. Three days later, the city streets were "choked with spectators" gathered to jeer at the king as his ornate coach carried him to Parliament, "most of them, according to *The Times*, 'of the very lowest order.'"[21] As the coach proceeded, the crowd yelled, "Down with George!," "No king!" and filthy insults. They threw mud and stones at the coach, and soon a projectile pierced its glass, which convinced George that he was being shot at. On its homeward journey, the coach was again pelted with stones and insults. The result of these indignities and the unsuccessful treason trials was a series of new laws, collectively referred to as the Gagging Acts, which sharply limited the permissible size of public meetings and redefined treason to include any "Words or Sentences to excite or stir up the People to hatred or Contempt of the Person of His Majesty."

None of these efforts at censoring political speech and preventing assembly suppressed anti-government discussion. Rather, they sharpened sentiment among the working and artisan classes that their government was both illegitimate and against them, and that their right to voice their grievances freely had to be protected at all costs.

STIRRED SPIRITS AND SEVERED HEADS IN FRANCE

King Louis XV's council decreed death in 1757 for anyone involved with writings that might "stir up spirits" (*"émouvoir les esprits"*) or diminish royal authority.[22] The decree was ignored, however, most notably by France's chief mid-century censor, Guillaume-Chrétien de Lamoignon de Malesherbes, who used his influence to allow an array of books that were very stirring indeed. Immediately after the start of the French Revolution in 1789, the National Constituent Assembly guaranteed freedom of speech and thought, unleashing a torrent of new publications. But censorship and executions for speech returned a few years later, and soon the government would lead a campaign of wanton book burning and iconoclasm targeting pre-Revolutionary art, all while attempting to preserve works for the new museum at the Louvre.

These contradictions only hint at the confused censorship policies of eighteenth-century France, where proscriptions rarely had any effect on reality, and modern and forbidden literature often overlapped. As Malesherbes recognized in 1788, not long after his tenure as censor had ended, "A man who had read only [formally approved] books . . . would be behind his contemporaries by nearly a century."[23] As true as that might have been, it did not eliminate the dangers that still attached to the thousands of condemned texts. An arbitrary punishment is no less bitter than one imposed under a rational set of rules, as a Paris bookseller and a grocery clerk learned in 1768 when they were caught dealing in forbidden books. They were publicly exposed in chains for three days, wearing signs saying "Purveyor of Impious and Immoral Libels," after which they were condemned to be galley slaves for years; branded with the letters "GAL," (an abbreviation of *galérien*, or "galley slave"); and then banished from France.

Prepublication licensing was over in England by the century's start, but in France the licensing bureaucracy was rapidly expanding. As the government struggled to keep pace with the explosive growth in publishing, the ranks of censors grew from 10 in 1660 to 180 in 1789.[24] Inspectors carefully reviewed each new book, then gave it either a full royal *privilège*—in effect, an official invitation to read it—or placed it in one of a series of nuanced categories on a spectrum descending from *privilège* to tacit permission (*permission tacite*), to simple permission (*permission simple*), to police permission (*permission de police*), and down to mere tolerance (*simple tolérances*), which amounted to an informal agreement that police would look the other way when the book was sold under the counter, and, finally, books that were forbidden in all circumstances.

The standards governing each of these classifications were vague; even the police would sometimes become confused. When, in 1771, a customs agent on the Swiss border asked a superior for guidance on what was banned, he received a telling reply: "I cannot tell M. Pion positively what is forbidden. In general, everything . . . opposed to religion, the state, and good morals cannot enter."[25] Many in the book trade ignored the licensing system and went straight to the underground market, because they knew their products would never be approved, and because an official imprimatur could hinder sales. Labeling a book sardonically as "printed at the expense of the Vatican," or "at the sign of liberty," or "chez William Tell" was simply good business, and if a few copies were found by police and set alight, so much the better for promotion. The authorities eventually realized that burning books publicly only increased sales of the clandestine editions that inevitably followed.

Between the extremes of official endorsement and outright illegality, it was rarely certain how a book might ultimately be classified. The decision could be based on more than a strict evaluation of the work's content. Take, for example, the century's most censored author, Voltaire, whose books were burned at least seven times, who knew the inside of the Bastille, and who was repeatedly forced to flee France on account of his writings. A book that was critical of him was precisely the kind of work to which the state would give its most enthusiastic commendation, yet on one occasion a censor begged Malesherbes to give such a work only a *permission tacite*. The censor feared attacks from the bilious *philosophe* and his partisans if his name appeared alongside a more fulsome seal of approval.

Aside from the censor's well-being or a book's potential for offense, works were also suppressed for not being good enough. A biography of Frederick II was rejected as little more than "a compilation without taste and without discernment," while a biography of the Prophet Muhammad was panned for being inadequately researched. A sentimental romance was turned down for being poorly written, and a mathematical text was refused because it failed to work out the problems sufficiently. A book could also be too boring or obscure for the state to care much about it one way or the other, as with certain philosophy texts. One book on Leibnizian metaphysics was written up as having the potential to be a "dangerous influence on religion," but the censor added that "it is merely a philosophical dispute," so there was no reason to prevent its circulation.[26]

As is richly described by Robert Darnton in *Censors at Work*, the lives of these French officials were harried and anxious. They were freelancers drawn from the ranks of authors, academics, doctors, and lawyers, and they were given few resources, little time, and often no money for their efforts. Given that censors usually inhabited the same milieus as the writers they evaluated, they were often acquainted with one another and corresponded to commiserate and work through suggestions for textual and stylistic changes. "Despite the occasional disputes," Darnton observes, "censorship, of the business-as-usual variety, drove authors and censors together rather than apart." What most worried censors was that they would miss a veiled insult or slight against a high-ranking minister or his mistress. To the outsider, the social and political machinations taking place at Versailles were virtually unknowable, and rather than make a ruinous error by missing a snotty or revelatory allusion, many censors rejected manuscripts about which they were unsure. Malesherbes stepped in when heightened discretion was called for and didn't hesitate to defer to the subject of the book. The Duc d'Orléans himself thanked Malesherbes for ensuring that "nothing concerning his father should be printed before he [the current duke] should be informed."[27]

Once a book was declared forbidden, an elaborate policing machinery went to work to prevent its printing, sale, and importation from abroad. Raids were common on illegal operations in the publishing houses and shops of the Latin Quarter, at the Palais Royal, and in the countless back rooms and slums throughout France where banned literature was produced or sold. Special police inspectors ferreted out participants in the illegal book trade, but sometimes they could not resist profiting from the expertise they gained on the job. One inspector organized the production of illicit books, confiscated a few to demonstrate that he was enforcing the law, and then sold the rest through illegal dealers. This went on for several years until he was denounced by one of his middlemen, after which he was thrown into prison; he died in a dungeon near Paris in 1778.[28]

Some of these "bad books" (*mauvais livres*) were printed illegally in France; most were produced on the numerous presses that ringed France from the Dutch Republic to Switzerland and were then sent across the borders via elaborate smuggling networks. The black market diverted so much revenue from the formal economy that Malesherbes tried to expand the legal trade by increasing the number of books given *permissions tacites* and *simples tolérances*. As Darnton writes, "economics mattered as much as politics and/or religion in the administration of censorship."[29]

Malesherbes was generally sympathetic to the French intellectuals of the Enlightenment, many of whom he knew personally, and whose works he and others in elite circles read avidly. He intervened on behalf of the Enlightenment's magnum opus, the *Encyclopédie*, a vast collection of articles chiefly edited by the prominent *philosophe* Denis Diderot and featuring contributions by literary outlaws such as Voltaire, Montesquieu, and Rousseau. Together, the multivolume work comprised the era's most thorough exposition of the principles of religious tolerance, rational inquiry, and democratic governance—very little of which lined up with church or state orthodoxy. Diderot's entry in the first volume, "Political Authority," made clear his lack of regard for the absolute monarchy under which he lived:

> No man has received from nature the right to give orders to others. . . . Power deriving from the consent of the peoples subject to it necessarily presupposes conditions that render the wielding of it legitimate, useful to society . . . and within certain fixed limits.[30]

The 1752 release of the *Encyclopédie*'s first two volumes was greeted with intense opprobrium, particularly by the Jesuits and the archbishop of Paris. The King's Council ordered the books seized for their tendency to "destroy the royal authority, set up the spirit of independence and revolt, and . . . raise the foundations of error, of corruption of morals, of irreligion, and of unbelief." The condemnations only drove interest in the work, and subscription sales jumped. Amidst the furor, Malesherbes quietly arranged a *permission tacite* for forthcoming volumes.

Safe for the moment, Diderot proceeded with his work, and publication of the *Encyclopédie* continued through to volume 7, which appeared in 1757. However, an article against religion in that volume managed to offend both Catholics and Protestants, and the king revoked the *Encyclopédie*'s tenuous license, citing "irreparable damage . . . to morality and religion." Having no choice, Malesherbes ordered the police to raid Diderot's offices and confiscate his vast trove of papers related to the enterprise. Before the raid, however, he warned Diderot to remove the files to a safe place; many of them ended up in Malesherbes's own home. Diderot continued his work in secret, and the last ten volumes appeared under a false imprint.[31] The entire *Encyclopédie* was placed on the Vatican's *Index of Forbidden Books*, where it remained until the twentieth century.

Most French readers, however, cared little about the writings of the philosophes. They spent their money on a subcategory of forbidden books that Malesherbes made no effort to protect called *libelles*, which reached full flower mid-century and into the early years of the Revolution. *Libelles* served up a frothy brew of gossip and sex, but over time they also dispensed news, though not the kind that would appear in today's *Le Monde*. Rather, these were tales of the private lives of the king, his wives and mistresses, and others in power. The result was what Darnton called an early form of "journalism disguised as contemporary history and biography," and while much of it was false, enough rang true that readers took *libelles* seriously and bought them in volume. Their depictions of corruption and perversity in Versailles reinforced each other, and they helped to heat up the crises that led to the Revolution.

Libelles could take the form of handwritten or printed broadsheets, which were revised as additional information was gathered or invented, or they could appear as books, sometimes reaching several volumes in length. By the 1780s they were longer and more complex than ever. The best-selling *La Vie Privée de Louis XV*, for example, ran to three volumes; along with gossip and humor, it gave readers an extraordinarily detailed account of the period's political history. But as much as anything else, it was sex that sold many *libelles* and sex they delivered in spades, particularly as it concerned Louis XV. One after another, they described in musky detail a king who was debauched yet impotent, preyed upon by perverse, low-born mistresses, and manipulated by courtiers. A verse from one *libelle*, referring to Louis's domination by his ex-prostitute mistress, Madame du Barry, pulled no punches:

Who'd imagine that a clique,
In the teeth of all critique,
Could turn a wanton, public whore
Into a brand new potentate?
Who'd ever think that, without shame,
Louis would give up the helm
To such a bitch, and let
Founder the imperiled ship of State?[32]

Louis died of smallpox in 1774, but the *libellistes* did not let him rest. One told of his departed soul's search for paradise, during which he asks directions from Saint-Denis (who had been decapitated) and Mary Magdalene, both of whom point him in the wrong direction. When he finally arrives at the heavenly gates, Saint-Pierre ridicules him for taking directions from "men with no brains and whores."

These publications, as well as those later directed against Louis XVI and Marie-Antoinette, who was accused of horrid perversions, portray a monarchy degraded and getting worse. Whether, or to what extent, the *libelles* contributed to the toppling of the monarchy is impossible to say, but they certainly didn't help the monarchs. More importantly, by putting all news about government outside the law, the French state ruled out self-restraint by those who reported on it. The growing appetite for news, especially of goings-on in Versailles, was matched by the novel and revolutionary idea that the public had a *right* to know how their country was being governed.

Censorship collapsed in the winter of 1787–88 with the crumbling of royal authority. In 1789, the Declaration of the Rights of Man and of the Citizen guaranteed freedom of speech and thought as the natural rights of all people. A surge of publications ensued, with greater press liberty than ever before in France—until equally unprecedented repression returned in 1792–93. In the convulsions of the Revolution's successive stages, one's opinions and writings could bring persecution and, all too often, execution if they were out of step with the ruling ideology of the moment. A 1793 decree, for example, ordered death for any person "guilty of advocating either a return of the monarch or attacks on property."[33] The casualties were many, including Malesherbes himself (beheaded in 1794 for his defense of Louis XVI), as well as journalists such as Jean-Paul Marat. Some repressed journalists and newspapers reappeared under new names, behaving, in the words of the historian Emmet Kennedy, "like mice toward cats, disappearing and reappearing, trying to avoid the final strike."[34]

In addition to persecution for political speech, the Revolution sparked explosions of iconoclasm and book burning, driven mainly by the urge to strike at symbols of the ancien régime and the Catholic Church. In August 1792, days after the monarchy was swept away and the mob tore statues of kings to the ground, a law was passed requiring more comprehensive obliteration: "All monuments containing traces of feudalism, of whatever nature, that still remain in churches, or other public places, and even those in private homes, shall without the slightest delay be destroyed by the communes."

And destroy they did. All "symbols of royalty, superstition, or ignorance" had to go. Even books stamped with the fleur-de-lys, a symbol of royalty, were sometimes included in the bonfires that were lit everywhere. In 1793, a bonfire lasting nearly an entire day consumed "all monuments of superstition," including the city's religious books. Marseilles's citizens told the city's librarian to destroy the library's collection because it was "useless or evil."[35] The Ministry of War made cartridges out of three thousand pages of documents relating to France's fifteenth- and sixteenth-century kings. Churches were also ransacked, and many were rechristened as "temples of reason." At the altar of the looted and desecrated Notre-Dame Cathedral, what the scholar Lynn Hunt called a "Carnival queen" was crowned goddess of reason and liberty.[36]

The goal was to obliterate symbols of the pre-revolutionary world, but there was also palpable hostility among many toward art itself. Many believed the arts were useless byproducts of luxury and vice. One deputy to the National Convention argued in 1793 that any inclusion of fine arts in the education of children would render France's future citizens cowardly, weak, and unsuited to life in a republic. While this never emerged as official policy, the distrust of art, at least of the pre-revolutionary variety, entered the ranks of artists themselves. Jacques-Louis David, among France's finest painters of the time, promoted bonfires of "attributes of royalty" and announced that the arts "will no longer prostitute themselves to celebrating tyrants."[37] Under David's guidance, the new Commune des Arts planned a ceremony in 1794 in which each member would join in the mutilation and burning of a portrait of the dauphin, Louis-Joseph. Those who refused to participate were presumed to have been infected by "counterrevolutionary" tendencies.

At the same time, a counternarrative was unfolding. Successive revolutionary regimes recognized that they presided over a treasure house of Western art, much of which was worth preserving for its own sake and for the glory of France. They established one of the world's preeminent museums, the Louvre, to house it. The process was chaotic and full of contradictions. The Monuments Commission was created in 1790 to collect objects of high artistic value, but it was understaffed and unpaid, and its efforts were continually undermined by decrees mandating destruction. For example, the commission made great efforts to preserve the tombs of France's kings at the Basilica of Saint-Denis, but in 1793, the Committee for Public Safety ordered the commission to destroy fifty of them: they were "monuments of idolatry" that "still nourished the superstition of some Frenchmen." The corpses of the sovereigns were dug up and thrown into pits.

The destruction fueled apprehension that France was eating its own heritage alive and degrading itself as a nation. As the historian Stanley Idzerda puts it, "Some courageous Frenchmen began to hint that the primrose path of iconoclasm leads to the hell of barbarism." Those engaged in government-sponsored iconoclasm were often compared by critics to the likes of Ostrogoths and early Christian fanatics. As the enormous scope of the losses came into focus, the ground shifted. Propagandists began to blame the wreckage on "the outrages of aristocrats," on "enemies of liberty," and on "English spies" who led people to destroy works "which attest the superiority of our arts and our genius." New laws were passed forbidding harm to items of high artistic or historical value, while still mandating the destruction of purely "feudal," "superstitious," or "royal" objects. The artifacts that survived this oxymoronic instruction were to be "taken to the nearest museum" for conservation.[38]

The Louvre opened in August 1793. It was there, and in the new Museum of French Monuments, that the Revolution's paradoxical relationship with art was put on display. In the museums' neutral halls, works that had been reviled as hateful emblems of "royalty, feudalism, and superstition" were now simply art, to be appreciated in a setting shorn of context. A member of the Monuments Commission revealed much when he recommended that a king's scepter from the royal tombs of Saint-Denis be preserved for the Louvre "not as a scepter, but as an example of fourteenth-century goldsmith work."[39] As Kennedy observes, these museums acted as "depositories in which to quarantine the past lest it exercise a pernicious influence on the present."[40]

FREEDOM FROM DEFINITION: SPEECH IN THE AMERICAN COLONIES AND THE UNITED STATES

Censorship in America followed a boomerang trajectory. Up until the middle of the eighteenth century, the colonial governments used all the weapons of English law to beat back criticism; during the revolutionary period, fear of anti-British riots managed to loosen restraints on the patriot press; and soon after the young United States adopted the First Amendment and its seemingly ironclad speech protections, Congress passed a sedition law that was so draconian King George III should have been impressed. But the boomerang didn't stop there. That same sedition law forced a national conversation on liberty of speech that eventually resulted in freedoms unheard of anywhere else—that is, until new crises sparked more repressions.

Before the American Revolution, the primary agents of speech repression were the colonial governors and governing assemblies. While there are no precise numbers, they likely brought hundreds of prosecutions for words taken as "affronts," "impudence," or "indignities."[41] It bordered on the obsessive. As the century opened, for example, the memory was still fresh of a Virginia printer who had been banned from the trade for publishing that colony's laws without permission. Most times, however, the assemblies were merely thin-skinned, as Boston's irrepressible James Franklin, the elder brother of Benjamin Franklin, found in 1722 when he wrote in his *New England Courant*, sarcastically, that colonial naval forces were waiting for nice weather before they left the harbor to engage pirates. He was summarily jailed for committing a "high affront to this Government." Upon his release, he redoubled his jibes, which brought him more censure and an order not to print anything without permission. Franklin ignored this command and went ahead with the *Courant*'s next issue. However, to avoid certain arrest, he went into hiding, leaving Benjamin, who was under no such restrictions, to run the paper in his absence.[42]

Colonial assemblies also didn't hesitate to punish mouthy members of government. Samuel Mulford—nicknamed Captain Fishhook for the snares he kept in his pants to ward off pickpockets—was expelled from the New York General Assembly in 1715 for publishing one of his speeches. The prickly legislator and whaler was incensed by the imposition of a new tax on whale oil and had accused the colony's governor of embezzling some of the tax revenue. By 1720, Mulford was back in the assembly, but he was soon expelled again for "rash expression," having accused his colleagues of running up too much debt.[43] A few decades later, a justice of the peace named Samuel Townsend was jailed for a "high Misdemeanor and most daring insult": he had sent the assembly a letter seeking relief for refugees quartered in Queens County. Townsend was only released after abjectly apologizing and promising not to speak out again.[44]

The doctrine of seditious libel was alive in colonial America but not particularly well; few such cases were brought. However, the convictions that were obtained in the eighteenth century's early decades made a chilling impression. Take the case of a Pennsylvania man, already under arrest in 1723 for deriding the king, who had the cheek to comment that neither the king nor his judges had any authority over him. At his trial, the judge asked the jury, "What severity can be too harsh for those who despise dominions, . . . who curse, asperse, and deny their supreme, true, and lawful and undoubted sovereign?" The answer: very little. The man was pilloried for two days, after which he was roped to a cart and dragged around in public, given forty-one lashes, and finally imprisoned until he repaid the costs of his prosecution. Observed Levy, "A sentence like this did not have to be repeated to have a lingering cautionary effect on the tongues of citizens."[45]

Against this background, the acquittal in the 1735 seditious libel trial of the New York publisher John Peter Zenger was extraordinary. His *New York Weekly Journal* had bitterly criticized the colony's governor, William Crosby, for incompetence and corruption. A conviction seemed a foregone conclusion; the law only let the jury determine whether the articles had in fact been published. It was then for the judge to rule whether they were seditious. If he was in fact as inept and corrupt as the *Journal* accused, Zenger would only be in deeper legal jeopardy. As the prosecutor told the jury, the truth of the accusations would be "an aggravation of the crime." Put another way, the law was not there to facilitate an informed public but to protect the aura of excellence upon which government was supposed to rest. Accurate criticism only made matters worse.

But Crosby was no match for the legal dream team behind Zenger, the face of which was the august Andrew Hamilton, nearly eighty years old with flowing white hair and a grandiloquent delivery that made his every word sound like Scripture. He startled the courtroom by confirming that Zenger had indeed published the attacks on Crosby, asserting that his client, like "every free-born subject," had been within his rights to do so—as they were correct. Defying the judge, and challenging the law, Hamilton told the jury that the "truth ought to govern the whole affair of libels," which the jury, not the court, should decide. If the charges made in the *Journal* were true, he argued, then that should decide the case in Zenger's favor. His concluding remarks made clear the implications:

> The question before the court and you, gentlemen of the jury, is not of small nor private concern. It is not the cause of the poor printer, nor of New York alone. . . . No! It may in its consequence affect every free man that lives under a British government. . . . It is the best cause. It is the cause of Liberty. . . . The laws of our country have given us a right to liberty of both exposing and opposing arbitrary power (in these parts of the world at least) by speaking and writing truth.[46]

Ten minutes later, the jury acquitted Zenger, and cheers erupted in the courtroom. The verdict did not change the law of seditious libel—that would not happen for some time—but its landmark symbolic status is deserved: a jury had, in effect, decided that it had the power to determine whether or not speech was seditious, and that truth was a defense. A book recounting the trial was read widely in the colonies and in England, and Hamilton's courtroom speeches became, along with Cato's *Letters*, the central Anglo-American defense of freedom of speech of the eighteenth century.

Yet even as a symbol, the Zenger verdict was insufficient protection for dissent. To confine liberty of expression to "speaking and writing truth" is to build a temple on a flimsy foundation, as one person's truth is another's deception; and "truth" excludes the biases and opinions that make up much of human discourse, which should not have to depend on objective proof to be protected. Nevertheless, while seditious libel prosecutions were a common occurrence in England, Zenger's victory helped to ensure that they were rare in the colonies for decades to come.

The revolutionary period did much for press freedom: between 1763 and 1775, the number of revolutionary newspapers doubled. Fear of mob violence acted as a check on many seditious libel prosecutions, and while the governing assemblies continued to go after critics on their own authority, nothing effectively stemmed rebellious expression. But even as the patriot press maintained its own right to liberty of speech, invoking the likes of Cato, Zenger, Junius, and Wilkes, it recognized no such right for publications loyal to the British. Loyalist newspaper offices were regularly attacked and proprietors threatened. As one exasperated Massachusetts justice expressed in 1767, the patriots were "contending for an unlimited Freedom of Thought and Action, which they would confine wholly to themselves."[47]

The danger of riots against censorship was immediate. For example, the 1765 Stamp Act—the hated duty imposed by Britain on newspapers and legal and commercial documents that stoked revolutionary sentiment—sparked furious opposition in the press; but authorities were often too intimidated by the writers and their supporters in the streets to attempt to muzzle them. The New York printer of one such newspaper was identified, but it was deemed imprudent to proceed against the printer for fear of "raising the mob which it is thought proper by all means to avoid." New York's lieutenant governor conceded "that considering the present temper of the people" it was an inopportune time to start any prosecutions.[48] And when charges were sought, grand juries did not always cooperate. In Massachusetts, authorities repeatedly sought indictments in 1771–72 against Isaiah Thomas, the publisher of the *Massachusetts Spy*—known as the "sedition foundry"—after the paper called the lieutenant governor a "perjured traitor" and the governor a "usurper," and accused King George III of corrupting government by appointing "every dirty booby" he could find. However, the grand juries refused to indict in each instance. Even if they had, government officers recognized that "in the present temper of the times, prosecutions [against Thomas] will be of no effect."[49]

One set of prosecutions, against Alexander McDougall, deserves a closer look. In late 1769, when the New York General Assembly voted to pay for the quartering of British troops in New York City, McDougall penned an anonymous broadside titled *To the Betrayed Inhabitants of New-York*, which called on the citizenry to "rouse" against unjust measures such as this and which he signed "A Son of

Liberty."[50] The assembly offered a large reward for the identity of the author. It was more than a knowledgeable printer could resist, and McDougall was arrested for seditious libel. Rather than pay bail for release pending trial, he remained behind bars, which only raised the case's profile among the colony's restive population. After several months of McDougall's confinement, a mob accompanied him from jail to court, but as the proceedings ground on, the key witness lined up to testify against McDougall died suddenly and the case fell apart.

The assembly had McDougall arrested again on a charge of libeling the assembly itself. He refused to enter a plea of guilt or innocence, to which the assembly responded by threatening to tie him to the ground and place increasingly heavy weights on his body until he either relented or died. McDougall persisted in his refusal to plead, and the torture never took place. Despite further threats, charges, and imprisonment, he was finally released after the legislative session ended. Now known as "America's Wilkes," McDougall went on to become a major-general in the Continental Army and a delegate to the Continental Congress. What had started as a protest against the quartering of British troops became a winning battle for the right to make such a protest. By thumbing his nose at authority and walking free, McDougall did much for the revolutionary cause.

While McDougall's record of anti-British rhetoric was sterling, he earned failing grades when it came to protecting speech he didn't like. In 1775, soon after hostilities with England began, he led a band of armed men to smash the press of James Rivington, a notorious Tory publisher. The following year, not long before independence was declared, McDougall led a team of vigilantes against Samuel London, a New York publisher who had printed a loyalist response to Thomas Paine's *Common Sense*. They broke down London's door, rousted him from his bed, and made him deliver the plates of the anti-Paine tract for destruction. If that was not intimidating enough, a communiqué issued soon afterward threatened "death and destruction, ruin and perdition" to anyone printing pro-British messages. No further loyalist publications were printed in New York.[51]

Once the war with Britain was won and the Constitutional Convention's delegates met in Philadelphia that sweltering summer of 1787, it was not clear what speech guarantees would result from their efforts. The signals were mixed. Back in 1776, the Continental Congress had urged the states to pass laws preventing people from being "deceived and drawn into erroneous opinion," which they had done.[52] Even states with free-speech clauses in their constitutions were not always taking those guarantees very seriously. Massachusetts saw indictments that same year of several people who had vocally supported the uprising known as Shays's Rebellion, including William Whiting, a prominent judge who was convicted of seditious libel.[53] Virginia's Declaration of Rights echoed Cato in declaring that a free press is a "great bulwark of liberty" that only despotism can restrain, but that didn't stop the commonwealth from later passing a criminal law against "idle and busy-headed people" who "forge and divulge false rumors and reports."[54]

Simultaneously, the convention's delegates were forging a federal government with sharply limited powers, utterly unlike that which existed in Britain. Those powers not specifically enumerated in the document did not exist, and the framers omitted any grant of authority to regulate or punish speech. That was the response given to South Carolina's Charles Pinckney when, a few days before the convention's close, he proposed to his tired colleagues that a clause be added to the document guaranteeing that the "liberty of the press" would be "inviolably preserved." Connecticut's Roger Sherman replied, "It is unnecessary. The power of Congress does not extend to the press."[55] Pinckney's proposal was rejected, and the convention was soon over.

Drafting the Constitution was difficult; so was getting it ratified by the states. There was widespread distrust of the federal government being created, which many feared would become a monster hungry to devour the individual liberties and state prerogatives for which the Revolution had been fought, at least in part. Opponents of ratification focused on the absence of a bill of rights explicitly limiting federal powers and guaranteeing rights such as freedom of speech and of the press. The responses to proposals for such a bill of rights included that it would block powers the Constitution hadn't granted to the federal government in the first place, that it was dangerous even to imply that such powers could exist, and that nothing in the Constitution limited speech.[56] The arguments failed to persuade opponents, and the reality set in that the Constitution would be ratified only if a bill of rights was soon added to it. That occurred in 1791, and the Bill of Rights became the first ten amendments to the Constitution.

The First Amendment reads:

> Congress shall make no law respecting an establishment of religion, or prohibiting the free exercise thereof; or abridging the freedom of speech, or of the press; or the right of the people peaceably to assemble, and to petition the government for a redress of grievances.

Heady stuff indeed, but the question remained as to how far the framers intended this "freedom of speech, or of the press" to extend. Amazingly, we don't know for sure—and neither, it seems, did many of them. Referring to the First Amendment, Benjamin Franklin admitted, "Few of us, I believe, have any distinct Ideas of its Nature and Extent."[57] The congressional debates regarding the Bill of Rights shed no wisdom, as there was almost no discussion of the speech and press guarantees. Surveying the framers' individual views, Levy surmises that the First Amendment was likely intended to align with then-current English law: no prior restraint of speech but still leaving the courthouse doors open to seditious libel prosecutions.[58] Other scholars, such as Zechariah Chafee Jr., argue that the framers, for whom Wilkes and Junius were "household words," surely intended "to achieve a new victory abolishing sedition prosecutions."[59] The most judicious assessment comes from law professor Geoffrey Stone, who states that despite the framers' lack of clear consensus on details, the First Amendment represented a broad principle: "It was an aspiration, to be given meaning over time."[60]

Much else in the Bill of Rights is no less ambiguously aspirational than the First Amendment. It is strewn with inexact clauses such as "due process," "equal protection," and "unreasonable search and seizure," that were intended to state principles and guide the development of policy as circumstances arose. But the infant republic's acrimonious politics forced the First Amendment into a stress test before any useful doctrine could take shape. It failed miserably. The swift emergence of bitterly opposing political parties and the pressures of potential war with France led to the passage of a law that Stone calls "perhaps the most grievous assault on free speech in the history of the United States."[61] With the Sedition Act of 1798, the dominant party in Congress, the Federalists, made nearly all dissident speech a federal crime, from the writings of a congressman to the ravings of a town drunkard.

Just as the French Revolution rocked British politics, its disruptive force radiated across the ocean to the US. As France went to war with Britain and much of Europe, the US sided tentatively with Britain, which among other things resulted in France's seizing American merchant vessels in 1796–97. War appeared imminent, and rumors spread of French spies subverting the US from within. These tensions only widened the jagged fissures within government. The Federalists, led by President John Adams and Alexander Hamilton, who represented elite propertied interests, locked horns with the Republicans, with Vice President Jefferson and James Madison as the most visible faces, whose constituency was mainly artisans and farmers. Unsurprisingly, the Federalists were troubled by developments in France, which vindicated their distrust of the common man, while many Republicans saw the French Revolution as extending the promise of American liberties. The acrimony was thus not just a struggle for political power—although there was plenty of that. It was also a contest over the nature of the new nation. Would it be, as the Federalists feared, a riotous place where the masses terrorized the well-to-do? Or, as the Republicans worried, one where the injustices of Britain were repeated?

As the crisis deepened, the press organs loyal to each side added new barbs to their already sharp rhetoric. The Federalist press called the Republicans treasonous French agents, while the Republican press charged the Federalists, especially President Adams, with no end of mental, physical, and political deficiencies. Enjoying a narrow majority in Congress, the Federalists struck against the Republicans and their supporters with passage of the 1798 Sedition Act, which mandated fines and prison for "false, scandalous, and malicious writings" that brought the president or Congress—but *not* the vice president—"into contempt or disrepute."

The Sedition Act was deeply partisan. Vituperation against Vice President Jefferson was allowed, but dissent was criminalized when directed against President Adams and his government. The law also expired on March 3, 1801, the last day of Adams's administration.

The debates over the adoption of the act followed predictable lines. The Federalists said it was well within the confines of the First Amendment, which, in their Blackstonian interpretation, only barred prior restraint on speech, not punishment for what one said. Besides, added Congressman Harrison Gray Otis, any government must be able to protect itself against "injuries and outrages which endanger its existence." Putting a finer point on the argument, a Federalist newspaper said the act was necessary because Republicans were "parricidal miscreants" who were "preying on the vitals of the country."[62] Taken together, the Federalists interpreted the act according to the British model forbidding seditious libel, which was still the law.

The Republican response from James Madison, who had written the First Amendment, is more illuminating. He flatly rejected the idea that Congress may punish speech along British lines, particularly since the American system, unlike a monarchy, made government and its officials answerable to the people. "If they fail to live up to their trusts," he asserted, then "it is natural and proper, that according to the cause and degree of their faults, they should be brought into contempt or disrepute, and incur the hatred of the people." Under the First Amendment, the federal government was "destitute" of authority to restrain the press or shield itself against "libellous attacks."[63]

The Republicans had the better argument, but not the power. Before the act expired, it was deployed against at least twenty-five Republicans, which led to fifteen indictments and ten convictions. The targets included Matthew Lyon, an Irish-born immigrant who had risen to become a vehemently Republican Vermont congressman. During his campaign for reelection in 1798, he wrote a letter to a Vermont newspaper accusing Adams of forgetting the public welfare "in an unbounded thirst for ridiculous pomp, foolish adulation, and selfish avarice." For that he was stuck in a filthy cell for several months, although he managed to win reelection during his incarceration. Also jailed were the editors of four of the five most important Republican newspaper editors and, for good measure, Luther Baldwin, a drunk from Newark, New Jersey. Baldwin was convicted for stating, upon hearing cannons give a sixteen-gun salute to Adams, "I do not care if they fired through his arse!" The longest sentence, lasting eighteen months, went to David Brown, a Massachusetts Revolutionary War veteran who had participated in setting up a liberty pole to which a sign was affixed reading "No Stamp Act, No Sedition, No Alien Bills, No Land Tax; downfall to the Tyrants of America."[64]

The Sedition Act controversy helped Jefferson win the presidency in 1800, and he pardoned all those who had been convicted. More significant for our purposes was that the controversy triggered a new, more expansive phase in American thinking about censorship and freedom of speech. In many ways, the act was the embodiment of the Zenger case: truth was a defense, and it was for the jury to decide whether words were in fact seditious. But in the face of the act's politically motivated enforcement, those niceties proved insufficient to protect dissident speech, or even to allow comments on the trajectory of a cannonball. The Republican response to the act crystallized the idea that free political discourse necessarily includes speech hostile to the government, which the First Amendment must secure.

Of course, no historical process is ever neat, and as these theories were percolating, the politics of vengeance continued. While Jefferson made passionate arguments against the Sedition Act, his commitment to the cause of free speech was revealed to be less than absolute after he took office. In an 1803 letter to Pennsylvania's governor discussing his irritation with the Federalist press, he confided: "I have . . . long thought that a few prosecutions of the most prominent offenders would have a wholesome effect of restoring the integrity of the presses. Not a general prosecution, for that would look like a persecution: but a selected one."[65] In 1806, six of President Jefferson's critics in Connecticut found themselves indicted for seditious libel, with his apparent blessing.[66]

CLASS WARFARE IN
THE NINETEENTH CENTURY

"The barbarians that threaten society," declared a French legislative deputy in the early 1830s, are the "[working classes] of our manufacturing towns."[1] In France, and throughout nineteenth-century Europe, elites were intent on choking off information that might stir working- and lower-class demands for political and social rights, which the upper orders equated with rebellion. Censorship of the press, the theatre, caricature, and, soon after the century's end, cinema was almost invariably driven by the morbid conviction among the governing classes that an informed populace would become an inflamed populace and lead to their own demise.

"Four hostile newspapers are more to be feared than a thousand bayonets," observed Napoleon Bonaparte. "If I allowed a free press, I would not be in power for another three months."[2] England's Lord Grenville warned in 1817 that the press's "wicked and blasphemous productions" did not merely risk changes in government; they questioned "whether government should exist at all."[3] In 1819, Austria's foreign minister, Klemens von Metternich, called the press a "scourge" and the era's "greatest and consequently the most urgent evil."[4]

Government survived, of course, and much of the censorship during this period turned out to be paranoid and ludicrous. Austria banned the word *"liberté"* on the sides of imported boxes of china, while Russian cookbooks could not refer to "free air" in ovens. But however overwrought were the fears of the elites, the faith among workers and their allies that a free press would solve society's ills was equally intense. In 1842, Karl Marx extolled an unregulated press as "the ideal world, which constantly gushes from the real one and streams back to it ever richer and animated anew"—a numinous sentiment that was hardened into a battle cry by the liberal German parliamentarian Georg von Bunsen: "The fight for the freedom of the press is a holy war, the holy war of the nineteenth century."[5]

By 1849, as revolutions roiled Europe, Marx was standing trial in Germany for publishing derogatory remarks about government officials. He came to see that "the first duty" of the press was to "undermine all the foundations of the existing political system."[6] And in 1910, the socialist *Hamburger Echo* invoked Napoleon's comparison of newspapers to weapons: "In waging war, we do not throw bombs. Instead, we throw our newspapers among the masses of the working people. Printing ink is our explosive."[7]

No one took these words as hyperbole, and no one underestimated the stakes when the lower classes demanded the right to read, watch, say, and write about what they pleased. In a period of rapid industrialization, rising literacy, and accelerating communications, and in the face of persistent revolt and labor unrest, what the common people thought became a matter of urgent concern to political leaders. Demands for liberty of expression played central roles in the political upheavals and demands for reform that shook England, France, Central Europe, and Russia. Yet instead of making their case to the masses, governments opted instead to bar and punish speech they feared would aggravate the public. As a French drama censor explained in 1849:

> In seeing passages with a political or social significance we asked ourselves: "Does that aim at causing the different classes to rise up against each other, to excite the poor against the rich, to excite disorder?" We asked ourselves in principle if it was possible to allow the ridicule on the stage of the institutions of the country, . . . and expose them to the laughter and mockery of the crowd. We had no trouble in answering no.[8]

While society was, for the most part, more forgiving of transgressive political and artistic expression by the end of the century than at its beginning, the process was turbulent. How could it be otherwise, when authorities viewed censorship as "a sanitary measure to protect society from the contagion of false doctrines, just like measures to prevent the spread of the plague," as a French aristocrat put it? Or when Spain's General Ramon Narváez declared, "It is not enough to confiscate papers; to finish with bad newspapers you must kill all the journalists"?[9] The loosening of speech restrictions was followed consistently by the imposition of new ones, or by redoubled enforcement of the rules that remained. In Germany, for example, a liberal press law was passed in 1874, but the next six months saw approximately eight hundred prosecutions against the press for libel and "slanderous insult."[10]

European censorship measures were consistently geared toward deflecting troublesome ideas away from the poor. A novel or story, for example, might be barred if sold at a low price but approved if priced so that only the well-heeled could afford it. Certain French and German plays could be performed in theatres catering to the upper and middle classes, but were forbidden in venues with poor and working-class audiences. Media consumed in groups or that did not require reading, such as caricature, remained of particular concern to censors. And with the arrival of the cinema—which was cheap, consumed in the dark, and immensely popular among workers and the poor—even countries that had long since abolished prepublication censorship rushed to reimpose it on the new medium.

Yet despite thousands of censorship bans, prosecutions, jail terms, and fines, the circulation of ideas and information was never effectively stopped. There was too much out there for authorities to chase down, and the systems of speech repression—plagued by varying degrees of corruption, maladministration, and pointed resistance—were often two steps behind the outlets they aimed to control. Even in Russia, then as now Europe's most restrictive jurisdiction, mid-century censors admitted that "there are no books which you could not get in St. Petersburg if you wanted them," and that "Russia is flooded with these publications."[11] The same was true everywhere else in Europe. Words and images surged through loopholes, swerved around prohibitions, and hopped over borders . . . and became all the more desirable for being forbidden.

Nineteenth-century censorship conflicts did not just pit elites against their social inferiors, however. Many in the upper classes feared that descriptions of "sinful" behavior would unravel the moral fabric knitting together their own stratum of society. Whereas men of standing considered themselves immune to bad influences from pornography, they felt very differently about their own women and young. Vice and social-purity societies sprang up like supercilious weeds to protect them from temptation, and to campaign for laws that would enforce a strict moral code. At least in Europe, the objective was not just to inoculate the lower orders from what Lord Mount Temple called the "loathsome contagious disorder of soul and body" resulting from depictions of lust.[12] Rather, obscenity censorship was also to prevent the moral corrosion of those worth protecting, including the respectable women the London *Daily Telegraph* spied "furtively peeping in at these sin-crammed shop windows, . . . guiltily bending over engravings as vile in execution as they are in subject."[13]

The lower orders were seen as licentious by nature. Their access to dirty books had to be limited because erotic stimulation supposedly sparked criminality, and that brought disorder and property loss. To keep the poor pacified, enormous efforts were also made to keep cheaply priced anti-Christian literature away from them, as uncritical acceptance of Christianity was thought necessary for them "to bear up against the pressure of misery and misfortune," in the words of a government prosecutor. Without the consolation of religion, they might not accept the bitterness of their lives in return for rewards in the hereafter. "The consequences" of this, the same lawyer argued, "are too frightful to be contemplated."[14]

Sexual material was discreetly available to men of means, but when it was circulated to others, the vice societies, police, and courts went to work. Most obscenity prosecutions resulted in convictions, mainly because the middle and upper classes—nostalgic for a halcyon world where moral lines were clear and coarseness was absent from polite society—supported them. In any event, formal court actions usually weren't necessary to purge sex or rough language from literature; publishers, librarians, and, often enough, writers did the censoring themselves. This was the era when the Bible and Shakespeare were purged of sections considered, in the words of Thomas Bowdler, "unfit to be read aloud by a gentleman to a company of ladies";[15] when Gibbon's *History of the Decline and Fall of the Roman Empire* was "Bowdlerized" to remove passages describing immoral behavior; and when the novelist and editor William Makepeace Thackeray expressed gratitude for living in an age when writers "no longer have the temptation to write so as to call blushes to women's cheeks."[16]

This sanitization of discourse worked poorly, particularly as it coincided with a new genre of dirty books in which fictional women of standing gave detailed, first-hand accounts of their tireless sexual ardor, all of it taking place in the same cozy, respectable homes that censorship was supposed to safeguard. The more women were, at least in theory, placed by men in sexless cages by the fireside, the more their desires were fetishized, and the more sales increased of forbidden books celebrating unbridled female lust. The bourgeois maiden or wife in heat became a standard trope of nineteenth-century pornography. So much for avoiding "blushes."

The Russian author Alexander Pushkin, whose masterpieces were regularly banned and mangled by censors, moaned, "Only the devil could have thought of having me born in Russia with a mind and talent," while the Greek poet Alexandros Soutsos bitterly observed, "The press is free so long as you don't write."[17] But these men *did* write. Authors, agitators, and pornographers everywhere found their audiences in the face of sometimes fearsome barriers, and in many countries a free press started to take shape.

BLASPHEMY, RESISTANCE, AND THE NATURE OF TRUTH IN ENGLAND

England was not a happy place in the early nineteenth century—not, at least, if one worked on the land or for wages. The price of victory in the Napoleonic Wars was economic depression and intense suffering among the most vulnerable. Wages plummeted and jobs disappeared, while bad harvests and protective grain tariffs propelled food prices upward. Many among the laboring classes were brought to the brink of starvation, and were radicalized. Far from trying to relieve the misery, Tory governments attempted, in the words of a House of

Lords committee, to ward off "general plunder and division of property."[18] This included the iron-handed censorship of rebellious speech, the banning of meetings among disaffected workers, and suppression of anything that smacked of sedition. At the same time, resentment among the lower classes seethed against the Church of England, which the historian Joss Marsh describes as "politically corrupt, bloated with wealth, scandalously disorganized, and apparently indifferent to the spiritual fate of the new urban masses."[19] Church officials were chiefly focused on augmenting their wine cellars, collecting tithes, and guarding their prerogatives. Their lack of concern for the suffering of workers and the poor exacerbated the latter's deep and growing sense of grievance and abandonment.

Elbowing into the unrest came the twopenny press, despite punitive taxes aimed at doing away with low-priced publications. William Cobbett's *Political Register*, which started in twopenny form in 1816 and soon reached a circulation of forty thousand, loudly voiced the discontents of its impecunious readers. Along with a bevy of imitators, the *Register* hacked at England's pillars of power, launching bitter assaults on the monarchy, Parliament, and limited suffrage. Its core message was simple and effective. As Cobbett wrote, "Good government is known from bad government by this infallible test: that, under the former the labouring people are well fed and well clothed, and, under the latter, they are badly fed and badly clad."[20] By this standard, the government was very bad indeed. The cheap press savaged the church, religious doctrine, and bloated prelates no less aggressively. They were all indissoluble components of the matrix of oppression.

Authorities also viewed church and state as codependent; an attack on one was regarded as an assault on the other. Since the French Revolution, radical politics in England and on the Continent had involved distrust of religious institutions and questioning the tenets of Christianity. In the view of a London judge in 1819, the Revolution had been a dark time when "the worship of Christ was neglected," which resulted in "the bands of society torn asunder, and a dreadful scene of anarchy, blood, and confusion."[21] France had been defeated, but the specter of religion's "neglect" in England remained wherever challenges to authority were raised. "Everything . . . in the nineteenth century," observes the British historian E. P. Thompson, "was turned into a battleground of class."[22]

Cobbett was certainly biased, but he was dead-on when he wrote that for England's bishops, political reform was revolution, "and revolution means a revolution like that in France, which . . . stripped the Church of all its property including its tythes."[23] England's legal machinery was designed to prevent that from happening, and it started by censoring irreligious speech. The same London judge who lamented the French Revolution's atheism didn't mince words when he scolded a radical publisher for criticizing religion: "You stand in a court where Christian religion must be observed as the law of the land," he thundered, "and where no man is allowed to revile it."[24]

In 1817, police arrested more than twenty pressmen. So began a decades-long run of hundreds of prosecutions against radicals for blasphemy, which prosecutors viewed as an easier sell to middle-class juries than seditious libel, although such charges were usually included. Yet the first accused blasphemer to be brought to trial, William Hone, was no crucifix-smashing rabble rouser. Rather, he was an obscure bookseller and antiquarian with an irreverent sense of humor whose cheap, politically barbed parodies of religion were deemed too incisive for the lower ranks. The Crown badly miscalculated by targeting him. Rather than putting him away in jail, the three trials it brought against him, on as many successive days, made him a celebrity for the cause of freedom of speech, with thousands of supporters and purchasers of his writings.

The first trial concerned Hone's *The Late John Wilkes's Catechism of a Ministerial Member*, a humorous takedown of the catechism, the Lord's Prayer, and the Ten Commandments, all laced with biting references to members of government. Hone told the jurors that he intended merely "to produce a laugh against the ministers," but the government focused on passages disparaging Christianity. The prosecutor emphasized that the *Catechism*'s cheap price placed it in the hands "of the lower classes" who were "ignorant and uninformed" and "not fit to cope" with such blasphemous messaging. Hone's parody must be barred because it would influence these readers to lose their reverence for Christianity and the church, and with it their obedience to law.[25]

In other words, poking fun at religion diminishes its soporific effect on the rabble, resulting in chaos.

Given the strong religious convictions of middle-class jurors, this should have been a winning argument, but in the end, three aspects of Hone's improvised, motor-mouthed defense strategy saved him. The first was his history lesson on religious satire. With maximum flair, he recited to the jury the writings of Martin Luther, John Milton, the dean of Canterbury, a minister of state, and others—each of whom had parodied Scripture, and none of whom had blasphemed. Hone also benefitted from the wit of his own works. As each offending phrase from his parodies was read aloud to the jury, bursts of laughter erupted in the courtroom, which none of the judge's threats could subdue. "Nothing," Marsh explains, "more earned Hone's acquittals than laughter."[26] Finally, Hone's own tireless performance won the day. He spoke for five hours almost nonstop, overawing the jury with his theatricality and his exhortations to stand up to an unfair legal system. He was acquitted after a jury deliberation of fifteen minutes.

The next two trials featured similar marathon presentations by Hone, but this time before a much larger audience who attended the trial and thousands more crowding the surrounding streets. By the third acquittal, the judge didn't bother trying to quell the applause in the courtroom. Hone, a single man in rumpled clothes with a sharp wit, managed to deflect the full weight of the Crown's legal power. With his victories, the use of humor to ridicule the church and government was no longer something that could reliably get one thrown in jail. At least laughter was more or less safe.

Hone never set out to be a warrior for free speech, much less for blasphemy. With little money and a dozen or so children to feed, he had no choice but to find creative ways to defend himself. Richard Carlile was a different character. A tinsmith-cum-atheist agitator and radical publisher, he found his life's purpose in fighting legal battles for freedom of speech and promoting the anti-church writings of Thomas Paine, particularly the long-proscribed *Age of Reason*, published in three parts in 1794, 1795, and 1807. "My whole and sole object, from first to last," he wrote in characteristically grandiose terms, "has been a Free Press and Free Discussion."[27] He paid a big price, spending a total of about nine years in jail, impoverishing himself and his family and sparking more than one hundred blasphemy prosecutions against himself and his supporters. But whereas Hone won his cause in a few days, Carlile obtained a measure of satisfaction through attrition. After nearly a decade of blasphemy prosecutions against Carlile and his followers, *The Age of Reason*, with its brutal criticism of Christianity and the Church of England, would remain in circulation.

Carlile's radicalization began after he lost his job as a tinsmith during the economic troubles of 1816. Soon he became a publisher himself, producing work by Hone and Paine among others, and speaking at mass meetings despite a stumbling oral delivery. By 1819, he had racked up sedition and blasphemy charges, but nothing had come to trial. That changed in August after the Peterloo Massacre, in which British cavalrymen trampled eleven workers to death at a mass protest in Manchester and injured hundreds more. Carlile, who had been scheduled to speak, escaped the melee to London in a mail coach. Within days, he released an impassioned account of the massacre in *Sherwin's Weekly Political Register*. The newspaper was immediately shut down and its press confiscated, so he published the same account in the *Republican*. This time he was arrested and put on trial, in a case that tied disbelief in the Christian God directly to radical politics. At about the same time as the Carlile trial, Parliament passed the notorious Six Acts, which imposed new taxes on the twopenny press and banned public meetings.

Carlile's account of Peterloo, with its demand that "the murderers are brought to justice," well fit the definition of seditious libel, but the prosecution focused on his reissuing, in a cheap edition, *The Age of Reason*.[28] Given the current climate, prosecutors believed that Carlile's anti-government utterances would not anger a jury as much as Paine's aspersions against God. Paine's attacks on Christianity and the Bible's "lies," "absurdities," "atrocities," and "contradictions" gave prosecutors much to work with. The book labeled Christians infidels, framed Christianity as a heathen mythology, and characterized the Immaculate Conception as an "obscene" tale of a young woman "debauched by a ghost." Religion itself was cast as a political weapon for crushing the common people.[29]

Carlile's prosecution was aimed at the effect of these ideas on lower classes. "The gospel is preached particularly for the poor," the prosecutor said, and the trial was "for the purpose of protecting the lower and illiterate classes from having their faith sapped" and their "deference to the laws of God, and of their country" diminished. Carlile tried to demonstrate that Paine's critiques of religion were in fact correct, but the judge stopped him: "I cannot let men be acquitted of . . . violating the law because they are unbelievers." When Carlile tried to show inconsistencies in the Bible, the judge again refused: "You cannot go into the truth of the Christian religion. . . . You are not at liberty to do anything to question the divine origin of Christianity."[30]

Carlile lost the case and was sent to jail, but his goal was achieved, at least for the moment. Court rules permitted him to read the entirety of *The Age of Reason* while on the stand, and the law allowed the publication of court proceedings. Carlile's wife, Jane, went into action, selling ten thousand copies of Paine's work in the form of a trial report in a matter of weeks. More importantly, Carlile's travails sparked widespread discussion on the meaning of freedom of the press. The question was not whether Paine's opinions were correct, but whether Carlile should be jailed for publishing them. A small army of supporters took up his cause, and Jane took over his Fleet Street printing shop and was jailed herself at least four times. Other supporters continued publishing the writings of Paine and Carlile; they were almost all summarily tried and convicted. So many of Carlile's shopmen and supporters ended up in Newgate Prison with him that they launched a magazine, *Newgate Monthly*, which managed to remain in publication out of Carlile's shop for two years.

One of Carlile's more pugnacious shopmen was Humphrey Boyle, who was tried in the Old Bailey in 1822 for selling Paine's blasphemous works and another pamphlet that characterized the Bible as obscene. Boyle described himself as a "humble mechanic" of "limited education," but he conducted his own defense with skill. He spoke passionately to the jury about the iniquities of government and the nobility of humankind's natural right to express itself. He ran into trouble, however, when, he attempted to show that the Bible was in fact laced with obscenities. "Shall I," he asked the jury, "instance that disgusting scene described as occurring between Lot and his daughters? Shall I take you to the bed-chamber of Onan and Tamar?"[31]

Before Boyle could dive into these passages, with their detailed descriptions of incest, misdirected human seed, and other sexual irregularities, the judge cleared the courtroom of women and youngsters, whose ears were evidently too delicate to hear material quoted from the same book that, just one year earlier in the Carlile trial, the court held up as an irreproachable work of divine provenance. The judge's refusal to let women and young people listen to the words of the Bible went far toward making Boyle's point that the book was obscene, but that irony was lost on the jury, whose members recoiled as Boyle carried on reading. He was convicted and sent off to prison. (Notably, Boyle's trial took place during the same year that Thomas Bowdler published a cleaned-up version of the Bible, which he promoted as safe for family consumption.)

In all, about two hundred English blasphemy cases were brought, nearly all against radicals whose ideas were deemed liable to incite the lower classes. By the middle of the century, the prosecutions had largely run their course, but in 1883, more insults to religion were raised that were too pointed for the Crown to ignore. The result of these cases set the tone for class-based evaluations of language well into the twentieth century. The main targets this time were G. W. Foote and *The Freethinker*, a cheap magazine he published. In its first issue, he described it as an "aggressive" "anti-Christian organ" dedicated to "wag[ing] relentless war" against "superstition in general, and against the superstition of Christianity in particular."[32] Foote and others involved with the publication were charged with blasphemy for eight *Freethinker* issues, in which God was described as bloodthirsty, barbarous, and despotic. While that charge was pending, Foote published a Christmas issue that broke all bounds. It accused the Gospels' narrators—Matthew, Mark, John, and Luke—of blasphemy and revived Paine's claim that God had produced an illegitimate son by raping the Virgin Mary. If that was not enough, it charged Jesus Christ with blasphemously claiming to be God. More charges and trials ensued.

The trials should have been easy wins for the prosecution—ever the provocateur, Foote demanded evidence of God's displeasure. Some convictions resulted, but Lord Chief Justice John Coleridge's charge to the jury in the third case derailed matters. Christianity, the judge said, was no longer quite the law of the land it had once been—indeed, a

Jew, Benjamin Disraeli, had become prime minister—so criticizing "the truth of Christianity" no longer sufficed to convict. But such criticism had to be made with delicacy: "I now lay it down as law that, *if the decencies of controversy are observed*, even the fundamentals of religion may be attacked without the writer being guilty of blasphemy" (italics added).[33] In other words, blasphemous speech was allowed if expressed in the "decent" language of the middle and upper classes.

The jury, not knowing what to make of this, could not reach a verdict, and as Foote had already been convicted in one of the previous trials, the case was dropped. But a new standard for irreligious speech had been established. Blasphemy became, in Marsh's words, a "class crime of language" based on the choice of words rather than the ideas behind them—a standard that was "impossible for the less educated to observe."[34]

Justice Coleridge's ruling in the *Freethinker* trial was classist in the extreme, but it nevertheless was an incremental reduction in speech restrictions. England had become a more pluralistic place, and some room had to be made for (well-phrased) opinions that would have been anathema in previous years. "Law grows," he stated, and its principles "have to be applied to the changing circumstances of the times."[35] That 1883 decision concerned speech about religion, but it came as the purpose and efficacy of censorship on other fronts was also being debated—not only by working-class radicals but also by intellectuals in society's upper reaches.

Most notably, the philosopher and later member of Parliament John Stuart Mill published his *On Liberty* in 1861, which advanced some of the most cogent arguments for why governments should tolerate the free flow of opinions and ideas, even immoral, impious, or wrong ones. Reduced to its basics, Mill's argument discerned only one reason why "mankind" might legitimately curb individual freedoms: "self-protection." That is, an individual's power over his or her own actions must be preserved so long as he or she does no harm to others or the state. Mill further argued that most speech restrictions harm society because they deprive it of potential sources of truth—what he called the source of "the mental well-being of mankind."[36] Echoing

Protagoras's statements about the limits of human understanding, Mill cautioned that an idea that seems preposterous or pernicious today might someday prove beneficial in ways we are presently incapable of grasping:

> If all mankind minus one were of one opinion, and only one person were of the contrary opinion, mankind would be no more justified in silencing that one person than he, if he had the power, would be justified in silencing mankind. . . . The peculiar evil of silencing the expression of an opinion is, that it is robbing the human race; posterity as well as the existing generation; those who dissent from the opinion, still more than those who hold it. If the opinion is right, they are deprived of the opportunity of exchanging error for truth: if wrong, they lose what is almost as great a benefit, the clearer perception and livelier impression of truth, produced by its collision with error.

With no certainty as to what is true, the state's "silencing of discussion," even of an erroneous opinion held by just one person, is a dangerous "assumption of infallibility." The truth must emerge through what Mill called the "process of a struggle between combatants fighting under hostile banners." Where Coleridge drew a line around "decencies" in controversies, Mill contended that that the law generally had no business regulating how ideas should be expressed.[37]

Mill's beautifully expressed pleas for tolerance go a considerable way toward contemporary ideals of free speech as a universal right, but he hadn't arrived there quite yet. In the first place, his main concern was not for those who express ideas, but to protect those ideas that have utility for society. Mill thought it wrong to silence opinions chiefly because doing so harms the common good, not because it violates an individual's freestanding rights to express themself.[38] Second, Mill's tolerance of ideas was calibrated to the position of those who expressed them. Revealing his core colonial elitism, he limited the reach of his free speech principles to societies such as Britain, where people had supposedly attained "the maturity of their faculties" and are "capable of being improved by free and equal discussion." Those in "backward states of society in which the race itself may be considered as in its nonage"—that is, the people whom Britain ruled—deserved none of the liberties he advocated. For such "barbarians," he believed, "despotism is a legitimate mode of government."[39]

Finally, who should decide whether an idea would cause harm, or even what the "truth" is? Unsurprisingly, Mill appointed people who resembled himself: "Philosophers and theologians," he said, are the only ones capable of guiding "simple minds" to sort out true from false notions and protect them from being misled.[40]

On Liberty remains one of the most influential tracts in the Western tradition advocating tolerance of minority opinions, but Mill could not help being a product of his time, place, and circumstances. To argue that *everyone* should be accorded full freedom of speech, he would have had to endorse the dismantling of British colonialism, which was unthinkable. And to claim that people should have the right to speak for their own benefit, regardless of whether society derived any tangible advantage from that, would have betrayed his allegiance to the utilitarian principles on which he built his thinking: unless an idea could have broad-based benefits, it wasn't worth much to him.

Another provocative British thinker weighed in on the censorship debate in 1883, posing a challenge to Mill and pushing the rationale for toleration of speech one step further. In *The Suppression of Poisonous Opinions,* Leslie Stephen—man of letters, mountaineer, and the father of Virginia Woolf—brushed away Mill's idea that censorship compromises truth, not because censorship is legitimate but because it doesn't work. For censorship to be effective, Stephen argued, not only must a "poisonous" work be destroyed, but the very ideas in the work, what he called the "mental phase," must be erased from people's minds. That task would require a much more far-reaching, and functionally impossible, level of persecution. "If so wild a hypothesis can be entertained," Stephen wrote, such an effort "would be equivalent to the suppression, not of this or that theory, but of thought" itself. And unless the state is capable of stifling thought, which it is not, it "may as well let it alone altogether."[41]

Stephen's essay makes a stronger case for the toleration of heterodox opinions than *On Liberty.* Mill's arguments presumed that speech suppression causes ill because it is effective; Stephen's thesis is grounded on the fact that such persecutions are by nature half measures. Yet he goes further: "Restraint of opinion, or of its free utterance . . . is the essence of persecution," he concludes, "and all conduct intended to achieve that purpose is immoral."[42] But even Stephen, as a man of his class and position, took part in a little nip and tuck on expression when he or his colleagues thought it necessary. As the editor of the *Cornhill Magazine*, he demanded multiple expurgations of Thomas Hardy's novel *Far from the Madding Crowd*. It was inappropriate in a publication established to be, in founder William Thackeray's words, "strictly limited to the inoffensive" and with "nothing which could be unsuitable reading for the daughters of country parsons."[43]

OXEN AT THE GATES: CENSORSHIP IN CONTINENTAL EUROPE

As in England, censorship on the Continent was one of a series of tools deployed by governing authorities to maintain dominance over the increasingly restive masses. Elites had good reason to be uneasy: the recent revolution in France, and the alarming uprisings in 1830 (France again), 1848 (multiple countries), 1871 (France once more), and 1905 (Russia) made plain the threat of politicized lower classes. While relaxation of speech restrictions followed each upheaval, they often proved temporary as the disruptive potential of unregulated speech revealed itself.

Power, as it was constituted in the nineteenth century, saw the populace as a threat. Enormous energy and resources were devoted to managing what the common people could read and express, and to preventing the dissemination of information that might lead to discontent. Denmark's King Frederick opined in 1833 that a peasant should learn only his duty to God, himself, and others. "Otherwise, he gets notions in his head."[44] More pointedly, the president of France, Adolphe Thiers, defined the purpose of education as instructing the lower orders that "when the poor have a fever it is not the rich who have sent it to them."[45] Spain's prime minister Juan Bravo Murillo rejected schools for the poor entirely, declaring, in 1851, "Here we don't want men who think, but oxen who work."[46]

Primary education for the masses remained mostly unavailable until late in the century, but literacy rates rose nonetheless, as did the speed and breadth of communications and industrialization. Emperor

Franz I of Austria refused in the 1830s to allow railway construction, lest "revolution might come into the country," but of course railroads were built in Austria and everywhere else. News soon traveled faster than steam locomotives. Yet power and wealth were still hoarded by the very few, and the poor, who worked and lived like animals, saw more clearly than ever what they were missing. They resented it. "The rightful demands of the laborers increased because the people of the land study more, know more, see more," testified a Hungarian peasant in 1890. "How can you blame us? We have learnt how to read and write. We would now like to wear better clothes, eat like human beings, and send our children to schools."[47] The "oxen" were no longer content to remain in their pens.

Just as education was denied to the poor, so too was the right to vote. The British historian Thomas Macaulay maintained that expanded suffrage would lead the populace to "plunder every man . . . who has a good coat on his back and a good roof over his head."[48] The result, declared the German historian Heinrich von Treitschke, would be "the superiority of . . . workers over employers."[49] Also restricted were rights to assembly and to form trade unions; most gatherings and organizations were forbidden, or required prior permission. Throughout the nineteenth century, unions, socialist organizations, and labor strikes were routinely and violently suppressed. As the historian John Gooch concludes, the "immediate concern" for European armies was to serve as "agents of domestic repression."[50]

Intertwined with these measures were mounting pressures on the press. French press laws had become so complex that at least ten books were published between 1830 and 1880 to help guide befuddled lawyers and journalists. A late-century Russian newspaper had to hire a specialist to help it make sense of the thousands of government circulars on public-affairs coverage; violation of any one of these could see the publication closed, or worse. France's new press law, in 1881, replaced an accumulation of more than three dozen laws comprising hundreds of separate clauses that had been adopted in the previous seventy-five years.[51] Even after this liberalization, the prosecutions—against obscenity, the press, caricatures, the theatre, and cinema—persisted.

Sometimes it was clear what was being banned in the press and in the arts. In Russia, playwrights and librettists were barred from depicting hundreds of specific subjects, including the Romanov tsars, the famine of 1892, and censorship itself. Not long after Napoleon abdicated in 1814, France expressly prohibited stage references to the disgraced emperor. But such specific prohibitions were rare, as most censorship standards fell somewhere between the vague and the absurdly vague. A late-century Berlin court upheld a ban on plays that might undermine "confidence in the administration of the law," including material that could imply that the government "does not grant the individual citizen his rights," while an Austrian law forbade all printed matter that might create "an unfavorable influence upon the people's morals, patriotism, or education."[52]

Such laws were ambiguous by design, giving authorities wide latitude to strike at any material they perceived as threatening the state or moral order, whether explicitly or by implication. A Swedish parliamentary committee determined that broad laws were required against publications "detrimental to public safety," because "there are modes of writing, using allusions, as well as allegories and irony which cannot possibly be anticipated in any detail" in a written statute.[53] At all events, writings directed at the lower classes were subject to the most exacting scrutiny. The files of German censors were stuffed with police warnings about written materials whose "style and cheapness" made them available to the "great mass of people"; Prussian censors targeted a book for removal from shops not just because it complained about injustices and "bad government" but because it was also written in a style addressed to "the less educated social strata," in whom it could induce "discontent with existing conditions."[54]

Such nebulous standards made life both easy and hazardous for censors. They were given wide discretion to decide what to suppress, but one misstep could bring harsh consequences. In 1842, a freshly jailed Russian censor begged the chief of the secret police to tell the tsar "how difficult it is to be a censor. We really do not know what is demanded of us. . . . We are never safe and cannot fulfill our obligations." The trepidation caused by this uncertainty, according to the Russian historian A. M. Skabichevskii, writing in 1892, "explains why censors were able to find the spirit of revolution even in cookbooks."[55] Censors even banned materials that caused no offense. In 1823, after the Austrian playwright Franz Grillparzer's drama *King Ottakor* was blocked for two years, he asked the censor what the problem with the play was. "Nothing at all," the censor replied, "but I thought to myself, 'One can never tell!'"[56]

An additional layer of ambiguity was added when states tried to accommodate the demands of the middle and commercial classes for materials that were off-limits to the poor. At various times, France, Germany, and Russia all exempted expensive works from prepublication censorship while imposing it on cheaper books, newspapers, and pamphlets. In Austria and Russia, a book could be banned when published individually at a low price, and permitted when sold as part of an expensive set, which happened with Tolstoy's mildly steamy novella *The Kreutzer Sonata*. The author's wife, Sonya, pleaded with the tsar to allow it to be published as part of Tolstoy's collected works, since, as the tsar himself noted, "not everyone could afford to buy the whole set."[57] At the same time, books with extremely troublesome subject matter could be allowed if the lower classes were deemed too ignorant to grasp them. This occurred, with delicious irony, in 1867, with the book that became the seminal text of communism: Karl Marx's *Das Kapital*. Russian authorities allowed it in both the original German and in translation, because it was "difficult" and "inaccessible," its socialist message deemed buried in a "colossal mass of abstruse, somewhat obscure" arguments.

Authorities were especially alarmed by media that did not require reading, particularly theatre, drawings, and caricature, which communicated to a broader and poorer audience than printed text did and carried a more powerful, visceral impact. In several countries, advance censorship of theatre and graphic art continued long after such controls had been dropped for press publications. As the nineteenth century progressed, printed text came to be regarded by authorities as the least threatening communications medium, because so many poor people remained illiterate or semiliterate. Print was consumed individually rather than in groups, and text required some degree of reflection to process its messages. With the emergence of the cinema at the end of the century, a panoply of controls was hastily imposed to restrict what was viewed onscreen. Even under relatively liberal political systems such as those in Sweden, Denmark, and France, unapproved films could not be presented.

Whether in theatre, opera, film, or even songs, the perceived threat of instant, unmediated communication was compounded by the fact that these forms were consumed collectively. They were thus, according to the scholar Robert Goldstein, considered "far more likely to provoke *immediate* action than printed matter typically read in the privacy of (often middle-class) homes."[58] As elaborated by an Austrian censor in 1795:

> Censorship of the theatre must be much stricter than the normal censorship of printed reading matter. . . . The impression made [by a dramatic work] is infinitely more powerful . . . because [it] engages the eyes and ears and is intended to penetrate the will of the spectator in order to attain the emotional effects intended; this is something that reading alone does not achieve. Censorship of books can . . . make them accessible only to a certain kind of reader, whereas the playhouse by contrast is open to the entire public, which consists of every class, every walk of life, and every age.[59]

And when this impressive experience is shared in darkened rooms by simple people, according to a French theatre censor in 1862, the risk of chaos results:

> An electric current runs through the playhouse, passing from actor to spectator, inflaming them both with a sudden ardor and giving them an unexpected audacity. The public is like a group of children. Each of them by themselves is sweet, innocuous, sometimes fearful, but bring them together and you are faced with a group that is bold and noisy, often wicked. The courage or rather the cowardice of anonymity is such a powerful force![60]

Preventing such electric currents kept theatre censors busy throughout the century. While special scrutiny was paid to inexpensive venues, plays performed before all strata of society were examined. Regardless of where they were performed, any play that impugned ruling authority would likely be censored. Austrian censors demanded that even fictional kings be depicted with delicacy. The producers of Shakespeare's tragedy *King Lear* were told in 1826 to rewrite the play so that Lear did not die at the end, even though the story was rendered incomprehensible as a result. The censor believed it was treasonable to show a king dying in a state of abject insanity.[61]

French censorship highlights the excesses of nineteenth-century speech suppression efforts as well as the ways in which writers and publishers circumvented them. It starts with Napoleon: Just two months after taking power in 1799, he shuttered fifty of Paris's sixty-three newspapers and barred new ones from opening. The population, weary from more than a decade of upheaval and looking for a measure of stability, barely resisted.

The police were assigned close control of the press, book publishing, the theatre, and booksellers, but for Napoleon—a control freak for the ages—this was not enough. The terms "usurper," "tyrant," and "social compact" were banned from print, as were references to French military defeats.[62] The existence of censorship itself was censored: in 1806, Napoleon rebuked his minister of police, Joseph Fouché, for allowing a book on conditions that implied that other books were being suppressed. That same year, he declared, "There is no censorship in France"—but the facts were plain, as were the falsehoods spewing from his regime in a stream of bulletins. "False as a bulletin" became a common saying.[63]

Napoleon also involved himself personally in the censorship of speech and the arts. Along with his duties as emperor and supreme military commander during a time of general war, he moonlighted as a censor, poring over texts of astronomy, poetry, history, and literature and ordering the suppression of works he found to "trouble the peace of the State." The works of the prominent astronomer Jérôme Lalande were suppressed on Napoleon's orders on account of the scientist's atheism, which the emperor believed was harmful to society.

No less pernicious, in Napoleon's estimation, were the ancient works of Tacitus. He banned them from schools, fearing that the Roman historian's critiques of tyrants would reflect badly on him. As for the officially approved plays that, according to the historian J. Holland Rose, were "remarkable only for fulsome adulation," they "were sometimes hissed off the stage."[64]

Over at least nine regime changes during the century, French censorship policy oscillated wildly. Despite the critical role of the underground press in mobilizing opposition, and the loosening of censorship that followed most changes in government, those taking power inevitably reimposed controls. Pamphleteers were effective in fomenting the 1830 revolution that brought in the July Monarchy of Louis-Philippe I. As promised, the king initially relaxed his predecessors' aggressive speech restrictions, even declaring in a charter that "censorship can never be reestablished." Yet massive crackdowns started the following year, including more than one hundred prosecutions against one republican opposition journal, *La Tribune*.[65] The censorship of caricatures also ping-ponged with each sudden shift in government. Requirements that caricatures be approved before publication were eliminated in 1814, restored in 1820, abandoned again in 1830, reestablished in 1835, abolished in 1848, brought back in 1852, eliminated once more in 1870, reinstated the next year, and then abolished in 1881.[66] Even during periods when censorship was suspended, caricaturists weren't safe. Honoré Daumier was jailed for six months for an 1831 illustration of Louis-Philippe sitting on a toilet-throne, gobbling food and tribute from the poor while defecating riches to his aristocratic supporters.

Censors had always been concerned about immorality, but now they focused primarily on suppressing the lower classes' access to political information. Targeted taxes, as well as fines and imprisonment of journalists and editors, ensured that for much of the century, approved press content was almost entirely apolitical. For example, the first French mass-circulation newspaper, *Le Petit Journal*, contained no political content, so it escaped steep taxation and thus could be sold at a low price. Even sensational news was suppressed, as lurid vice and crime stories were thought to stimulate the latent criminality of the underclasses.[67] Yet the state's elaborate censorship machinery was not as effective as it might first appear, particularly when it came to the ultracheap end of the printing trade. Corruption and inconsistent enforcement carved holes in the system that savvy publishers and rogue operators exploited repeatedly.

One such printer was Antoine Chassaignon, who published from a filthy little shop on Paris's Left Bank. He specialized in *canards*, single sheets catering to the lower classes and featuring tales of violent crime and executions. Because of their low price, *canards* were the most accessible source of news for a broad stratum of the population, and it was government policy to regulate them carefully. Yet Chassaignon operated without a license for eleven years, and despite multiple arrests, he stayed out of jail and in business. One of his arrests, in 1842, involved the sale of a banned work, *Les Aventures du Duc de Roquelaure*. Two thousand copies were discovered at his shop, after thousands more had been distributed via street peddlers. He was provisionally sentenced to one month in prison and a heavy fine, but neither penalty stuck. After he managed to have the sentence suspended and his case put on ice for two years, the evidence against him had decomposed beyond recognition: the police had left him in charge of the offending sheets, which he wisely placed in a damp corner of his shop. With nothing but moldy paper to use against him, the charges were thrown out.

Chassaignon's case is curious, but not an anomaly. Rather, it shows that laws alone are not enough to stifle the press. They must be consistently enforced, and in nineteenth-century France, they often were not. "For every example of newspapers destroyed by fines and famous editors and authors jailed for publishing . . . questionable works, there is a counterexample of printers and peddlers evading the law," writes the historian Thomas Cragin. As press restrictions multiplied, so did the number of unlicensed printers, acquittals on technicalities, payoffs, and breakdowns at every level of the system. "With such consistent failures to enforce press laws," Cragin concludes, "one can hardly imagine many printers troubling themselves about them."[68] That is not to say that French press censorship was entirely ineffective—the thousands who were silenced, jailed, fined, and bankrupted would beg to differ. But most censorship systems can be breached, and the more complex they become, the more opportunities present themselves for doing so.

CHAINING THE DEVIL: DIRTY BOOKS IN ENGLAND, FRANCE, AND THE UNITED STATES

The nineteenth century's preoccupation with censoring sex aligns with the class-driven suppression of other types of speech. In England, cheap pornography was feared for its supposed ability to unleash what the historian M. J. D. Roberts characterizes as "the potential animality of the working classes," and to stimulate their "criminal appetites."[69] But smeared onto these concerns was a thick layer of paradoxical sexism: obscenity law was also deployed to protect middle- and upper-class English females from their own libidos. Much of the legal assault on sexually arousing materials was based on the assumption that exposing women to pornography would rouse in them a slumbering dragon of lust, to the destruction of family, home, and all that is well and good in society. On the following page an 1801 illustration depicts what many feared a book like Matthew Lewis's lurid gothic novel *The Monk* might incite a respectable lady to do when no one is watching. Even the cat is overwhelmed.

Many of the men who worked to prevent such a nightmare scene from taking place seemed to have spent quality time alone with such images, as pornography celebrating the febrile sexual appetites of middle- and upper-class women was consumed in considerable volume. The law aimed to guard good wives and daughters from exposure to anything that would spark the same kinds of desires their husbands and fathers fantasized about.

A key group driving English obscenity prosecutions was the Society for the Suppression of Vice, a collection of moneyed do-gooders dedicated, according to one satirist, to "suppressing the vices of persons whose incomes do not exceed £500 per annum."[70] The society dedicated itself against smut with the zeal of the righteous and scored several big hauls. In 1845, it nabbed a London dealer with 12,346 obscene prints, 393 books, and hundreds of copper plates and lithographic stones for reproducing even more. But its efforts only highlighted the

Pub.d Feb.y 26.1801 by R.W.Fores 50 Piccadilly.

Tolios of Caricatures lent out for the Evening

LUXURY
or the Comforts of a Rum p ford.

large quantity of pornography in circulation. One of the society's nemeses was the leading Holywell Street pornographer William Dugdale, whose booklist featured the perennial bestseller *Memoirs of a Woman of Pleasure* (popularly referred to as *Fanny Hill*), as well as titles such as *The Bed-Fellows or the Young Misses Manuel, The Confessions of a Young Lady, The Ladies' Tell-tale*, and the magazine *The Boudoir*, all explicit accounts of the sex lives of fictional well-born women and girls. While the society consistently secured convictions against Dugdale, it failed to inflict lasting damage on his business. By mid-century, it had become evident that going after pornographers with one-by-one lawsuits was not working; a change in the law was needed to empower magistrates and police to seize and destroy obscene materials wherever they were found.

The society's wishes were fulfilled in 1857. In yet another of its suits against Dugdale, Lord Chief Justice John Campbell, who had never presided over an obscenity case, was awakened to the scale of the porn trade and was horrified. He sentenced Dugdale to a year in prison, for which Dugdale threatened him with a knife, and then ran to the House of Lords. "Cackling like an old hen," according to one account, Campbell reported what most everyone already knew, that the "sale of poison more deadly than prussic acid, strychnine, or arsenic—the sale of obscene publications and indecent books—was openly going on." He introduced a bill allowing police, on a magistrate's order, to break into any premises where such materials were kept or sold and "burn or otherwise destroy them" then and there. The society had found its key ally.[71]

The proposed law, called the Obscene Publications Act of 1857, or Lord Campbell's Act, drew resistance from some lords who were concerned that it could be used to censor legitimate art and literature. Campbell replied that he sought only to enforce "common feelings of decency," the contours of which were self-evident. By way of example, he held up a copy of *Lady of the Camellias* by Alexandre Dumas fils. Campbell said the book (about the proverbial prostitute with a heart of gold and which later became the basis for Verdi's opera *La Traviata*) was "polluting," but nevertheless would be allowed because it was not written for the "single purpose of corrupting . . . morals." In the charged atmosphere surrounding the bill—which M. J. D. Roberts describes as a press-driven panic over the "moral leprosy" porn was causing in women and youth—that was enough to assuage concerns. It had to be. There was intense pressure on lawmakers to do *something* to stop pornography's effect on "pure minds." The bill became law, and in various forms remained so for a century. Later that year, Justice Campbell recorded in his diary that Holywell Street's pornography business had been shut down after "several assaults." That was true for a short time. Dugdale continued his trade under a series of fake names, often changing locations and selling his wares by mail, until his death in prison in 1868.

The broad reach of Lord Campbell's Act was set a decade later, when the definition of obscenity was finally, if poorly, articulated. This time the Court of Queen's Bench considered *The Confessional Unmasked*, a pamphlet about the "depravity" of Catholic priests and the licentious questions they "put to females in confession." The pamphlet was tame compared to much of the stuff still being sold in London, and it was more intended to knock Catholicism than to arouse, but one Lord Chief Justice Alexander Cockburn seized on it to make a lasting mark on obscenity law. He made no secret of his own opinions, comparing the circulation of pornography to carrying a child with smallpox through the streets. Yet the pox infects without regard to its victims' social position, whereas Justice Cockburn assumed that pornography only contaminates certain groups of people—those, presumably unlike himself, whose moral foundations were shaky to begin with. He stated:

> I think the test of obscenity is this, whether the tendency of the matter charged as obscenity is to deprave and corrupt those whose minds are open to such immoral influences, and into whose hands a publication of this sort may fall.[72]

This 1868 decision, *Queen v. Hicklin*, set the standard for British and, later, American obscenity law well into the twentieth century. Under what became known as the Hicklin test, an entire work could be banned if even one isolated passage tended to "deprave and corrupt" any segment of the population whose minds were believed to be vulnerable. *Hicklin* was a censor's wet dream, as it gave authorities astoundingly broad latitude to target any works they found objectionable. And while Justice Campbell might only have meant to ban works of pornography when he rammed his bill through Parliament, Hicklin invited censorship of serious works of art, literature, and even scientific inquiry.

In fact, the Hicklin test was no test at all. As the scholar Harry White points out, it "merely formulated a prevailing prejudice regarding class [and gender] differences and recommended that obscenity rulings be guided by it."[73] Consider the 1877 arrest and prosecution of the publishers of a birth control manual, *The Fruits of Philosophy*. The book had been available for decades in pricy editions, but Charles Bradlaugh and Annie Besant provoked authorities by releasing it as a sixpenny pamphlet. Bradlaugh lamented in court that "it is a horrible thing to put us in danger of imprisonment for giving information to the poor, which may with impunity be given to the rich." Besant argued that the book helped impoverished women guard their health by explaining to them how to have fewer children.[74] These arguments did them no good. The "lewd, filthy" book was found to "deprave public morals" by facilitating sex for pleasure among the lower classes. The conviction was set aside on a technicality, but it was nevertheless used later to label Besant an unfit mother and revoke her custody of her young daughter.

Lord Campbell's Act and the Hicklin test were also used to censor books that seemed to cause no harm in their original languages, but became dangerous when published in low-priced translations. Among these were three works by Émile Zola, for which the English publisher Henry Vizetelly was charged in 1888. Vizetelly pleaded guilty and withdrew the books. Facing financial ruin, he then released them again, although without the passages he surmised were objectionable. This brought more charges, and a jail sentence. *The Times* cheered the convictions: "Assuredly most people will agree that the publication of cheap translations of the worst of Zola's novels is a grave offence against public morals, and that it is a good thing that the law should be invoked to restrain it." Significantly, Zola's books themselves were not the source of harm. Had Vizetelly republished them in the original French, the readership would have remained limited to the well-educated, and no one would have cared. It was what the scholar Marcelle Wong calls Vizetelly's "infringement of the de facto censorship of the language barrier"—that is, his release of foreign ideas to an unschooled domestic audience—that did him in.[75]

Chancy scientific materials were also kept away from general audiences. Most notably, *Sexual Inversion*, a book cowritten by the physician and sexuality researcher Havelock Ellis, came under fierce attack upon its release in 1898. The study involved the case histories of twenty-seven gay people, "inverts" in the parlance of the day, and was meant to challenge the assumptions behind a recent statute prescribing two years in prison for people who commit "gross indecencies." In a bitter irony, the law responded by labeling the study obscene and suppressing it. The London bookseller George Bedborough was charged with inflicting on society a collection of "lewd, wicked, bawdy, scandalous, and obscene" pornography. According to the indictment, *Sexual Inversion* was not meant to advance knowledge or spark discussion, but to stimulate "disordered and lustful desires" and bring readers into "a state of wickedness, lewdness, and debauchery."[76]

Like Vizetelly, Bedborough had little choice but to plead guilty, but debate over the case typified the period's science-versus-smut controversies. While some in the scientific community defended *Sexual Inversion*, others were ambivalent. The prominent British medical journal *The Lancet* opined that the book's subject matter "touches the very lowest depths to which humanity has fallen," but concluded that it was nevertheless a legitimate inquiry, written in a "purely dispassionate and scientific style." What chiefly bothered *The Lancet*'s editors was that a nonscientific publisher had released it. This put the book "into the hands of readers totally unable to derive benefit from it as a work of science and very ready to draw evil lessons from its necessarily disgusting passages." While a work dealing with an "odious" subject such as homosexuality is not necessarily indecent, *The Lancet* argued, it could become so "if offered for sale to the general public with the wrong motive." By taking the work out of the ivory tower and placing it into "dirty hands," Bedborough had transformed Ellis's genuine scientific efforts into illegal filth.[77]

Just as Zola's literary naturalism became obscene when translated into English, Ellis's study on homosexuality became illegal when released to the general public. In both cases, it was the readers who had changed, not the works, and "lewdness," "wickedness," and "debauchery" were ascribed to the broader public that received them. This protean definition of obscenity is exactly what the Hicklin test was meant to achieve: a work's legality depended less on its contents than on who consumed it. The law can "chain the devil of impurity," wrote William Coote, the leader of Britain's National Vigilance Association.[78] By endorsing Lord Campbell's Act and later driving the Zola prosecutions, the NVA sought to accomplish just that, but selectively. The devil was to be shackled in the people who were believed to be most susceptible to his mischief.

The year 1857 was a busy one in the history of censorship. As Parliament passed Lord Campbell's act, France saw prosecutions of two works that are now fixed in the canon of Western literature: Gustave Flaubert's *Madame Bovary* and Charles Baudelaire's *Les Fleurs du Mal* (*The Flowers of Evil*). As in Britain, it was the audience for *Bovary* rather than the book's contents that spurred the charges. Novels at the time were read primarily by women—a group, as the scholar Elisabeth Ladenson points out, regarded as "essentially infantile," lacking men's capacity to distinguish fiction from reality.[79] Flaubert himself deployed this trope in the book, which ties Emma Bovary's problems to her consumption of novels. The impossible ideals she absorbs from books drive her away from her husband, into the embrace of other men, and on a path to ruin. When Emma finally kills herself, she does so by swallowing arsenic, imagining the painless, picturesque death she has read about in fiction and plays. However, she dies in agony, with the poisonous taste of ink—literature itself—in her mouth.

The government focused on the bad example set by Emma's adultery, coupled with the absence of characters who forcibly argue against infidelity—or, indeed, of any admirable characters at all. "Who," asked the prosecutor, "are the readers of M. Flaubert's novel? Are they men interested in political or social economy? No! The light pages of *Madame Bovary* fall into even lighter hands, into the hands of girls and sometimes married women." Given the purportedly impressionable minds of the novel's readership, Flaubert should have elevated rather than debased his audience's morals and avoided using his talents to invite women and girls to emulate "nature in all her nudity and crudity." Flaubert's attorney agreed that literature should uplift, but he maintained that the book did so by showing the ruin that comes from vice.

This argument worked to the extent that Flaubert was acquitted, but the judges were not appeased. The novel still "merits severe blame," they wrote, for failing to "beautify and enhance the spirit by elevating the intelligence and purifying the morals," and Flaubert was wrong to have produced a book reflecting "vice" and "disorder" rather than serving as an antidote to it.

Flaubert recognized early that the controversy was the promotional opportunity of any young writer's dreams. The hubbub surrounding the prosecution against this, his first novel, helped to launch his career. Just before the trial, he gushed in a letter to his brother that "everyone" was now interested in *Bovary*. "If my book is bad, the trial will serve to make it seem better; if on the contrary it is to last, this will be its pedestal."[80] Two months after the proceedings ended, the novel was published in unexpurgated form, and fifteen thousand copies sold almost immediately. Excerpts from the trial were regularly included in later editions.

Women were not Baudelaire's target audience. The poet himself asserted that his poems—about putrefaction, lost innocence, and corruption of mind, body, and spirit—were "not written for my wives, my daughters, or sisters." Women in nineteenth-century Europe were seen, at least by men, as too intellectually insubstantial to contend with serious poetry. As the prevailing myth went, the works of the great poets lined the bookshelves of educated men, for whom they were a passage to lofty contemplation. *Les Fleurs du Mal* was the first volume of serious poetry whose author was brought up on obscenity charges in France, and the trial, following soon after the *Madame Bovary* case and with the same prosecutor, Ernest Pinard, in charge, continued the debate about the uses of literary realism. True, the poems were addressed to readers who believed themselves more resilient than female consumers of novels, but Baudelaire's insertion of what the judges called "vulgar realism" into the elevated realm of poetry made his transgressions even more transgressive. "The reader holds his nose; the page stinks," complained one critic. *Bovary* erred in exposing women to the world without cautionary messages; *Les Fleurs du Mal* offended by smearing mud and waste onto the walls of literature's most treasured palace.

The prosecutor Pinard, smarting from his loss against Flaubert, exhorted the judges to halt "these growing tendencies," the "unhealthy fever" that had arisen "to depict everything, to say everything, as though the law against offending public morality had been suspended, and as though morality did not exist." The judges obliged, and Baudelaire gave them much to condemn. However, unlike *Bovary*, which concerned something as common as an adulterous marriage, the six Baudelaire poems the court condemned reflected nothing of this world. One poem involved the sucking of hemlock from a woman's "pointy breast" ("La Léthé"); another included a threat to make "a wide and gaping wound" in a woman's "astonished flank" ("Á celle qui est trop gaie"); while still another described sex with a female vampire ("Les Métamorphoses du vampire"). Regardless of the unreality of what they depicted, the poems were, in the end, considered too sexual, too strange, and in the judges' words, led to an "excitation of the senses."[81] The suppressed poems could soon be found in France in illegal editions, but it would take nearly a century before a French court officially reversed the ban. And despite France's removal of most press restrictions in 1881, about fifty obscenity cases per year were brought through the end of the century, most resulting in convictions.

Most accounts of nineteenth-century American responses to pornography center on the morals crusader Anthony Comstock and the 1873 federal law informally bearing his name, which criminalized the use of the mail to transmit anything remotely "indecent." The focus is understandable. Comstock, colorful and maniacal in his enforcement of that law, for several decades ran a pitilessly effective censorship machine. But there was considerable obscenity suppression in the United States before he left his Brooklyn dry-goods business to purify America. In the pre–Civil War years, particularly in New York City, repeated action was taken against pornography, much of it of the variety celebrating the passions of middle- and upper-class females. The prosecutions diminished the street trade in such literature, but not the demand. The business largely shifted to the safer mail-order model, which allowed it to expand both in volume and geographic reach. By the time Comstock arrived, bundles of porn were being posted throughout the country from New York.

Unlike those in Britain and France, pre-Comstock American enforcement efforts were not primarily focused on protecting women, youth, or the lower classes from the malign influence of sexually arousing materials. Rather, police and the courts were interested in suppressing anything with a tendency to corrupt anyone's morals. This was the standard adopted in what appears to be the United States' first reported court case dealing with pornography, *Commonwealth v. Sharpless* (1815), in which the Pennsylvania Supreme Court affirmed the conviction of six men who had charged money to view a painting in a private home of a "man in an obscene, impudent, and indecent posture with a woman." Such an exhibition, the court held, "tends to the corruption of morals," which "weakens the bands by which society is held together." Similarly, at about the same time, the Connecticut Supreme Court declared: "Every public show . . . which outrages decency, shocks humanity, or is contrary to good morals, is punishable."[82]

But if women were not a central focus of the law, they were certainly on the minds of consumers. The first New York obscenity indictments were brought in 1842 against several men for trafficking in obscene prints and "fancy" books, as explicit pornography was called, many of which were first-person accounts of fictitious women slaking their prodigious sexual appetites. A selection of the titles gives the picture: *Memoirs of the Life and Voluptuous Adventures of the Celebrated Courtesan Mademoiselle Celestine of Paris*; *The Curtain Drawn Up, or The Education of Laura*; and *The Confessions of a Voluptuous Young Lady of High Rank*. The indictments included excerpts from the offending works, such as this dramatic passage from the generously titled *The Cabinet of Venus Unlocked in a Series of Dialogues between Louisa Lovestone and Mariana Greedy, Two Cyprians! Of the Most Accomplished Talent in the Science of Practical Love*:

> Oh, what rapturous exquisite delight as I took it, when it rushed in and filled the whole deep cavity where I felt it swell and throb as if it would burst with its exertions within. I strained and struggled with him to the utmost of my strength, and seemed inspired beyond my natural powers in every effort. I screamed with excessive ecstasy, and, oh! God of burning lust! At the last flush and overwhelming flow of bliss that gushed into me from him, my senses were wholly entranced and the whole world of love seemed swallowed up in the heavenly sweet delirium.[83]

For obvious reasons, prosecutors soon stopped including such quotations in their indictments.

The rise in the number of prosecutions after these cases made the retail distribution and sale of porn a risky proposition. Jail sentences and stock seizures could only be prevented with expensive bribes. In 1858, the publisher Frederic Brady was held in the notorious New York jail called the Tombs and had his entire stock confiscated after street peddlers identified him as their supplier. He bribed his way out of jail, but his business suffered. He and other publishers soon turned to the relative safety of mail-order sales. The new model worked well, as there were many "gentlemen at a distance" (in the words of one publisher) ready to pay for stimulation in a plain brown wrapper.[84] Publishers also tailored new products to the mails, such as *Venus' Miscellany*, a subscription magazine that featured presumably apocryphal letters from respectable women detailing their florid sexual exploits with various combinations of men and women.

This, and much more, is what Comstock devoted his life to eradicating. A failure in business and "devoid of humor, lustful after publicity, and vastly ignorant," as the historian Paul Boyer describes him, Comstock found his calling pushing through prosecutions of porn dealers. His first efforts brought him wealthy patrons, and by 1873 he had teamed with the YMCA to form the New York Society for the Suppression of Vice, the first American organization of its kind. Its objective, as he put it, was hunting down pornographers "as you hunt rats, without mercy." Other anti-vice societies, backed by titans of industry and finance, soon sprang up in most cities. They had a decisive influence on the law and the day-to-day decisions of editors, publishers, booksellers, and librarians, most of whom adopted the narrow strictures on speech the societies demanded. Their goal was no less than the extirpation of all the sexual influences corrupting society.[85]

The New York Society for the Suppression of Vice was not the only such organization, but Comstock's dedication to his cause was especially intense: it was based on firsthand experience. He had masturbated so compulsively in his younger days that he feared being driven to death. The rest of his life appears to have been an effort to atone for past transgressions. In his book *Traps for the Young* and other publications, he declared, "Satan is more interested in the child than many parents are."[86] The devil's chief weapons were books and pictures aimed at bringing young readers into a "state of excitement," leading to masturbation, the "secret vice" that, along with the lust that drives it, "defiles the body, debauches the imagination, corrupts the mind, deadens the will, destroys the memory, sears the conscience, hardens the heart, and damns the soul."[87]

In 1873, Comstock brought this message to Washington, DC, where he pressed for a federal law criminalizing the use of the mail to transmit these secret entertainments. To illustrate the scope of the problem, he set up a "chamber of horrors" in Vice President Schuyler Colfax's office, where he exhibited items that had purportedly been mailed to students. These included fancy books and lowbrow magazines, devices to aid in sexual potency, and other "abominations." As legislators toured and retoured the show, examining the displays with all the thoroughness the gravity of the matter required, they were reminded by the bill's sponsor, Representative Clinton Merriam of New York, that such "low brutality" threatened to "destroy the future of the Republic."[88] The *New York Times* applauded the proposed law, as did anti-vice societies and the grandees who supported them. The Comstock Act was signed by President Ulysses S. Grant that year.

Like Lord Campbell's Act, the new law, formally called the Act for the Suppression of Trade in, and Circulation of, Obscene Literature and Articles of Immoral Use, prohibited much more than explicit material. In addition to the "lewd" and "lascivious," everything "indecent" or "immoral" was barred from the mail, as well as contraceptives and information regarding birth control or abortion. Comstock was later appointed as postal inspector, and the act, along with American court decisions adopting the broad Hicklin test for obscenity, gave him almost limitless power to strike against Satan's merchants. By the end of Comstock's forty-year run as the nation's chief censor, he claimed to have confiscated sixteen tons of "vampire" literature, organized more than four thousand arrests, and secured the convictions of enough people to fill sixty train coaches. In addition to erotic materials, he seized and burned illustrated playing cards, physiology textbooks, sex toys, abortion and birth control devices and information, marriage guides, and a good deal of serious literature. "Garbage smells none the less rank and offensive," he wrote, "because deposited in a marble fount or a gold or silver urn. . . . Decaying matter breeds disease, whether confined in costly receptacles or ash-barrels."[89] Under the Comstock Act, works by Chaucer, Tolstoy, James Joyce, William Faulkner, Ernest Hemingway, and William Burroughs, among many others, were banned.

THE FEELINGS OF SLAVE OWNERS AND THE DIVISIONS WITHIN THE UNITED STATES

The mail delivered a serious political crisis in 1835, when Northern abolitionists sent mass mailings to Southerners advocating, in strident terms, the end of the "peculiar institution" of slavery. This brought a furious reaction from Southern, and many Northern, lawmakers and citizens, and drove several events that tested state and the federal governments' readiness to censor political speech. The abolitionists had touched a raw nerve: the question of whether new states and territories would allow slavery was volatile, and the compromises reached thus far had only prompted ever more vexing disputes. More immediate was the prospect of violence by Southern Blacks, who vastly outnumbered the white population. A slave revolt was only narrowly avoided in South Carolina in 1822, and in 1829, a free Northern man of color, David Walker, sent pamphlets urging slaves to rebel. Two years later, the enslaved Virginia preacher Nat Turner led a revolt of African Americans that left sixty whites dead and sowed panic throughout the South. Virginia's governor, John Floyd, blamed the uprising on abolitionist literature.

Terrified that the next revolt might be successful, and convinced that Northern meddlers were stoking Black discontent, Southern states locked down discussion of abolition within their borders. Alabama, for example, decreed death to anyone distributing writings "tending to produce conspiracy or insurrection . . . among the slaves of colored population," while Virginia passed a law imprisoning anyone circulating materials with the intent of "persuading persons of colour . . . to rebel or denying the master the right of property in their slaves."[90] In North Carolina, it was a crime to teach slaves to read. Yet after the 1835 mass mailings, such laws were seen as insufficient. Postmasters in Southern and certain Northern states embargoed abolitionist literature, an action with which Amos Kendall, the US postmaster general, agreed, while President Andrew Jackson—a slave owner who believed abolitionists should be killed—proposed a federal law prohibiting the use of the mail to deliver "wicked" and "inflammatory appeals addressed to the passions of the slaves." After intense debate in Congress, the proposed legislation failed. A majority agreed that the federal government did not have such expansive powers to regulate abolitionist speech in the mail, even if the states did.

Southern lawmakers also demanded that Northern states ban abolitionist speech, which seemed possible given the threat to public order posed by mob attacks on abolitionists in the North. In 1835, William Lloyd Garrison, the publisher of an abolitionist paper, *The Liberator*, was led by such a mob half naked through Boston's streets with a rope around his neck; soon afterward, Elijah Lovejoy, another abolitionist and the publisher of *The Observer*, was murdered in Illinois. Many Northern politicians reviled abolitionists. New York's governor, William Marcy, presided over a meeting that denounced abolitionists as "disturbers of the public peace" who were "disloyal to the Union." But despite broad-based anti-abolitionist sentiment, not one Northern state passed laws banning such speech. Typical was the response of Governor George Wolf of Pennsylvania. He agreed that the abolitionists' crusade smacked of "dangerous and alarming" fanaticism, which stood to "kindle a fire which it may require the best blood of the country to quench," but he still maintained that "legislation cannot be brought to bear upon it without endangering other rights and privileges." These included "freedom of speech and of the press," which "must not be infringed upon or controlled by enactments intended to remedy some temporary mischief."[91]

Southern states had more success in censoring discussions of abolition in Congress, at least temporarily. Antislavery petitions were pouring into the Capitol, creating new channels for abolitionist ideas to spread and, it was feared, encouraging slaves to revolt. No less urgent were the fragile emotions and self-esteem of slave owners, who resented being ridiculed for owning other human beings. According to South Carolina's slave-owning senator John C. Calhoun, the petitions "contained reflections" that were "injurious to the feelings" of himself and others like him. "We must not . . . permit those we represent to be thus insulted on that floor"—namely, of Congress.[92] In 1836, the

House of Representatives sought to restore "tranquility to the public mind" by passing a resolution not to consider any such petitions, which became known as the Gag Rule. For seven decidedly untranquil years, the receipt of such petitions and the discussion of slavery and abolition was barred in the House. Nevertheless, the number and breadth of petitions increased sharply—now including demands to eliminate the Gag Rule itself as a curb on free speech.

In the end, the Gag Rule only managed to increase support for the abolitionist cause and focus attention on the right to discuss the issue.[93] By 1859, a broad defense of free speech about slavery was part of the platform of Abraham Lincoln's Republican Party. The efforts to ban abolitionist literature under federal law, and the other efforts to ban it in the Northern states, were rejected not because a court said so but because of what Professor Michael Kent Curtis identified as the "revered—if somewhat undefined—place freedom of speech and press occupied in the hearts and minds of many Americans." The abolitionists believed, as Curtis put it, that "truth would vanquish error, and freedom of speech would destroy slavery."[94] As the Civil War would show, it was not as simple as all that.

Speech repression in the South only grew worse in the years leading to the war. An 1849 Virginia code imposed prison terms and fines on anyone who "by speaking or writing maintains that owners have no right of property in slaves," and Louisiana imposed twenty-one years' hard labor on those indulging in conversation having "a tendency to promote discontent among free colored people, or insubordination among slaves."[95] In Arkansas, three men were hanged merely for owning copies of Hinton R. Helper's *The Impending Crisis of the South: How to Meet It* (1857), a book arguing for the end of slavery on economic rather than moral grounds, and for the right to protest against it. As the South hurtled toward a rupture with the Union, Georgia made dissent against secession a crime punishable by death.

Once the war began, harsh speech controls were imposed in the North and in the areas controlled by the Union armies. Resistance to the war in the North was often strong, particularly among opponents of conscription and, later, the emancipation of enslaved African Americans. The postal service was closed to "treasonable correspondence," a category that included many "disloyal" newspapers. In the face of what Lincoln and military authorities saw as efforts supporting the Southern rebellion, the writ of habeas corpus was repeatedly suspended and martial law declared in many areas. The most extreme of these measures, from September 1862, applied nationwide against "all persons discouraging volunteer enlistments, resisting military drafts, or guilty of any disloyal practice affording aid and comfort to rebels against the authority of the United States."[96] Thousands of opponents of the draft and the war were arrested and held in military prisons without trial.

Many of those jailed were individuals whose outbursts could have had no possible effect on the war effort, such as an Illinois man who said that "anyone who enlists is a God Damn fool," and a New Jersey man who announced that a man who enlists is "no better than a goddamned nigger."[97] Hundreds of newspapers were also shuttered for running articles critical of the war. Authorities saw these not as exercises of free speech but as incitements to treason. Among the editors who were indicted was E. N. Fuller of the Newark, New Jersey, *Evening Journal*. In 1864—already three years into the conflict with only more bloodshed in sight—he was charged with inciting insurrection and discouraging army enlistments. Here is an excerpt from his offending editorial:

> Mr. Lincoln has called for another half million of men. Those who wish to be butchered will please step forward. All others will please stay home and defy old Abe and his minions to drag them from their families. We hope that the people of New Jersey will at once put their feet down and insist that not a man shall be forced . . . to engage in the Abolition butchery. . . . This has gone far enough and must be stopped. Let the people rise as one man and demand that this wholesale murder shall cease.[98]

Such arrests raised the question as to whether someone who encourages disregard for the law shares some measure of guilt with the one who in fact breaks it. Fuller's exasperation with the carnage, and his expression of disgust at another round of conscriptions, is quite different from refusing enlistment. But he urged others to "defy old Abe," and without sufficient troops, the Union's fighting strength would have been diminished and its very existence arguably put deeper into jeopardy. Should the citizenry's right to speak out be protected even when it may put the country in danger? Or, as Lincoln wrote in 1863 about a case against another man arrested for advocating against the war, "Must I shoot a simple-minded soldier boy who deserts, while I must not touch a hair of a wily agitator who induces him to desert? . . . I think that in such a case, to silence the agitator, and save the boy, is not only constitutional, but, withal, a great mercy."[99]

Supreme Court justice Arthur Goldberg noted in a 1963 draft-dodging case that, while "the Constitution protects against invasions of individual rights, it is not a suicide pact."[100] Fair enough, but the line between protection of speech and the maintenance of national security is never easy to draw, and decisions about whether to silence agitators are all the more vexing when the nation is hemorrhaging blood. Upon ordering his soldiers in 1863 to close the offices of the sharply critical *Chicago Times*, Union major-general Ambrose Burnside stated, "Freedom of discussion and criticism which is proper . . . in time of peace becomes rank treason when it tends to weaken . . . confidence of the soldier" in the government in times of war.[101] Many disagree. Geoffrey Stone expresses the opposing point well: "To stifle free speech about [whether and how to conduct armed conflict] at the very height of wartime is arguably to suppress the right when it is *most* critical to the well-being of society."[102] For it is then that the population, especially those called to fight and possibly die, need to make informed judgments; and it is then that John Stuart Mill's defense of minority opinions—the obnoxious ones that may advance truths no one presently grasps—must be taken most seriously.

Despite the repeated suppression of speech by civilian and military authorities during the Civil War, there was still no shortage of virulent criticism in circulation about Lincoln, the war effort, and the emancipation of slaves. But the key issue behind wartime abridgements of speech—the extent to which governments may invoke a national crisis to censor dissent—would arise again and again, into the present day.

6

TROUBLE IN MIND
The Early Twentieth Century

Nineteenth-century censorship was marked by elites' fears of challenges to their wealth and privilege from the underclasses. During the first half of the following century, speech suppression battles were engaged on a much wider and more explosive field. World War I changed the geopolitical order suddenly, fundamentally, and forever. The conflict erased four empires, resulted in the eventual creation of more than a dozen new nations, sparked the Communist revolution in Russia, and poisoned the ground on which an even more transformative global conflagration would be fought a couple of decades later. When the Great War began in August 1914, authorities predicted that it would be brief. Soldiers marched to battle confident they would be home safe by Christmas. Four years and forty million casualties later, the very notion of trusting governance in the traditional mold struck many people as absurd. They had been told too many lies, suffered from too much incompetence at the hands of their leaders, and witnessed too much gruesome death.

At a time when war was no longer waged just between armies but by and against entire populations, the task of managing public opinion became more intricate. Media were harnessed to incite frenzies of hatred against enemies, and censorship of speech and opinion became more penetrating, widespread, and, ultimately, futile. Photographs of American and British soldiers killed in battle were totally suppressed, yet no one believed that death on a massive scale was not taking place; meanwhile, American propaganda films showing wounded soldiers whose "only sorrow" was "that they can fight no longer" were too ridiculous to take seriously.[1] And the mass arrests of people whose wrongdoing consisted of expressing opposition to the war only drew further attention to their message.

The war refined the scope and techniques of censorship for the coming decades, but what was, and remains, missing was any unified theory or consensus as to why some forms of speech should be censored more than others. What the legal scholar Thomas Emerson wrote about the US Supreme Court's approach applies to most democracies: namely, that it has "totally failed to settle on any coherent approach or to bring together its various doctrines into a consistent whole."[2] Instead, there have been waves of ad hoc repression to meet short-term policy objectives, sometimes followed by after-the-fact repentance—and then by more of the same when the political waters again become choppy. It was in the context of the US' most excessive suppressions of World War I–era political speech that the Supreme Court, while *affirming* the convictions of harmless dissenters, fitfully developed many of the conflicting theories that have come to ground the present day's broad speech protections. Speech regulation is as messy as speech itself.

At the same time, the arts everywhere were at the mercy of local authorities with nearly unchecked power. In the century's first decade, Lewis Carroll's *Alice's Adventures in Wonderland* (1865) was banned in many American schools for its imagined promotion of sexual fantasies and masturbation. In 1931, the book was also forbidden in China's Hunan Province because of the story's talking animals. "It is disastrous," the Hunan governor said, "to put animals and human beings on the same level." Later, it was banned again in the US for the bad example set by its hookah-smoking caterpillar.[3] The courts usually went along with such censorship and, whether the suppression took place in fascist Germany, New York City, or Manchester, England, few people rose to defend the targeted works. In 1929, Ernest Hemingway's *A Farewell to Arms* was banned in Boston for being too sexual, not long before it was thrown onto bonfires by the Nazis for its pacificism. And while Americans were denouncing the Nazi book burnings, John Steinbeck's *The Grapes of Wrath* was being set aflame in several states, even as New York City policemen heated their head-quarters by incinerating confiscated sexy books and photographs.

The lack of a coherent theory behind censorship makes it situa-tionally driven and, to varying degrees, arbitrary. Published images of dead American soldiers would be allowed two years into the US' in-volvement in World War II, but with severe restrictions, and then only to manipulate public opinion and demonize the enemy—images of GIs leering at prostitutes remained banned. And as American authorities aggressively censored information about the death and suffering from the nuclear attacks on Hiroshima and Nagasaki, they disseminated gruesome accounts and photographs from liberated Nazi concentra-tion camps. Only the enemy does evil.

"The first casualty when war comes," US senator Hiram Johnson reportedly said in 1917, "is truth."[4] In a half century wracked by rev-olution and armed conflict, truth was something to ration like a scarce resource, and to kill when expedient. The era's depredations brought fervent affirmations of the value of free speech, such as Article 19 of the United Nations' 1948 Universal Declaration of Human Rights: "Everyone has the right to freedom of opinion and expression; this right includes freedom to hold opinions without interference and to seek, receive, and impart information and ideas through any media and regardless of frontiers."[5] However, without a genuine commit-ment to these ideals, or a readiness to tolerate obnoxious opinions, they remain mere words on paper. "If liberty means anything at all," George Orwell wrote in 1945, "it means the right to tell people what they don't want to hear."[6] By this measure, liberty was in short supply. And so was the ability to express oneself on transgressive subjects such as sex and birth control, especially in cinema.

SEX AND CINEMA IN THE PRE-WAR YEARS

Restrictions on the press and political speech had been relaxing some-what before World War I, but tight morals controls remained, especially on materials crossing into radioactive subjects such as homosexuality.

Since 1872, for example, the British government had recognized the right of "public address" at Speakers' Corner in London's Hyde Park, but only if the rules of "decency" were observed. This did not include public defenses of same-sex love or sympathetic words about Oscar Wilde. The memory was fresh of Wilde's 1895–97 imprisonment for "gross indecencies," a sentence that had been greeted by cheers in the press and in the streets. In 1908, one Herbert Blyth ascended a platform at Speakers' Corner to vent about the wrongs that had been done to Wilde. When Blyth addressed homosexual behavior, two nearby policemen promptly arrested him for using indecent, obscene language.[7]

Pornography was easy to obtain in fin-de-siècle France, although trouble with the police was always possible. Depictions of homosexuality, especially lesbianism, were quite risky, notwithstanding that gay sex had been legal among consenting adults for more than a century. "At the very time the law ignored lesbianism as a reality," explains the scholar Nicole Albert, "it felt compelled to sue writers for giving sapphism a name and for granting it visibility." Absent special certification, women were not even permitted to wear men's clothing in public. The tame, lesbian-themed novel *Zé' Böim* (Gomorrah) had sold quietly for a dozen years without police attention until 1889, when the publisher used a new cover featuring a languid woman wearing only stockings on her parted legs, and with a flash of light where her crotch would be. The publisher's entire stock was seized. Two years later, the book went on sale again, this time with an image of a cat's head masking the woman's genitalia. The humor was lost on police. The publisher fled, but he was fined heavily and sentenced in absentia to more than a year in prison.

The Parisian music-hall scene was famously bawdy, but representations of sapphism remained taboo there as well. In 1907, at the Moulin Rouge, the writer Colette staged a pantomime performance with her lover, the Marquise de Morny, called *Rêve d'égypte* (Dream of Egypt). De Morny played a male archaeologist who happens upon a female mummy, played by Colette, who seductively unwraps herself and then kisses "him." The immediate uproar was front-page news. Under pressure from de Morny's family, police threatened to close the venue if the two women performed together again. The marquise withdrew, but Colette performed the following night with another person. This time, the show was closed. Another music hall, the Little Palace, staged *Rêverie d'éther* (Ether Daydream) in 1908, in which two women in minimal costume performed in a state of "ether inebriation and lesbian passion." The actors were fined for appealing to the "grossest, most excessive and dangerous lubricity" and "nervous passions."[8]

In the United States, Anthony Comstock and his allied anti-vice and "social hygiene" groups continued with their own excessive passions. Their aim was to eliminate materials that, as the Boston-based Watch and Ward Society put it, spread "moral diseases which lead to misery and crime." The society pushed through a successful obscenity prosecution against Elinor Glyn's frothy best-selling romance novel *Three Weeks* (1908), in which a young Englishman finds love in Venice with a married Russian woman. On appeal, the Massachusetts Supreme Court rejected the publisher's argument that the absence of explicit sex rendered the book non-obscene, holding instead that it may be banned due to an "impure" theme, even when it only discloses "details of the way to the adulterous bed."[9]

It wasn't just evocations of immorality that drew the attention of censors. Public-health activists such as Margaret Sanger, founder of what became Planned Parenthood, were also targeted under the Comstock Act, which classified birth control and abortion information as obscene. Sanger devoted her indefatigable energies to assisting America's poorest women, whose unwanted pregnancies and self-induced abortions endangered their health. Sanger published a sex education column, "What Every Girl Should Know," for *The Call*, a socialist newspaper. The column was suppressed; a blank box was put in its place that read "What Every Girl Should Know—nothing, by order of the United States Post Office!"[10] Undaunted, Sanger put out a "militant-feminist" publication called *The Woman Rebel*, in which she continued to "advocate the prevention of conception" and counseled women to "look the whole world in the face with a go-to-hell look in the eyes." Several of its issues were halted as obscene, and she was indicted. She fled to Europe, but not before distributing a hundred thousand copies of *Family Limitation*, a pamphlet offering detailed contraception information.

In 1915, while Sanger was in exile, Comstock engineered the arrest of her husband, William, for selling *Family Limitation*. The highly publicized trial resulted in a conviction, but it also served the broader purpose of charging a national debate on birth control, one that continues to the present day.[11] Returning to the US, Sanger opened the nation's first birth-control clinic, in Brooklyn, in 1916. It was shut down ten days later, but the movement she started, and the cause of women's reproductive freedom, was just getting started.

Sexual and other moral questions were front and center as censors contended with the advent of cinema and its uniquely powerful effects on audiences. To hype his new Vitascope, Thomas Edison hired two stage actors in 1896 to recreate for the screen the canoodling from the Broadway show *The Widow Jones*. Edison's catalog described the twenty-second film *The Kiss* this way: "They get ready to kiss, begin to kiss, and kiss and kiss and kiss in a way that brings down the house every time."[12] As expected, it brought howls of outrage. "Such things demand police interference," fumed one critic.[13] The critic's wishes were amply fulfilled, as cinema soon became the definitive mass entertainment. Film censorship was swiftly imposed in the US and Europe. Writing about Germany, the historian Gary Stark describes concerns behind film censorship throughout the West: it "sprang from upper-class fears of the urban lower classes," as widespread movie consumption was thought to "deprave and disorient" them, "undermine their attachment to traditionally sanctioned values, and lead to moral, perhaps even to social, anarchy."[14] On the silver screen, a kiss was *not* just a kiss.

The first American film censorship rules came out of Chicago in 1907, where more than a hundred thousand people were already visiting nickelodeons every day. Under the city's new ordinance, police could bar a film if it was "immoral or obscene, or portrays depravity, criminality or lack of virtue . . . or tends to produce a breach of the peace, or riots, or purports to represent any hanging, lynching, or burning of a human being."[15] Similar state laws followed, which the US Supreme Court upheld against First Amendment challenges in 1915. The court held that cinema merited no free-speech protections because it was "a business pure and simple," and films should not "be regarded as part of the press of the country or as organs of public opinion." Given that movies were "capable of evil . . . the greater because of their attractiveness and manner of exhibition," and were capable of exciting a "prurient interest," laws preventing such ills were needed.[16] That ruling, which stood until 1952, left movies open to a panoply of actual and threatened government controls that the industry would try to avoid by strict self-censorship.

The tendency of early film stock to explode sparked Britain's first regulations on film content. The 1909 Cinematograph Act empowered localities to impose safety rules on movie theatres, but it was soon used to govern the moral content of what was being shown as well. Faced with the reality of censorship and a confounding array of local standards, members of the film industry formed the British Board of Film Censors (BBFC, much later called the British Board of Film Classification) to impose a "voluntary" scheme of film censorship. No film would be passed unless it was "clean and wholesome and absolutely above suspicion," a broad standard that covered subcategories for sex, politics, violence, and derogatory representations of the armed forces and the empire.[17] However, the BBFC never had direct power to censor films itself: it only offered advice to local authorities, which did have this power.

In Germany, courts engaged in deft intellectual footwork to allow film censorship. The law had been liberalized in the late nineteenth century to bar censorship of "pictorial representations . . . reproduced mechanically or chemically for purpose of public distribution." Read literally, the law would *preclude* film censorship—but that would have left movies ungoverned, which was unacceptable. Films such as *Sinful Love*, *Queen of the Night*, and *Death in the Nude* were enticing masses of lower-class patrons, raising the risk, according to Württemberg authorities, of "severe agitation, high excitability and even mental disorders." The courts held that the law did not apply to movies, as audiences viewed not the celluloid film itself but the image it incorporated, which was in turn an illusion created by light passing through the film. Thus, no tangible "pictorial representations" were displayed. Police were in put charge of reviewing the movies that more than one million Germans were viewing daily. These included *The Cheap Meal*, a 1913 comedy short, which was refused. In it, an angry diner offended by a nasty waiter stomps out of a restaurant without paying the bill. It was feared that the film would encourage others to do the same.[18]

Censors also targeted politically sensitive subjects. The first recorded act of European political film censorship occurred in Russia, in 1896, when incompetence on the part of authorities resulted in the Khodinka Field disaster, a human stampede in which hundreds of people who had gathered to celebrate the inauguration of Nicholas II lost their lives. Anyone documenting the event had their cameras and film seized, and the press was forbidden to mention what had happened. In Prussia, a film about the 1910 Portuguese revolution was banned for fear that it would glorify revolt, as was the 1913 movie *The Enemy Is Here*, about a hypothetical Franco-German war that was thought to depict the German army in a negative light. That same year, as tensions at the border increased, French authorities urged local officials to suppress movies in which characters appeared in German uniform.[19]

The subversive potential of film deeply concerned ruling authorities, yet the danger was largely hypothetical. Escapism, not politics or revolution, was the preoccupation of pre-war cinema, and no early movies came close to posing a true challenge to entrenched power. In any event, it wasn't films or news articles that threatened governments. It was war. That came in 1914, with the pistol shot that ended the life of Austria's Archduke Franz Ferdinand. As blood splattered across Europe and other parts of the globe, information became ordnance—to be deployed, siloed, or falsified as conditions demanded. As governments enlisted entire citizenries in the fight, the small space that had been opening for expression and dissent in previous decades was shut tight.

PURITY THROUGH BLOOD: CULTURE, NEWS, AND DISSENT DURING THE GREAT WAR

The geopolitical causes of World War I have been debated in thousands of publications, but none of them mattered on the ground at the time. War on a massive scale was on, and the minutiae of international alliances, colonial contests, and trade disputes were sterile abstractions to those being asked to join the fighting or otherwise make sacrifices. Something more elemental—like hatred—was required to motivate people to risk everything. Belligerent governments ignited multimedia propaganda machines to bombard their populations with messages demonizing the enemy as murderous, perverted subhumans while exalting the nobility of their own national causes and characters.

To the Allies, the German "Hun" was portrayed, in Boyer's words, as "an obscene, lustful brute who laughed as he mutilated virgins and impaled infants on his bayonet."[20] Germans were also accused of spreading the "infection" of homosexuality, using agents provocateurs to foment labor unrest, and stupefying British troops with cocaine and opium—an ironic charge, given that in 1917 the British dropped opium-laced cigarettes behind Turkish lines.[21] Germans were told they were defending their fatherland against maniacal aggressors. The kaiser's government accused Russians of destroying Prussian villages and massacring civilians, and circulated accounts of Belgian women and priests abusing wounded German soldiers. The Allies were also denounced for using "savage"—that is, dark-skinned—colonial troops from Africa and Asia to fight civilized—white—peoples.[22]

The war was promoted as more than an opportunity to vanquish a depraved enemy. It was also embraced on all sides as a blood-drenched purification rite leading to personal and collective renewal. A feeling had taken hold that something vital had vanished amid decades of rapid industrialization and social division—a sense of unity and purpose lost, of collective spirit adrift. To many middle- and lower-class youth, the world in 1914 appeared as filthy as the Thames, as dark as the skies above the Ruhr, and as hopeless as the bitter, short lives of miners and industrial workers. The war would solve all this, and a restoration of spirit would emerge in a clash of blood and iron. This sentiment was also common among the cultured elites. Reflecting on the "wave of diseased degeneracy" that pervaded British art and society, the sculptor W. R. Colton stated in 1914 that "it was high time that war should come with its purifying fire."[23]

The English poet Rupert Brooke wrote immensely popular sonnets in a series titled *1914* that reflected the depth of this yearning. In "Peace," he spoke for legions of Britain's young men when he thanked God for delivering the war, which "caught our youth, and wakened us from sleeping . . . to turn, as swimmers into cleanness leaping" away "from a world grown old and cold and weary," populated with "half-men" with "their dirty songs and dreary." Many British volunteers left for training with copies of Brooke's poems in their kits.[24]

For the German writer Ernst Jünger, whose unsparing wartime novel *Storm of Steel* (1920) later became a favorite during the Third Reich, the war, with its gore and deprivation, was a cleansing ordeal bringing personal and national strength. His description of the heady excitement of the war's first days read:

> We had come from lecture halls, school desks, and factory workbenches, and over the brief weeks of training, we had bonded together into one large and enthusiastic group. Grown up in an age of security, we shared a yearning for danger, for the experience of the extraordinary. We were enraptured by war.[25]

Thomas Mann called the war "a purification, a liberation, an enormous hope," while Stefan Zweig described the excitement as news of the war's outbreak spread in Vienna's streets, when "a city of two million . . . in that hour felt that they were participating in world history . . . and that each one was called upon to cast his infinitesimal self into the glowing mass, there to be purified of all selfishness."[26]

For the US, which joined the fighting in 1917, the war was no less a rite of national cleansing and a contest of absolute good against pure evil. In his message to Congress calling for a declaration of war, President Woodrow Wilson accused the German government of conducting "warfare against mankind," against which the US would conduct a "vindication of right."[27] Soon, articles appeared, such as those by an army public relations officer, Harold Hersey, assuring the nation that the war had "recreated" soldiers into men of "clean motives and higher desires," and "superhuman beings" overnight: "How much sweeter and cleaner would our home lives be if we were to live like these boys do?"[28] Social reformers and vice societies took the cue and pushed for redoubled morals censorship at home to bring the national character in line with the new, morally irreproachable fighting men. "Gradually," Boyer observes, "the belief took hold that the civilian population, deprived of the purification of the trenches, should nevertheless seek its own spiritual renewal."[29]

A surge of local anti-vice campaigns broke out across the country, many backed by new anti-obscenity and morals legislation. The October 1917 issue of Margaret Anderson's magazine *The Little Review* was banned from the mail for its inclusion of Wyndham Lewis's short story "Cantelman's Spring-Mate," which concerns a British conscript who gets a young English girl pregnant and then cruelly abandons her. The offending sex scene goes thusly:

> On the warm earth consent flowed up into her body from all the veins of the landscape. The nightingale sang ceaselessly in the small wood at the top of the field where they lay. He grinned up towards it, and once more turned to the devouring of his mate. He felt that he was raiding the bowels of Nature.

It's likely such a passage would not have invited suppression had the war not backgrounded it, but a later scene in which Cantelman bashes in a German's head "with the same impartial malignity that he had displayed in the English night with his Spring-mate" sealed the story's fate.[30] The link between killing and sex was too close. Postal authorities confiscated the issue, a move Anderson unsuccessfully challenged in court. Judge Augustus N. Hand—who would later affirm lifting censorship of James Joyce's *Ulysses*—was uncomfortable with the suppression of works of "permanent merit," but he was hesitant to undermine the government's position in wartime. "I have little doubt that numerous really great writings would come under the ban if the tests that are frequently current were applied," he wrote.[31]

Most wartime American literary censorship resulted not from court action but from intimidation and complicity. The War Department gave the American Library Association lists of books that did not belong in libraries, and they were followed to the letter. Most writers were "caught up in the exaltation of the moment," writes Boyer, "and to the few who were not, publishers' doors were firmly closed. . . . In a time of national stress, American writers were expected either to offer superficial escape . . . or to provide yet another channel for glorifying the Allied cause and reinforcing the national impulse toward a higher, purer life. To the vice societies, all this seemed to be the realization of their most fondly cherished dreams."[32]

Similar cultural and, in many cases, sexual cleansing efforts were underway in all combatant countries. During the course of what the scholar Samuel Hynes calls the British assault on "dissenting sex— that is, homosexuality," Rose Allatini's inexplicit novel *Despised and Rejected*, which followed the wartime experiences of a gay consci- entious objector and a lesbian woman, was banned for its threat to the nation's moral health and military success. The publisher's stock of D. H. Lawrence's *The Rainbow*, with its frank treatment of het- ero- and homosexual desire, was seized and destroyed in Britain soon after its 1915 publication. According to one reviewer, "A thing like 'The Rainbow' has no right to exist in the wind of war." The book's decadent sexiness made it "one more symptom of the sex problem that the war had been sent to cleanse, and by writing it Lawrence had man- aged to subvert the war effort without mentioning it," writes Hynes.[33] No meaningful distinction was made between the war in the trenches and the metaphorical war against sexuality in fiction.

In Germany, the wartime imposition of martial law was an oppor- tune pretext for authorities to further tighten control over the cinema. Out went films "not in keeping with our earnest times due to shal- lowness or banality," including those concerning the "lives of whores and criminals . . . [that] for want of any larger idea, comprise a chain of crazy, outlandish, exaggerated, and often meaningless scenes"; and in came movies "suited to maintain high morals and to cultivate love for the fatherland."[34] Military commanders across Germany banned "junk" movies from their districts, as well as garish movie posters that were deemed unsuitable to the "gravity of the present times."[35] The film historian Wolfgang Mühl-Benninghaus explains that these mea- sures were taken to reestablish an imagined "'spiritual harmony' that was lacking before the war . . . [and restore a] 'healthy national soul.'" In this sense, the war was not merely to defeat enemies in battle, but also to regain a national purity that had been lost.[36] In such a climate, even a film such as the lowbrow 1914 thriller *Detective Braun*, which had been approved before the war, was now banned. Films of quality were also refused when they clouded the clear lines authorities wished to mark. *The Iron Cross* concerned German and Belgian families who were friends before the war but now must endure their sons fighting against each other. It ended by asking where all the suffering will end . . . and was refused by censors.

Addressing the war's human cost, the British prime minister, David Lloyd George, told the *Manchester Guardian*'s editor in 1917, "If people really knew, the war would be stopped tomorrow. But of course they don't know, and can't know. The correspondents don't write and the censorship would not pass the truth. What they do send is not the war, but just a pretty picture of the war with everybody doing gallant deeds."[37] For Britain and the other combatant states, censorship was weaponized to support propaganda campaigns and to keep people ignorant of the true price they were paying, until, as Lloyd George put it, the "knock out" of the enemy was delivered.[38] In the process of controlling the wartime news, newspapers were raided and closed, dissent was equated with treason, and a true understanding of the conflict was prevented.

Expansive laws thrown into place at the war's beginning (and later in the US, after it joined the fray) led to the organization of elaborate censorship machines. Their practices varied, but each was geared to keep reporters away from anything other than government-sanctioned and cleansed information and, if they somehow managed to obtain genuine news, to prevent them from publishing it. Authorities also controlled the news and discussion at home that had bearing on the war and suppressed any speech that might distress people or weaken morale. Add to that new, wide-ranging prohibitions on sedition—typical were New Zealand's criminalization of words that "excite disloyalty" and the US law against speech that could bring the government into "disrepute"—and the foundation for what the conservative and later Nazi jurist Carl Schmitt called state intervention in "all spheres of human existence" was laid.[39]

Winston Churchill, then first lord of the Admiralty, expressed the British government's view about war reportage when he told editors, "The best place for correspondence about this war will be in London," and that it should be "fought in a fog."[40] As soon as the fighting began, in August, all the undersea cables surrounding Britain except those that were British-owned were cut, and all communications entering the country were intercepted. Britain's secretary of state for war, Lord Horatio Kitchener, banned correspondents from the area surrounding the British Expeditionary Force. The hasty passage of the Defence of the Realm Act greatly magnified the state's power to control information and punish its misuse. France and Germany passed similar restrictions, with the result that virtually all civilian and military news, cables, and correspondence were inspected and censored. Nevertheless, some reporters pressed on to the front line, exposing themselves to both enemy fire and retribution from their own governments. The British journalist Philip Gibbs, who defied Kitchener's ban by surreptitiously signing up with the Red Cross in France, was thrown in jail briefly when the subterfuge was discovered and told that he would be shot if caught again.[41]

By late 1915, France and Britain had established a system whereby accredited correspondents could sometimes report from the front, but only under close supervision. Every word they wrote was reviewed by field censors, who also checked that they did not conceal messages with invisible ink. Once approved, British reports were transmitted by the army to the War Office and then to newspapers and agencies. Only army officials could take photographs on the front lines, and, as in the United States, no images of their own dead made it to newspapers. Severe punishment awaited any unauthorized British photographer caught violating the rules. The war artist Paul Nash complained, "I'm not allowed to put dead men into my pictures because apparently they don't exist."[42]

Self-censorship by news organizations added to the sanitized picture. "The guiding idea behind the censorship," Gibbs later wrote, "was to conceal the truth . . . from the nation, in defense of the British High Command and its tragic blundering." Nevertheless, he and his colleagues were complicit: "There was no need of censorship of our dispatches. We were our own censors."[43] C. P. Scott's *Manchester Guardian* initially opposed the war, but he wrote that, once hostilities began, he saw the media's role as less to present the truth than to fall in line with the war effort: "The whole future of our nation is at stake and we have no choice but do the utmost we can to secure success."[44] Ernest Hemingway was characteristically blunter in his assessment, calling the war "the most colossal, murderous, mismanaged butchery that has ever taken place on earth," and adding, "Any writer who said otherwise lied. So writers either wrote propaganda, shut up, or fought."[45]

The close control of war news led, at times, to peculiar results. When the Germans conquered Fort Douaumont during the Battle of Verdun, French censors buried the news. When French troops later recaptured the fort and trumpeted their success in an official communiqué, people were surprised to learn that the Germans had ever held it. During Germany's "Turnip Winter" of 1916–17, when food shortages caused panic, the crisis couldn't be entirely denied, but it was minimized. The government censured a newspaper for publishing an advertisement that suggested too obviously the desperation caused by the diminished food supply: "Fat Dogs Wanted."[46] At times, news reports from France, Germany, and Austria were so heavily censored that nothing would appear of them in newspapers except blank spaces where the articles would have been. Some Austrian newspapers protested by inserting the word "*Zensur*" in the blank spaces, but in Germany such protests were forbidden, as they only highlighted the fact that information was being withheld.

Censorship resulted in disinformation, either by omission—such as strict restrictions on casualty reports—or by affirmative falsehoods. The first day of the bloodiest defeat in British history, at the Somme on July 1, 1916, was framed as a victory. The report (by Gibbs, who was nowhere near the front lines and who relied on official sources) surely brought anxious families some relief as they read it over breakfast:

> Our troops, fighting with very splendid valor, have swept across the enemy's front trenches . . . and have captured villages and strongholds which the Germans have long held against us. [German] dead lie thick in the track of our regiments. . . . And so, after the first day of battle, we may say: It is, on balance, a good day for England and France. It is a day of promises in this war, in which the blood of brave men is poured out upon the sodden fields of Europe.[47]

Missing from this inspiring account: the British suffered more than fifty thousand casualties that single day, including twenty thousand dead— the most catastrophic one-day losses for any army during the entire war.

The United States was no less active in controlling news from the front. "Every war story" reaching the American public, according to the historians James Mock and Cedric Larson, "had been censored somewhere along the line—at the source, in transit, or in the newspaper offices."[48] All journalists were required to swear an oath not to publish anything helpful to the enemy. They also had to post a ten-thousand-dollar bond to ensure their fidelity to the rules, which included a selective ban on accurate reporting. When tractors were shipped from the US to France instead of motorcycles, and trucks arrived without engines, the *New York Tribune* published an article by Heywood Broun headlined "Supply Blunders Hamper First U.S. Units in France."[49] Broun was barred from the theatre of war and the ten thousand dollars the paper had deposited on his behalf was forfeited.

Government authorities were also not above using censorship to advance personal ends. Most cynically, when the Bolsheviks announced in 1918 that they would dishonor bonds that had been issued by the tsarist government, this information was kept secret in France for more than a week so that wealthy bondholders could dump their securities before their value collapsed.[50] In England, Lord Kitchener was embarrassed by a 1915 report in *The Globe* that he intended to resign, so he had police enter the paper's premises to confiscate the next day's edition as well as its printing equipment, and the paper's operations were suspended. As the historian Deian Hopkin dryly observes, "It was felt necessary to make an example of the paper to prevent yet more serious incidents."[51]

All governments invaded the private correspondence both of men at the front and civilians. In Austria-Hungary, letters to soldiers mentioning food shortages at home were intercepted so as not to "negatively affect their spirits," while in Italy and Germany, soldiers could be court-martialed for letters containing "exaggerated and false information." The British relieved the burden of reviewing millions of letters from soldiers with the Field Service Post Card, known as the Whizz Bang or the Quick Firer. This form allowed only anodyne, prepackaged remarks concerning a soldier's health, whether he was leaving the front, and whether the addressee's latest letter had arrived. The soldier was allowed only to strike out whichever lines did *not* apply; nothing could be added. That left no room for remarks such as, "I have been blinded by gas" or "My commanding officer is a sadist." One former British soldier, George Coppard, recalled that before starting extended shifts in bomb craters on the front, where there was "a pretty mean chance of survival," soldiers were ordered to fill out Whizz Bangs with the message "I am quite well" undeleted.[52] And speaking of wellness, to protect morale, news blackouts in the warring countries restricted reporting about the massive influenza outbreak in 1918. Since Spain, which was neutral, was not under such strict censorship, its media became the main source of news about the pandemic, resulting in the disease being labeled the Spanish flu.

By 1918, five thousand people were working for the British government to censor civilian mail and telegrams. Among their most important prey were influential war opponents such as Bertrand Russell, who was jailed for several months for an article that attacked the Allied rejection of a German peace proposal. When portions of the piece later appeared domestically, he was jailed for six months.[53] It wasn't only anti-war correspondence that incurred penalties; merely sending letters could sometimes bring terrible consequences. As propaganda-driven hostility toward Germans spread in New Zealand in 1914, the respected businessman and German consul, Eberhard Focke, wrote to his brother in Germany to say that they would not be able to correspond during the war. The letter was intercepted, and Focke was sent to the notorious Somes Island internment camp for violating the ban against corresponding with enemy nations. He remained there until after the war.[54]

Domestic censorship was particularly pointed in the United States, where people of German ancestry made up one-quarter of the population, including eight million who had been born in Germany. Many German Americans were not enthusiastic about the conflict, and pacifists, anarchists, and socialists spoke out loudly against it. Many other Americans had been indifferent about the war during its first three years, before the US entered it, and were not convinced of the wisdom of joining in. In the six weeks after the US declared war, on April 7, 1917, only 73,000 men enlisted in the armed forces.[55] Faced with such ambivalence, the government worked overtime to whip up xenophobic hatred against Germany and Germans, and to crush anti-war sentiment and speech.

President Woodrow Wilson had little patience for dissent and didn't mind encouraging animosities to drum up support for the war. In his April 1917 message to Congress requesting a declaration of war, he announced, falsely, that Germany had "filled our unsuspecting communities and even our offices of government with spies and set criminal intrigues everywhere afoot." When Wilson later proposed the most sweeping laws restricting political speech since the 1798 Alien and Sedition Acts, he made clear that disloyalty "was not a subject on which there was room for . . . debate," and those who were disloyal "had sacrificed their right to civil liberties." This sentiment became government policy. War dissenters can expect no "mercy . . . from an outraged people and an avenging government," said Wilson's attorney general, Thomas Watt Gregory.[56]

The task of building patriotic outrage went to George Creel, head of the Committee on Public Information (CPI), a sprawling agency established in 1917 to manage the government's propaganda and censorship operations. The CPI produced movies such as *The Kaiser: The Beast of Berlin*, which depicted supposed German atrocities. Its pamphlets, sponsored speeches, editorials, and news releases stoked the belief that German spies and saboteurs were everywhere. When the government asked Americans to spy on their fellow citizens and report instances of disloyalty, hundreds of thousands of complaints were filed by individuals and volunteer groups with names such as the Sedition Slammers. Amid the hysteria, vigilantes attacked German Americans and ransacked their homes and businesses. Nor were other Americans spared. In Illinois, a mob wrapped a man accused of disloyalty in an American flag and murdered him in the street.[57]

In several American states and communities, the use of foreign languages was restricted. German, the most commonly spoken language after English, was the main target. Iowa's "Babel Proclamation" was among the most extreme of such restrictions, requiring that only English be spoken in public, in schools and places of worship, on trains, and even on the telephone. Governor William Harding declared that the First Amendment "is not a guaranty of the right to use a language other than the language of this country—the English language."[58] At least eighteen thousand people were charged in Midwestern states for violating English-only laws.

Speaking German was even dangerous when addressing a pet: in 1918, "detectives" overheard German voices coming from an open hotel window. They made their way to the room to find one Leo Derringer, an unregistered alien, speaking to his parrot in German, which responded in kind. Derringer was jailed, and the bird sent to what Mock called a "loyal" pet store.[59] For its part, the federal government passed the Trading with the Enemy Act (TWEA) in 1917, barring the publication of articles in foreign languages unless translations were first filed with the postmaster for review. In one instance, the elderly editor of a German-language paper in Eau Claire, Wisconsin, published an editorial criticizing the US Army's smallpox vaccination program. As he had not filed a translation beforehand, he was indicted for violating the TWEA—and for espionage. Despite evidence of senility, he was sentenced to a year in federal prison, where he died.[60]

Sweeping new federal sedition laws, the first in the US in more than a century, further fueled the suppression of dissent. Under the Espionage Act, enacted in June 1917, a large fine and up to twenty years in jail awaited those who "willfully cause or attempt to cause insubordination, disloyalty, mutiny or refusal of duty" in the armed forces, or "willfully obstruct the recruiting or enlistment service of the United States."[61] Eleven months later, in what became known as the Sedition Act, it became a crime to "willfully utter, print, write, or publish any disloyal, profane, scurrilous, or abusive language about the form of the Government of the United States" and its armed forces or "language intended to incite . . . resistance to the United States" or to support its enemies.[62] In effect, disfavored opinions were criminalized regardless of whether any tangible crimes or threats to the government resulted from them. States followed with their own prohibitions. More than two thousand prosecutions were brought during the war, mostly against a series of unfortunates who had done nothing more than express opinions about the conflict.

The pacifist Reverend Clarence Waldron received a fifteen-year prison sentence for handing five people a pamphlet that read "Surely, if Christians were forbidden to fight to preserve the Person of their Lord and Master, they may not fight to preserve themselves, or any city they should happen to dwell in," and "Under no circumstances can I undertake any service that has for its purpose the prosecution of war." A socialist Russian immigrant named Rose Stokes told a women's club and later published in a newspaper: "I am for the people, and the government is for the profiteers." The judge said these words violated the Espionage Act, as they "chill enthusiasm, extinguish confidence, and retard cooperation of mothers, sisters and sweethearts." Stokes received a ten-year prison sentence.[63] A German American who had not bought war bonds was sought out by a vigilante committee, whose members demanded to know why. His reply—that he did not want either side to win the war—resulted in his arrest.[64] And a Minnesota man was charged with violating the state's espionage act for telling a group of women who were knitting socks for servicemen, "No soldier ever sees these socks." The comment was interpreted as an attempt to obstruct the war effort by discouraging the women from knitting.[65]

It could also become a crime to invoke inconvenient historical events. Robert Goldstein, the German American producer of a 1917 movie about the American Revolution, *The Spirit of '76*, was fined and sentenced to ten years in prison for violating the Espionage Act. The film depicted familiar highlights of the US' origin story, such as Paul Revere's ride and the signing of the Declaration of Independence—but it also depicted British troops bayoneting women and children in what is known as the Wyoming (Pennsylvania) Valley Massacre. The court found that the film would "make us a little bit slack in our loyalty to Great Britain in this great catastrophe." It mattered not that the massacre had in fact occurred. "History is history, and fact is fact," the judge allowed. "But this is no time . . . for those things that may have the tendency or effect of sowing dissension . . . and of creating animosity or want of confidence between us and our allies." As for Goldstein's loss of personal liberty, the judge told him, "Count yourself lucky that you didn't commit treason in a country lacking America's right to a trial by jury. You'd already be dead."[66]

If the main purpose of censorship during this period was, as Goldstein's judge emphasized, to hasten "the day when the success of our arms shall be a fact," then the Allies' victory in 1918 should have brought a reduction of paranoia. It did not. The "war to end all wars" left the world more unsettled than it had been when the conflict began. As the United States contended with widespread labor unrest and anti-Communist hysteria, more draconian new speech restrictions were imposed, and the Supreme Court issued a series of key opinions that shaped the censorship landscape for the rest of the century.

THE SUPREME COURT WEIGHS IN AMID ANTI-RADICAL HYSTERIA

The armistice and subsequent treaties brought peace abroad but no peace of mind at home. The US government abruptly canceled contracts for war materials, causing work shortages and decreased wages. Unemployment also rose as returning troops filled the labor market. Bitter strikes resulted, raising the specter of a leftist revolution like the one that had recently struck Russia. The press was thick with stories—often correct, other times exaggerated or false—depicting Bolshevik rule as an apocalyptic mixture of chaos, property confiscations, and unchecked brutality. These stories amplified American fears of homegrown radical movements, often led by immigrants, that celebrated the Russian Revolution and advocated the overthrow of capitalist rule. In the agitated recesses of the popular imagination, the subversive German spy was replaced by the Communist revolutionary. In 1919–20, at least 1,400 people were arrested, and hundreds were imprisoned, for displaying the red flag as a symbol of opposition to the US government.[67]

Throughout 1919, disturbances and acts of domestic terrorism broke out across the country. In late April, a bomb exploded at the home of Thomas Hardwick, a former US senator, and mail bombs addressed to the likes of Supreme Court Justice Oliver Wendell Holmes and oil baron John D. Rockefeller were intercepted. On June 2, bombs detonated simultaneously in eight cities, one of which damaged the home of Attorney General A. Mitchell Palmer, who called the attacks an "attempt of an anarchist element of the population to terrorize the country." Soon, federal and state authorities organized strike forces to stamp out radical organizations, as well as what Palmer called the "constant spread of a disease of evil thinking." The targets were mainly people who had been born abroad. At least one labor newspaper, the anti-capitalist *Seattle Union Record*, was raided and closed.[68]

In what became known as the Palmer Raids, thousands of people were arrested and deported in 1920. Writing about a raid in Detroit, the historian Robert K. Murray described those rounded up as "plain, ignorant foreigners who were completely unaware of why they were being so treated."[69] On January 2 alone, some four thousand people were rounded up in dozens of cities, resulting in thousands of deportations. That the most basic legal protections were denied to these people, both in their personal treatment and the ransacking of their homes for books and papers, caused little concern. The *Washington Post* expressed the prevailing sentiment in a January 4 article entitled, "The Red Assassins": "There is no time to waste on hairsplitting over infringement of liberty." Besides, those who were captured had, according to Palmer, "sly and crafty eyes" and "lopsided faces, sloping brows, and misshapen features," which he called signs of "cupidity, cruelty, insanity," and "the unmistakable criminal type."[70] In other words, they were less than fully human and therefore undeserving of American rights and liberties.

This was the setting when the Supreme Court started its review of wartime and post-war speech prosecutions and issued its first-ever major First Amendment decisions. In a series of opinions between 1919 and 1927, it ruled for speech restrictions every time. Yet as these cases progressed, Justices Holmes and Louis Brandeis, among the court's most brilliant members, became uncomfortable with the excesses being condoned. They started to issue separate dissents and concurrences that, in their scope and eloquence, laid the intellectual groundwork for the broad protections that later took hold.

The court first examined the case of the general secretary of the Socialist Party of America, Charles Schenck, who had been jailed for conspiracy to violate the Espionage Act after he oversaw the circulation of leaflets urging conscripts to resist the draft. Conscription was unconstitutional, the leaflets said, and draftees were "little better" than convicts. The Court affirmed Schenck's conviction in a unanimous, confounding 1919 opinion authored by Holmes. Using language that remains among the most famous in American legal history,

Holmes presented a compelling standard for drawing the limits of political speech in a time of war, even as he refused to apply it to the case at hand:

> The character of every act depends upon the circumstances in which it is done. The most stringent protection of free speech would not protect a man in falsely shouting fire in a crowded theatre and causing a panic. . . . The question in every case is whether the words used are used in such circumstances . . . as to cause a clear and present danger that they will bring about the substantive evils that Congress has a right to prevent.[71]

Few would dispute that causing a panic in a crowded theatre may be forbidden, and Holmes's analogy of such a scenario to disruptions of the war effort makes at least some sense. What he omits is that Schenck's leaflets had no such effect, much less did they constitute a "clear and present danger" of one. There was no evidence that they caused anyone even to consider refusing to enlist; in fact, they only appear to have filled up waste receptacles. Under Holmes's oft-quoted paradigm, Schenck's conviction should have been reversed, yet neither Holmes nor the other justices were inclined to protect his speech—or his liberty. The mere "tendency" of the pamphlets to cause illegal draft resistance was, in the end, enough.

No less shameful was the court's treatment of Eugene Debs, the leader of the Socialist Party of America, and the party's perennial presidential candidate. Debs had been convicted in 1918 for a speech denouncing the war as a capitalist plot and supporting several people who had been convicted under the Sedition Act for aiding others in refusing induction. He did not directly advocate draft dodging, but he told the crowd, "You need to know that you are fit for something better than slavery and cannon fodder." Again, the court unanimously affirmed the conviction, and again Holmes wrote the opinion. Just one week after the Schenck decision, the "clear and present danger" standard was now nowhere to be found. Rather, Debs was deprived of his right to speak because the jury had found that his words had the "natural tendency and reasonably probable effect" of obstructing recruitment.

Despite the absence of proof that Debs's speech had caused anyone to dodge the draft, his ten-year prison sentence was upheld.[72]

Holmes began to reconsider his position over the following months. "I fear we have less freedom of speech here than they have in England," he wrote to a friend.[73] His evolution is reflected in the court's next major political speech case, *Abrams v. U.S.* The targets were a group of Russian Jewish immigrants who opposed US military action against the Bolsheviks. The defendants had been charged under the Sedition Act for throwing from New York City windows English- and Yiddish-language leaflets that attacked capitalism, urged munitions workers to strike, and passionately supported the Russian Revolution. "AWAKE!" the English-language pamphlet read. "Awake, You Workers of the World!" The Yiddish-language pamphlets called on people to "spit in the face of the false, hypocritic military propaganda." After a trial marked by the presiding judge's expression of anti-immigrant and anti-Semitic beliefs, the defendants were convicted and given sentences ranging from three to twenty years.

The court affirmed the convictions, but this time Justices Holmes and Brandeis dissented. Holmes wrote that the defendants "had as much right to publish as the Government has to publish the Constitution." Revisiting the "clear and present danger" test, he argued that the "publishing of a silly leaflet" was merely "expressions of opinion and exhortations" and posed no danger of inciting criminality. Yes, the leaflets had been distributed in a time of war, but even then the government "certainly cannot forbid *all* effort to change the mind of the country." (Italics added.) Holmes went on to present one of the classic statements on the nature of speech and its protection:

> The ultimate good desired is better reached by free trade in ideas— that the best test of truth is the power of the thought to get itself accepted in the competition of the market. . . . That, at any rate, is the theory of our Constitution. It is an experiment, as all life is an experiment. . . . While that experiment is part of our system, I think we should be eternally vigilant against attempts to check the expression of opinions that we loathe . . . unless . . . an immediate check is required to save the country.[74]

The notion of "free trade" in ideas—the phrase was later refined by Justice William O. Douglas as a "marketplace of ideas"[75]—in which the collective wisdom purchases the good ones and leaves the bad ones to rot on the shelf, would come to infuse First Amendment law, but for the present the court was not done upholding speech convictions. In *Whitney v. California* (1927), Charlotte Whitney had been found guilty under a state law against advocating the violent overthrow of government. Whitney's crime was helping to establish the Communist Labor Party, which supported "revolutionary class struggle." The court allowed the conviction, yet Brandeis wrote a separate opinion, joined by Holmes, that advanced a definitive statement on the right to dissent. His words are as stirring now as they were nearly a century ago:

> Those who won our independence believed . . . liberty to be the secret of happiness and courage to be the secret of liberty. They believed that freedom to think as you will and to speak as you think are means indispensable to the discovery and spread of political truth; that without free speech and assembly discussion would be futile . . . that public discussion is a political duty; and that this should be a fundamental principle of the American government.

Brandeis then tied these principles to government restrictions on speech, affirming the "clear and present danger" standard and stating that unless the danger is imminent and serious, the targeted speech should be allowed. Only in the most extreme and urgent situations can the government interfere with speech. Otherwise, "the remedy to be applied is more speech, not enforced silence. Only an emergency can justify repression."[76]

In the subsequent decades, the expansive approach to speech in the Holmes and Brandeis opinions entered American jurisprudence. With starts, stops, and detours, the "clear and present danger" standard would be invoked and refined, leading to a seminal 1969 decision in *Brandenburg v. Ohio*. In that case, the court upheld the Ku Klux Klan's right to rally for "revengeance" against Jews and Blacks, and protected "mere advocacy" of violence unless it incited "imminent lawless action." By the 1970s, the right to protest US involvement in wars was also guaranteed, in theory if not always in practice. But that was all far in the future. During the interwar period, censorship was imposed on more than purely political expression—although politics was never far from the censors' concerns.

CULTURAL CENSORSHIP BETWEEN THE WARS IN GERMANY AND BRITAIN

Over its fourteen-year existence, Germany's Weimar Republic hosted one of history's most astonishing outpourings of creative and intellectual energy. Expressionism in art, film, and literature bloomed; the Bauhaus redefined architecture and design; Jews from Albert Einstein to Erich Fromm sat on university faculties; and modernism in all its vivid forms came into its own. Even Joseph Pilates refined his exercise techniques there. Yet this all took place amid economic collapse, volatile politics, and street battles among anarchists, Communists, and extreme-right groups such as Adolf Hitler's National Socialist German Workers' Party (NSDAP). All of them exploited the Weimar Republic's on-and-off commitment to protecting free expression. The paradoxes of Weimar censorship are many, but we will focus on cinema, starting with a film released in 1919 about homosexuality.

Just one day after Germany's 1918 defeat in World War I, its acting government, the Council of People's Deputies, took the extraordinary step of decreeing that censorship was abolished at the national level. It would soon be reestablished, but in the interim, a spate of films was released that would have had no previous hope of approval. These included dozens of "educational" movies with titles such as *Paradise of Prostitutes*, *Virgins' Hell*, and *Soul Sellers*.[77] While these films were to various degrees pornographic, *Different from the Others—Anders als die Anderen*—stood out as an earnest, if melodramatic, plea for the decriminalization of homosexuality. Alternately presenting the bitter life and suicide of a delicate young gay man and a lecture by a prominent researcher and sex reform advocate, Magnus Hirschfeld, the film contained no depictions of sex. Rather, it called for tolerance and political action. It closed with Hirschfeld admonishing viewers to redeem the protagonist's tragic death by working toward the repeal of Germany's anti-sodomy law. Lest the message be lost, the final shot shows Hirschfeld crossing the law out of a statute book.

Upon its release in Berlin, *Different from the Others* drew impressive crowds, but various German states found ways to bar it; it became Exhibit A (along with *Vow of Chastity*, a film about randy priests) for morals advocates in their efforts to reestablish national cinema censorship. In April 1920, after ten minutes of debate, the new Reichstag did just that. Movies would henceforth need permits before release, and no film would be allowed if the new censorship boards found that it could disturb order, injure religious feelings, was immoral, or endangered Germany's image or international relationships. *Different from the Others* was then banned, in part because, as the cultural historian James Steakley characterized it, "the film might sway 'wavering' audience members to act out slumbering homosexual propensities."[78]

As Weimar politics became increasingly charged in the 1920s, censorship boards succumbed to pressure from above by government and military officials, and from below by citizen action and street demonstrations. In general, films with Marxist or pacifist messages came under more severe scrutiny than those advancing a conservative or militaristic perspective, although there was much dithering by censorship authorities. On March 24, 1926, a permit to show Sergei Eisenstein's silent film *Battleship Potemkin* was denied: the film was declared a danger to public safety because it showed some attacks by sailors on officers. Two weeks later, that decision was reversed on condition that those scenes be removed. Agitation from the political right against the film's "Bolshevist" tendencies continued after its successful April 29 premier, and the film was again banned—that is, until it was reapproved with additional cuts. The expurgated film was a hit, running for more than a year at one Berlin cinema alone.

Germany's political polarization had substantially hardened by 1930, when the American anti-war film *All Quiet on the Western Front* came up for approval. Before even submitting the film to censors, Universal Studios cut scenes in which German soldiers attack their sadistic officer and blame the kaiser for the war. The edited movie was approved, but on the second day of its Berlin release, Joseph Goebbels and about two hundred Brownshirts rose in the theatre, shouting, "Jews out!" and "Hitler is at the gates!" In the melee that followed, the Brownshirts threw stink bombs and released white mice in the theatre. In Berlin, large Nazi demonstrations against the film continued over subsequent days. Such disturbances, and intense pressure from the military, resulted in the revocation of the film's permit. The censorship board now found that its "one-sided depiction" of German cruelty would "endanger the German image."[79] The film was later passed, with further cuts, for private screenings, and then for the public—with still more footage removed. Universal agreed to distribute only the butchered version to other countries.

By 1932, with the Weimar government teetering and the Nazi Party gaining ever more influence, a Communist agitprop film, *Kuhle Wampe or Who Owns the World*, made with the close participation of Bertolt Brecht, was bound to run into trouble. The film showed unemployment lines, government callousness toward workers, boorish bourgeoisie, and most everything else a Communist audience would expect. It ends with the question "Who is going to change the world?" to which the answer is, "Those who do not like it." The censorship board barred its release, concerned it would depict the state as "incompetent and worthy of destruction."[80] Heavy lobbying from the Left and Right ensued, along with large leftist protest rallies, which resulted in a compromise: the film was released with substantial cuts. However, while censorship-driven edits did not dampen demand for *Battleship Potemkin* and *All Quiet on the Western Front*, the cuts made to *Kuhle Wampe* rendered the film, which already bent narrative conventions, even more difficult to sit through. It floundered at the box office. The following year, the Nazis took power and *Kuhle Wampe*, *Battleship Potemkin*, and *All Quiet on the Western Front* were among the first films to be banned outright.

After the chaos of the 1920s and early 1930s, the Nazi Party seemed, to many Germans, the one group capable of establishing order and reaffirming a distinctly national identity against racial and cultural degradation. No one was more horrified by the cultural developments taking place during the Weimar Republic than Hitler. By the time the aimless corporal ascended to the leadership of what became the Nazi Party, the use of force to compel cultural homogeneity was already central to its program. The party's 1920 manifesto stated: "Newspapers which violate the public interest are to be banned. We demand laws against trends in art and literature which have a destructive effect on our national life."[81] While many of their early supporters were likely against such draconian measures, Hitler's and the party's intentions were always out in the open.

As the party gained power and legitimacy, it moved quickly to control speech. When, in 1930, Wilhelm Frick became Thuringia's minister of the interior—the first time a Nazi Party member assumed a senior post in a German state—he issued a decree, "Against Negro culture, for German racial heritage," which rescinded licenses for performance venues allowing "Negro" music, dance, or theatre. Other of Frick's prohibitions included the works of Igor Stravinsky, Brecht, and Kurt Weill. Erich Maria Remarque's novel *All Quiet on the Western Front* (from which the film was derived) was suppressed, and Weimar's Castle Museum was ordered to remove artworks by Otto Dix, Wassily Kandinsky, Oskar Kokoschka, and other modernists.[82]

Within a few weeks of being appointed chancellor in January 1933, Hitler persuaded President Paul von Hindenburg to issue an emergency decree granting the government power to shut down the free press, including Communist and Social Democrat newspapers. The following month saw the Reichstag fire, which the Nazis blamed on the Communists and used as a pretext for more drastic suspensions of civil liberties and the establishment of a dictatorship. Liberal newspapers were soon closed or taken over by the Nazi Party, while editors and journalists were made responsible to the state. As control was consolidated over the arts, media, and political speech, the need for censorship as such dissipated. Everyone who worked in the cultural or communications fields was required to affiliate with the Reich Chamber of Culture (itself attached to Goebbels's propaganda ministry) and to abide by its rules. No one interested in their own career or safety published works outside approved channels, much less against the regime. At the same time, the state hermetically sealed the population from the "infection" of foreign news. In 1933 alone, some 250 foreign newspapers were banned.[83]

Controlling expression was just one element of the Nazi policy of *Gleichschaltung*, which meant the synchronization of all aspects of German society. The accumulations of the past had to be systematically cleansed as well, and that involved fire. The signature early events in this process were the massive book bonfires of May 1933. For weeks beforehand, Nazi youth groups combed libraries and bookshops, compiling lists of "un-German" and "degenerate" volumes. On May 6, hundreds of thousands of books were seized, including twenty thousand volumes in a raid on Magnus Hirschfeld's Institute for Sexual Science in Berlin. Approximately one hundred students "arrived in trucks, early in the morning, playing a brass band," wrote the British author Christopher Isherwood, and after smashing their way into the building, they poured ink on the books before taking them away.[84] The raid was reported by Nazi newspapers as an "energetic action against a poison shop" to "fumigate" an institute run by "the Jew Magnus Hirschfeld."[85]

On May 10, those books and hundreds of thousands of others—including the works of Marx, Mann, Proust, and Einstein—were set alight in dozens of simultaneous bonfires throughout Germany. The carefully staged media events stressed national rejuvenation through the murder of "poisonous" texts and the ideas they contained. In Frankfurt, the books were hauled to a central square in manure carts pulled by oxen adorned with garlands and then burned to the music of Chopin's "Funeral March." In a live radio broadcast from Berlin, Goebbels expanded on the fires' significance:

> [You students] have done well in the middle of this night to throw into the flames these unspiritual relics of the past. It is a strong, great, and symbolic performance. . . . Here the spiritual foundations of the November [Weimar] Republic sink to the ground. But out of these ruins will arise the phoenix of a new spirit. . . . The past lies in the flames. . . . Today under this sky and with these flames we take a new oath: the Reich and the Nation and our leader, Adolf Hitler—Heil! Heil! Heil!

In the same address, Goebbels called the bonfires "a performance" of Germany's rebirth to "all the world."[86] However, until the war actually began, Germany still paid attention to the impression it made on the world stage. When the nation staged the 1936 Summer Olympic Games, it sought to project a dazzling image of a renewed, united Germany while masking some of its worst excesses. It also engaged in a form of reverse censorship to hide signs of its most virulent anti-Semitism. The vulgar propaganda mouthpiece *Der Stürmer*

disappeared from the streets of Berlin during the games, and the om-
nipresent anti-Jewish slogans, as well as signs banning Jews from businesses and the like, were removed from view.

With the war's commencement, the destruction of the books and
other cultural treasures of Germany's enemies became prime objectives
for bombing raids. Twenty million books were destroyed, including
six million on London's Paternoster Row, the wholesale booksellers'
district, in 1940. Using the *Baedeker Tourist Guide to Britain* to locate
cultural targets for destruction, the Germans destroyed many more in
1942, including the Gulson Library in Coventry. Once Czechoslovakia
fell to German control, Czech geography and history books, as well as
others with passages contradicting German territorial claims over the
country, were destroyed. In Poland, where cultural elimination was a
key element of Nazi operations, private book collections other than
those held by ethnic Germans were forcibly appropriated. To further
eviscerate Polish culture, and to prevent the formation of a cadre of resistance leaders, the Polish educated classes were murdered en masse.
"In my area," said one Nazi administrator, "whoever shows signs of
intelligence will be shot."[87]

Nowhere was Nazi book destruction more tied to the extermination of a people than in the case of the Jews. Everywhere German
forces went, they rounded up Jewish books along with Jewish people,
and the same fate was often meted out to both. When the great Talmudic library of one of Lublin's most important yeshivas was set aflame
in 1941, a brass band was brought in to mark the celebration. As the
books burned, the sounds of the horns and the soldiers' cheers clashed
with the anguished cries of Jewish onlookers.

Not all Jewish books were burned: in one of the more peculiar
aspects of Nazi censorship, the party established pseudo-scholarly research institutes such as the Institute for the Study of the Jewish Question in Frankfurt ("the Frankfurt Institute")—essentially, a place for
Jewish studies without the "pollution" of Jews—which it filled with
confiscated Jewish books. Books routed to the Frankfurt Institute included volumes from the collections of the great Jewish libraries of Vilnius, Lithuania. With the arrival of German troops in Vilnius in 1942,
Lithuanian Jews were shot or herded into a ghetto, and the looting
of the libraries began. The Jewish librarian Herman Kruk was forced

to oversee the libraries' dismemberment and the preparation of the collections for transport. He and his assistants managed to hide about five thousand items, including Theodor Herzl's diary, letters of Tolstoy and Gorky, drawings by Chagall, and dozens of ancient manuscripts.

Kruk died in a camp in Estonia, but when Soviet troops arrived at the city in July 1944, with them were some of his assistants who had escaped eastward the previous year. They located quantities of the hidden books and established a new Museum of Jewish Art and Culture to house them. That project was short-lived, however, because the Soviets closed the new museum in 1948. But portions of the collection had already been smuggled to a new yeshiva in New York. The rest of the remaining collection was kept in a closed repository in Lithuania until the post-Stalin era, and its existence did not become public knowledge until 1988. A few years later, much of this remaining material was shipped to New York.[88]

Old habits die hard in Britain, especially when one doesn't wish to break them. Much of Britain's cultural censorship continued into the decades following World War I, affecting most forms of cultural expression. The state and its surrogates banned books, prints, films, plays, even postcards, and opened mail looking for forbidden materials. All the while, the government maintained the public fiction that censorship did not exist. According to its deceptively narrow definition, "censorship" meant only preventing something from being published in the first place. The rest was merely law enforcement. Since no official carried the title of censor, and creative works (apart from plays) were not subject to government preapproval, it could be denied, as a matter of public relations, that the state's routine seizures and suppressions constituted censorship.

In a 1938 note to police about a confidential list of books to take off the market, the Home Office stressed the importance of not "giving the impression" that it or police "are acting in any way as censors, or have any power to 'ban' a book."[89] Going further, the home secretary and morals crusader William Joynson-Hicks (known as Jix) promised strong enforcement against indecency—including Shakespeare's "coarser" passages, "when published cheaply"—but stated that these actions would not "fetter" anyone's right "to write what the spirit moves them to write." He claimed that he was merely fulfilling his duty to carry out the law and took pains to affirm, "I am not a literary censor."[90] With that doublespeak in place, the reality of literary censorship ground on.

Regarding cinema, the deep links to the government of the British Board of Film Censors (BBFC) ensured that it acted as a private body in name only. Decrying BBFC censorship of newsreels, Member of Parliament Geoffrey Mander complained in 1938 that it was "extremely convenient" for the BBFC to appear separate from the government "because . . . the Government can say, 'They have nothing to do with us; they can do anything they like.'"[91] Film censorship focused mainly on suppressing depictions of sex, bolstering established institutions and authority, and stopping the spread of working-class militancy. The BBFC's 1919 annual report explained that "nothing should be passed" that demoralizes audiences, glorifies crime, incites contempt of religion or marriage, or invites the ridicule of "Public Characters." The BBFC also "very carefully considered"—that is, censored—"subjects which are calculated to foment violent social unrest." Soon it was censoring films that showed "equivocal situations between white girls and men of other races" and "British possessions . . . as sinks of depravity," or which contained "inflammatory subtitles and Bolshevist Propaganda." As the BBFC's president told the Exhibitors' Association in 1937, "We may take pride in observing that there is not a single film in London today which deals with any of the burning questions of the day."[92]

That Soviet films such as *Battleship Potemkin* were taboo for general audiences (but not for elites) is not surprising. Such films were deemed inflammatory for the laboring classes. Film censorship also supported British foreign policy, most reprehensibly its appeasement of fascism and Nazi Germany. "Nothing anti-fascist is permitted," said Mander.[93] In 1933, the year Hitler came to power, the proposed anti-Nazi films *A German Tragedy* and *City Without Jews* were refused. The following year, Al Rosen's screenplay for *The Mad Dog of Europe* was turned down because, according to the BBFC censor, it was "pure anti-Hitler propaganda" and thus was "unsuitable," as was the American Michael Mindlin's documentary *Hitler's Reign of Terror*.

In 1936, a remake of the German classic *The Cabinet of Dr. Caligari* was refused, in part because it included a comic waxwork effigy of Hitler, which the BBFC censor thought "quite unnecessary." In 1937, Joris Ivins's *Spanish Earth* was cut because it reported that Germany and Italy were intervening in the Spanish Civil War. And in 1938—the year Neville Chamberlain infamously returned from Munich claiming that Hitler wanted peace—the American newsreel *Inside Nazi Germany* was banned because "it would give offence to a nation with whom we are on terms of friendship and which it would be impolitic to offend."

The censorship of anti-Nazi films continued until Britain declared war in 1939, after which all things anti-German were allowed. Roy Boulting's film *Pastor Hall*, about the Nazi persecution of a clergyman, had been refused at the script stage during appeasement; now it could be produced.[94] Britain also changed its tune on the Soviet Union. The Ministry of Information published "Arguments to Counter the Ideological Fear of Bolshevism," a manual for journalists that downplayed Soviet atrocities and recommended propaganda painting a "positive picture of Russia."[95] This was too much for George Orwell, who stopped providing commentaries for the BBC in 1943 and wrote the anti-Soviet satire *Animal Farm*. The book was banned in Britain until after the war, raising Orwell's disgust at the "prevailing orthodoxy['s]" demand for "uncritical admiration of Soviet Russia."[96] In 1949, he published *Nineteen Eighty-Four*, which described a world where history is falsified and lies become truth.

British obscenity censorship came in two broad varieties: the dreary grind of mail and customs interceptions, seizures, fines, and imprisonments, and what the scholar Nicole Moore calls "spectacle censorship."[97] The first category brought little public concern, because pornography had no public defenders. Even D. H. Lawrence—no stranger to obscenity—wrote, "I would censor pornography, rigorously," as it was an "insult" to "sex, and to the human spirit."[98] Volumes of porn were intercepted in the mail, while dealers were routinely fined and sometimes imprisoned. Copies of seized materials were sent to restricted collections in various libraries and repositories, and police kept others for reference. The rest were destroyed.

As for works of literature and art, the question was not whether obscenity laws were well-advised, but whether prohibitions should apply to them. The merits of Joyce's *Ulysses* (1922) would be dissected by US courts, but in England, the director of public prosecutions read only a few dozen pages before declaring it obscene. Smuggled copies were routinely intercepted by customs authorities and incinerated, until 1936—that is, once the American courts had finally allowed the book, declaring it "somewhat emetic" but "nowhere . . . aphrodisiac."[99] Lawrence's *Lady Chatterley's Lover* (1928) would wait until after a sensational 1960 trial to be published in unexpurgated form in Britain, but an exhibition of his semi-erotic paintings in 1929 hardly eased his repeated run-ins with the law. The twenty-five watercolors, depicting nude, blissed-out men and women communing in a vaguely Arcadian landscape, drew twelve thousand visitors to London's Dorothy Warren Gallery in the show's first six weeks, whereupon Scotland Yard raided it. Thirteen of the works, each with visible fragments of pubic hair, were "arrested"—a prime example of spectacle censorship.

Obscenity charges were brought under the Obscene Publications Act against the Dorothy Warren Gallery. At the trial, the octogenarian magistrate, Frederick Mead, refused the gallery's request to allow experts, including the writer and critic Lytton Strachey, to opine on the paintings' artistic merits. "It is utterly immaterial whether they are works of art," Mead said. "The most splendidly painted picture in the universe might be obscene." He found them obscene: "I would destroy these pictures, as I would destroy wild beasts."[100] The images weren't destroyed. Rather, they were returned on condition that they be removed from England. Sometime later, Lawrence's wife brought many of them to Taos, New Mexico. Finally, in 2003, reproductions of some of the watercolors were put on display in London at the Waterstones bookshop in Piccadilly, but the censorship was still not over. The bookshop moved the exhibition from its public café to a room on the sixth floor. "We are not in the business of censorship," said a spokesman. "But the coffee bar area is a family space and we don't want to cause offence to anyone."[101]

Experts were also barred from testifying at the much-publicized trial of Radclyffe Hall's *The Well of Loneliness* (1928), likely the first novel in English to treat homosexuality as its central subject. The semiautobiographical bildungsroman treats lesbianism with great sympathy, but also as pathology. The female protagonist, Stephen, refers to herself as a "freak" and the result of God's cruelty: "He let us get flawed in the making." Despite the absence of explicit language or scenes, the novel's subject matter and its plea for acceptance—"Give us . . . the right to our existence!"[102] Stephen begs at the book's end—drew a sharp critical response. It was declared toxic. James Douglas's review in the *Sunday Express* was headlined "A Book That Must Be Suppressed." Taking his cue from Lord Campbell's comments back in 1857, Douglas stated that he would rather give "prussic acid" to a youngster than the book. "Poison kills the body," he wrote, "but moral poison kills the soul."[103]

The controversy made *The Well of Loneliness* a bestseller in England. Within a few months, copies were seized, and Jix initiated legal action for obscenity against the British publisher, Jonathan Cape. The defense lined up a roster of eminent literary figures to testify to the book's merits, but the magistrate wanted none of it; the novel should be banned and destroyed because the theme was perverse and such "horrible, unnatural" acts were not sufficiently condemned by the author. On appeal, the judges found the book "disgusting" without even reading it. It was not republished in England until 1949, although it was soon allowed in the United States after another series of legal proceedings. At the time of Hall's death in 1943, thousands of copies of the novel were being sold each day in various languages around the world. One woman who read it in Polish claimed she survived the Nazi concentration camps with the hope it provided for love from another woman.

IMAGERY AND DECEPTION DURING WORLD WAR II

German war correspondents and photographers were part of the military, and like all troops they were required to swear allegiance to the führer. Their job was propaganda, and the narratives they provided amounted to, as the literary historian and World War II veteran Paul Fussell put it, "nothing but fairy stories of total heroism, stamina, good-will, and cheerfulness." That included total suppression of images of German war dead. "As far as the German home front knew, soldiers' bodies were not dismembered, decapitated, eviscerated, or flattened out by tank treads until they looked like plywood."[104]

The American attitude toward war reportage was summarized by Admiral Ernest King, chief of naval operations: "I wouldn't tell the people anything until the war is over, and then I'd tell them who won."[105] While American journalists were not controlled as tightly as their German counterparts, military authorities censored all reports from the theatres of war. Most reporters did not object: they saw their role as supporting the war effort, not as exposing its flaws or emphasizing the suffering (or cruelty) of American forces. John Steinbeck explained how he and other war correspondents followed rules that were both "imposed and . . . self-imposed":

> We were all a part of the War Effort. We went along with it, and not only that, we abetted it. Gradually it became a part of all of us that the truth about anything was automatically secret and that to trifle with it was to interfere with the War Effort. By this I don't mean that the correspondents were liars. . . . It is in the things not mentioned that the untruth lies. . . . There was a general feeling that unless the home front was carefully protected from the whole account of what war was like, it might panic. Also, we had to protect the armed services from criticism, or they might retire to their tents to sulk like Achilles.[106]

The result was what Fussell called a "systematically sanitized and Norman Rockwellized" presentation, whereby the superiority of German weaponry, the horrors of exploding bodies, the vomiting of terrified GIs during battle, and the immense toll of it all were not transmitted home.[107]

Throughout the US' involvement in the war, photographs from the battle zones were controlled to manipulate public opinion and to prevent race, class, or ethnic disturbances. The censoring could be nonsensical, as in the withholding of an image showing a general fishing during a break in hostilities (evidently, generals always worked). It could be racist, too, as with the ban on photos of Black GIs overseas mixing socially with white women. Such images, General Dwight D. Eisenhower believed, would "unduly flame racial prejudice." To guard against what the army called the "tendency on the part of the negro press to unduly emphasize" African American sacrifices, photographs of wounded Black GIs were proscribed, as were images of the race riots on American military bases.[108]

Pictures of the dead were of acute concern to American censors. Images revealing American abuses of the enemy's lifeless bodies were forbidden, as were photographs of GIs making necklaces with the teeth of dead Japanese. For the first two years of the US' involvement in the war, all images of dead or severely disfigured American soldiers were confiscated and kept in a secret military file informally called the "Chamber of Horrors." None were published. But by 1943, military authorities were concerned that recent American military successes were generating overconfidence at home, and with it, absenteeism in factories. The public needed to be girded for further sacrifice, and for more waves of casualties. It was decided to start releasing images of the dead, and in September, *Life* magazine published photographs of three fallen soldiers on a beach in New Guinea. The impact was powerful and was soon being capitalized on. The following month, some personnel involved with selling war bonds wired the government with the urgent request: "Please rush air-mail gruesome photos of dead American soldiers for plant promotion third war loan."

An additional reason for unlocking the Chamber of Horrors was to bring home the reality of Japanese atrocities. Such images would, in the words of Elmer Davis, the director of the Office of War Information, "nullify any voices that might be raised here if we should undertake bombing of Japanese cities."[109]

Of course, the US did bomb Japanese cities, with massive civilian casualties. Its firebombing campaigns started in 1944, and the attacks on the urban population continued until atomic bombs were dropped on Hiroshima and Nagasaki in August 1945. Initially, Japanese authorities censored their own media about the nuclear strikes. Acting on instructions to "bury the news" of the Hiroshima bombing "in some obscure place," it was reported only that the city had been "slightly damaged." More accurate Japanese reports started to emerge after the attack on Nagasaki, mainly to stress US callousness in using a "new-type" bomb against civilians, and to label as hypocritical the US' claims to moral superiority. When Japan surrendered on August

15, the emperor emphasized the use of "cruel bombs to kill and maim extremely large numbers of innocent people." Yet that unpleasant fact was lost in the US' euphoria over its victory, which it saw as a moral no less than a military achievement.

Military and civilian authorities did their utmost to ensure that the true toll of the damage, particularly the deadly effects of radiation exposure on civilians, remained obscure. For weeks after the attacks, no Western report emerged on the health effects of the atomic bombs. American occupation authorities placed southern Japan off-limits to correspondents. However, in the face of US denials of harmful radioactivity, the Australian reporter Wilfred Burchett made his way to Hiroshima and filed an alarming report on September 5, headlined "The Atomic Plague," for London's *Daily Express*. Written as a "warning to the world," it gave the first accounts of the agonies of survivors, and the radiation's "uncanny after-effects." People who at first appeared uninjured were now losing their hair and flesh; bleeding from their ears, noses, and mouths; and dying in large numbers. American top brass denied the report and told Burchett that his eyes had been deceived: "I'm afraid," a brigadier-general said to him, "you've fallen victim to Japanese propaganda."[110]

The first American reporter to reach Nagasaki was George Weller of the *Chicago Daily News*. His moving September 8 and 9 dispatches on the effects of "Disease X" as a result of the nuclear attack, whereby victims were suffering the same symptoms as those described by Burchett, were buried by American military censors. (Carbon copies of the articles were discovered by Weller's son in 2003 and were published in Japan two years later.)[111] Japanese and American newsreel footage from both locations was also seized by US authorities and kept under wraps in military facilities for decades.

As the occupation forces locked down control on news from Japan and on the speech of the Japanese, including bans on criticism of the Allies, articles critical of the bombings disappeared and the stories of the *hibakusha*, or bomb-affected people, were suppressed.[112] Research data by Japanese scientists, and records of the symptoms of the ill and dying that were produced by Japanese doctors, were confiscated and kept classified for decades. None of it could be published in Japan, even though it might have helped local doctors struggling to aid the *hibakusha*. The lockdown on information also contributed to the spread of misinformation among the dazed population, such as the widespread belief that their conditions were communicable.

The level of censorship imposed on the Japanese citizenry is astounding. A personal account by a fifteen-year-old Nagasaki girl, *Masako Does Not Collapse*, which described "bodies like peeled peaches" and a river "filled with corpses, legs," was suppressed by occupation censors for fear that it "would disturb public tranquility in Japan" and "implies the bombing was a crime against humanity." A line in another book, suggesting a child "study earnestly and become a great scientist, since your parents were made victims of the atomic bomb," was removed because of concerns it could cause resentment of the Allied powers. And Takashi Nagai's book *The Bells of Nagasaki*, which draws on the author's ordeals as a survivor of the bomb attack in that city, was held up by censors for two years. It was then allowed on condition that "The Sack of Manila," an American-prepared description of Japanese atrocities in the Philippines, be appended to the work. Without this appendix, censors believed the "Jap military acts that were provocation of motive" for dropping the atomic bombs would not be shown. *The Bells of Nagasaki* would not be released in Japan until 1949, the same year the Japanese public was first permitted to read John Hersey's blockbuster, *Hiroshima*, a series of long survivor interviews first published in the *New Yorker* in 1946, and the work most responsible for bringing home to the world the brutal effects of the bombings.[113]

The reasons for censorship by occupation forces in Japan are many, and predictable: to prevent accusations of war crimes, to mislead the world as to the true murderous capacity of the new weapons, to keep a defeated population docile, and to drive the narrative that the bombs were necessary to end the war and save Japanese and American lives. According to Lieutenant Colonel Daniel McGovern, who directed US military film crews in Hiroshima and Nagasaki and then kept watch over sequestered American and Japanese footage for decades, the films were hidden because the military was "sorry we had dropped the bomb. . . . They didn't want the general public to know what their weapons had done—at a time they were planning on more bomb tests. We didn't want the material out because . . . we were sorry for our sins."[114] For the good of our souls, this explanation is the most palatable. Sin requires redemption, and redemption requires some degree of contrition.

By the twentieth century's halfway mark, the world had been blown up beyond recognition, and in the following decades it would transform again several times over. With the advent of true mass communication, the nature of information and its transmission, the ability of ordinary people to speak directly to billions of others, and the role of private companies in mediating communications have altered both the meaning of speech and the methods and purposes of controlling it. It is to this brave and cowardly new world that we now turn.

7

SCREAMING AT THE CROWD
IN THE CONTEMPORARY ERA

Over the course of one hundred days in 1994, Hutu civilians in Rwanda joined soldiers and militias in savagely murdering eight hundred thousand Tutsis. If the slaughter had a soundtrack, it came from Radio Télévision Libre des Milles Collines (RTLM), a Hutu radio station that played anti-Tutsi hate music, punctuated with broadcasts calling for a "final war" to "exterminate the cockroaches" and giving out names, addresses, and even automobile license plate numbers of intended Tutsi victims. One announcer called out, "You have missed some of the enemies. You must go back there and finish them off. The graves are not yet full!"[1] Samantha Power, author and later US ambassador to the UN, called these broadcasts "a crucial instrument . . . of the genocide."[2] Killers carried machetes in one hand and radios tuned to RTLM in the other.

Back in Washington, President Bill Clinton and his advisors dithered. Stung by the recent "Black Hawk Down" debacle in Somalia, and determined not to become ensnared in an ethnic civil war, they did little other than evacuate Americans. They considered jamming RTLM's radio signal in the hopes of stemming the tide of murder, but they did not even do that. "Radio jamming gets debated," Power reported, "and the response is, 'if we actually jam hate radio, it violates freedom of speech.'"[3] Two RTLM executives later received lengthy prison terms for crimes against humanity, but at least their right to spew hatred had been protected.

This episode occupies a maddening corner of the post–World War II censorship universe, in which the right to express even despicable views can trump the prevention of harm, and the power to suppress speech depends on control of the medium. While technology's influence on speech would soon explode—in many ways, technology has now *become* speech—the hatred corroding the human soul remains constant. Technology amplifies hateful speech, and no Western democracy other than the US tolerates it officially. Just two years before the Rwandan genocide, the Supreme Court cemented the US' outlier status by ruling in favor of a person who set a cross aflame in front of an African American family's home. The court found that burning crosses was "reprehensible," but there was no need to "ad[d] the First Amendment to the fire."[4] That ruling may not have been on Clinton's mind when he considered jamming RTLM's signal, but the assumptions behind it almost certainly informed his thinking.

The right to freedom of expression in the modern US is exalted to the point where most speech is protected unless violence or lawlessness is imminent. If vicious remarks cause pain, fear, or loss of dignity, the law, with few exceptions, simply does not care. Mindful that waves of extreme and hateful social media posts swell revenues, major American Internet companies (at least initially) adopted the same stance. One Twitter executive referred to the platform as the "free speech wing of the free speech party."[5] In a 2016 company memo, a Facebook executive—justifying the company's relentless drive toward growth—allowed, "That can be bad. . . . Maybe it costs someone a life by exposing someone to bullies. Maybe someone dies in a terrorist attack coordinated on our tools."[6]

The ramifications of such positions dominate today's censorship battles, particularly online. The postwar years have witnessed a breathtaking expansion of speech rights across the West, but with the Internet's upending of the marketplace of ideas, many of the victories are starting to look like liabilities. People who took strong libertarian positions for speech against injustice or corruption may well be less tolerant when invective is aimed at them. The Internet was first embraced as a "technology of freedom" letting all voices be heard in equal measure, but with time the management of online speech by self-serving corporations—whose readiness to manipulate people is matched by their platforms' susceptibility to exploitation—has wiped the bloom off the online rose. The Internet is *the* transformative phenomenon of modern life, but it is marred by hate, threats, data privacy breaches, and fake news driven by bots, troll armies, and unseen actors.

The US Supreme Court stated, in 1971, that "free expression is powerful medicine" for a diverse society, and if the resulting "verbal cacophony" disturbs, the noise is "not a sign of weakness but of strength." Unregulated speech places responsibility on the population "in the hope that . . . such freedom will ultimately produce a more capable citizenry and more perfect polity."[7] This is lofty rhetoric, and it is probably still true. But when "speech" becomes the enemy of free expression—when citizen speakers are reduced to online "users" whose scarce attention is manhandled for profit; when tsunamis of online garbage are weaponized to drown out voices and dilute truth (what Steve Bannon, Donald Trump's 2016 campaign manager, called "flood[ing] the zone with shit"[8]); when algorithms decide whose voices are heard or magnified; and when corporations frame their buying of elections and burying of climate change information as free speech—it may be time to rethink some cherished assumptions. That reassessment has begun even in the US. A 2019 survey showed that about half of Americans—and a higher percentage of millennials—believe the First Amendment is outdated and should be rewritten to reflect "the cultural norms of today," while one of the key American legal protections for unrestrained discourse on social media platforms is under review.[9]

There is little agreement at this point about what censorship *is*, much less whether it is a good or bad thing. Traditional forms of speech suppression (book burning, targeting journalists, authors, dissidents, and the like) have continued, often on a broad scale. Postcolonial state authorities have also taken aggressive measures to sanitize their pasts and clear the collective mind of anything questioning their legitimacy, while even countries embracing broad speech protections have felt the pull toward repression.

Unless a right is absolute, its reliability ceases. Once substantial exceptions or qualifications are introduced, the law balances the right against other imperatives. Freedom of speech is enshrined in German law, for example, but only as measured against its toll on human dignity. It is illegal there not just to advocate Nazism or degrade minorities but also to give someone "the finger" on the street. Britain prides itself on protecting free expression, but swearing is prohibited on many (gentrifying) streets because it causes "distress," and a man was arrested for inciting hatred after uploading a video of his dog making the Nazi salute.[10] In France, the fashion designer John Galliano was prosecuted for anti-Semitic remarks made in a bar.

These are not outlying cases. The European Court of Human Rights recognizes freedom of expression as a foundational right but will still condemn "any remark" against the "values" underlying the Convention on Human Rights, including words that "spread, incite, promote or justify hatred based on intolerance."[11] In other words, intolerance is not tolerated as it is in the US, and free speech exists to the extent that what is said is broadly acceptable. That is also the case in other democracies, and not just regarding hateful expressions. Australian authorities muzzled a student newspaper for a story on the benefits of shoplifting to alleviate poverty. The country's highest court recognized the value of press freedom, but not when the press "instructs" on matters of even petty crime.[12]

In the book accompanying a 1984 New York Public Library exhibition about censorship, the historian Arthur Schlesinger concluded that it "has lost its moral advantage, at least in democratic nations," which he posited against "those vast regions of the world sadly sunk" in "fanaticism."[13] What a difference a few decades make. European and other nations now aggressively punish expressions of racism and intolerance; Google censors its search results, and the BBC buries news to gain entry into foreign markets; and students demand that microaggressions be suppressed. The certainties of Schlesinger's universe concerning censorship have been erased. Who would have thought that we would be nostalgic for 1984?

POLITICAL SPEECH UNDER PRESSURE

"A totalitarian state is in effect a theocracy," wrote George Orwell, "and its ruling caste, in order to keep its position, has to be thought of as infallible." Such a state demands "the continuous alteration of the past" and "in the long run . . . a disbelief in the very existence of objective truth."[14] In light of the mass of disinformation that plagued the 2016 US presidential election and the UK's Brexit referendum that year, "post-truth" became the Oxford Dictionaries' "word of the year." "We've Entered a Post-Truth World—There's No Going Back Now," read the headline of Matthew Norman's November 8, 2016, column in *The Independent*. That may recently have become so in the democratic West, but Orwell's dark assessment has long been the case in postwar authoritarian states.

Between the 1960s and 1990s, the suppression of dissent was routine throughout much of Latin America. A "climate of terror" followed Brazil's 1964 right-wing military coup, the aim of which, according to the sociologist Clóvis Moura, was to "switch off the national memory" by eliminating anything remotely challenging the junta's legitimacy. *A New History of Brazil*, an elaborate academic project to present unofficial versions of Brazilian history, was seized and burned and its authors prosecuted for infusing "Marxist tendencies" into the text.[15] A year earlier, the Peruvian military fueled a large bonfire with one thousand copies of Mario Vargas Llosa's novel *La ciudad y los perros* (The time of the hero), which probed the moral effects of authoritarianism. And the 1973 military overthrow of Chilean president Salvador Allende's government brought savage crackdowns. Soldiers raided homes and businesses, flinging "leftist" and "subversive" books and magazines out of windows and setting them ablaze, including the works of Pablo Neruda and Gabriel García Márquez. As Neruda lay dying from cancer, troops sacked his house, burned his books, and stole his money. The regime continued burning books until its collapse in 1990.

The South African apartheid state used cruel and transparently desperate means to quell dissent. Steven Biko, who founded the anti-apartheid Black Consciousness Movement, was literally shut up. In 1973, he—like hundreds of others—was subjected to a banning order under which he could speak to no more than one person at a time and could never be quoted. His movements were also sharply restricted. (He violated the ban by visiting Cape Town and was arrested for terrorism and tortured; he died of massive brain injuries.) Biko's mistreatment received worldwide attention, but the salient point is that the banning order was less about what he said than the fact that it was he who said it. Having devoted himself to the human rights of black South Africans, his every word was viewed as an act of terrorism. Nothing he said, on any subject, could be heard publicly.

Colonialism and independence have been hazardous subjects for dissidents, intellectuals, and artists. In 1962, as it fought to keep its African possessions, Portugal declared the British historian Charles Boxer persona non grata and banned his books. The towering figure in Portuguese historiography had disputed the official line that Portugal had always maintained good relations with its African subjects, and argued that most Portuguese colonizers were white supremacists.

After more than a decade of bitter conflict, Algeria became independent from France in 1962, but the fighting left French nerves raw. Gillo Pontecorvo's 1966 film *The Battle of Algiers* was banned in France for being sympathetic to Algerian independence and criticizing the torture perpetrated by the French. The movie was also banned in Uruguay in 1968 for fear that it would encourage guerrilla movements there. In 1996, French police seized an issue of the Algerian daily *Liberté* because of an article, "When the Seine Rolled with Corpses," about a 1962 Paris demonstration for Algerian independence that ended in a bloodbath.[16]

Descriptions of contemporary colonial violence have also been widely censored. In 1989, the Arabic edition of Israeli author Dror Green's *Stories of the Intifada*, which described Israel's occupation from the perspective of the occupied, was banned in the West Bank and Gaza. Green had difficulty finding a Hebrew-language publisher for the book, but unlike the Arabic edition, it was not officially suppressed. Hebrew-reading Israelis may not have wanted to read the book, but no one questioned their right to do so. However, one of the collection's stories, "The Train of Wonders," sealed the book's fate for Arabic readers. The story, which Green insisted was based on an incident he had witnessed, described in excruciating detail the cruelty of Israeli soldiers toward Palestinian passengers who were left to bake nearly to death under the desert sun in an unventilated bus. That was damning enough, but when Green compared the situation in the bus to the suffering of Jews in railway carriages on the way to Nazi death camps, the entire book was deemed too incendiary for Palestinian consumption.[17]

Even in former colonies, the subject of colonialism has been closely controlled. Colonial rule was almost invariably replaced by regimes that proved no less repressive. If descriptions of life under foreign rule or of anticolonial resistance reflected poorly on the new states, however obliquely, they were likely to be censored. Indonesia is an example of this. In 1977, more than two decades after it gained independence, authorities banned Fons Rademakers's *Saijah and Adinda*, a film adapted from a nineteenth-century novel that depicted the complicity of the Indonesian gentry under Dutch colonial rule. The government feared the film would give the impression that Indonesians were victimized by their own people rather than the Dutch—which could raise uncomfortable questions about the present.

The Indonesian novelist Pramoedya Ananta Toer, who fought as a young man against Dutch colonialism and subsequently criticized postcolonial Indonesian elites, spent much of his adult life in prison. In 1965, Pramoedya was put in the infamous Buru Island penal colony, where he was denied pens and paper for the first seven of his fourteen-year sentence. He nevertheless composed the four novels known as the Buru Quartet in his head, which he recited to his fellow inmates in the evenings. He called the books "my lullaby for my fellow prisoners, to calm their fears." When Pramoedya was finally allowed to write, the texts, which trace the birth of the Indonesian nationalist movement, were put to paper. They were smuggled out of Buru Island by a priest and published to acclaim and translated into dozens of languages. Citing its "Marxist-Leninist teachings," the Indonesian government banned the Buru Quartet. In truth, the authorities were concerned that the books would evoke analogies between Dutch abuses and the brutality of President Suharto, who ruled from the mid-1960s until 1998.[18]

For many Westerners, the definitive setting for twentieth-century censorship was the Soviet Union and its client Eastern European states. Yet apart from the common understanding of a monolithic system of terror-based information control, the censorship practices there were full of contradictions, even in the USSR itself. From Vladimir Lenin's 1917 "Decree on the Press," which prohibited publishing any "bourgeois" articles criticizing the Bolsheviks, to Nikita Khrushchev's 1962 decision to allow the publication of Alexander Solzhenitsyn's *One Day in the Life of Ivan Denisovich* and other indictments of Stalinism, to Leonid Brezhnev's strangling of political discourse and expulsion of Solzhenitsyn, and on to Mikhail Gorbachev's policy of glasnost ("openness"), the USSR's censorship policies were mercurial and in many cases arbitrary. Among the outrages, hundreds of dissidents were thrown into mental hospitals and tortured with cruel and bizarre "treatments." The writer and biologist Zhores Medvedev was accused of suffering from "incipient schizophrenia" and "paranoid delusions of reforming society."[19] His "symptoms" included his work exposing the quack science that led to massive crop failures and famines under Stalin.

Thanks to the opening of archives and the scholarship of Dominic Boyer and others, we can examine quotidian censorship practices in an important corner of the Soviet-dominated Eastern Bloc: the German Democratic Republic (East Germany). There, the Communist Party continued the Nazi Party's practice of defining itself as the sole voice of German *Kultur*. The party devoted immense energy to regulating the information and culture industries, as any deviation from its positions risked, according to Boyer, "a relapse into the dissonant, hybrid, and thus regressive" mentality of the West—particularly of capitalist West Germany. As in most Communist regimes, the GDR's constitution guaranteed freedom of the press, but that was a false promise. A centralized system of control managed all aspects of media production. There were no press censors as such; journalists were instead expected to know the day's party line and reflect it in their reports. This led to pervasive self-censorship, what journalists called *Schere im Kopf*, or "scissors in the head." "The reality," as one reporter described it, "was that 'to show life as it really is' meant photographing [party leader Erich] Honecker forty times at a rally."

Erich Honecker did more than pose for cameras. From his position as what Boyer called "the ultimate intellectual arbiter of the will of the *Volk*," Honecker spent much of his time writing articles and bulletins and revising the work of others, down to punctuation. Once he had completed a report, nothing could be changed, not even spelling errors or obviously inadvertent inaccuracies. In addition to receiving instructions from Honecker, journalists were bombarded with advisories as to which subjects to stress and which to avoid, such as this list from the mid-1980s:

- Nothing about . . . lawn bowling, villas, or boulevards. (They awaken desires we are not capable of satisfying.)
- Do not photograph the fruit on the tables at official receptions. (Otherwise the people will become envious.)
- Nothing about Bratwurst-kiosks. (People are already eating enough meat.)
- Nothing about homemade gliders. (People may think to escape.)
- Nothing about Formula 1 racing. (We cannot afford it.)

These dictates were simple to follow, but sometimes journalists stumbled into "political errors" for which they could pay a dear price. In one case, a reporter mentioned potholes in East Berlin's streets, which was not in itself a dereliction, but became one when the West German press picked up the story to make the GDR look shabby. A much worse error occurred in 1953, when a hastily inserted notice about Stalin's death in *Die Tribüne* called him a "champion for the preservation and consolidation of war in the world." For inadvertently using the word "war" instead of "peace," the paper's chief editor was fired and the supervising editor was forced under torture to say that Western spies had ordered the error. Both the supervising editor and the typesetter were sent to prison for espionage. Another journalist later commented, "Each of us knew that it could have just as well been us. . . . We knew then that none of us were safe."[20]

"THOUGHTS WE HATE": POLITICAL SPEECH IN THE UNITED STATES

Led by a Supreme Court intent on smashing speech restrictions, the postwar US has become, despite bouts of backsliding, among the least regulated speech environments the world has ever known. The same legal precedents have been applied to protect racists as well as demonstrators for minority rights. Justice Thurgood Marshall, a towering figure in the civil rights movement and the Supreme Court's first Black justice, joined in a 1969 opinion protecting a white supremacist's call for violence against African Americans.[21] How long these extraordinary achievements will remain intact is none too clear, however, as several initiatives are underway that call such near-absolutist First Amendment norms into question.

It starts with protecting thought itself. Recall that during World War I and its aftermath, the law penalized people for their sentiments as well as their actions against the government. Nonconformist ideas were often equated with disloyalty, sedition, or espionage. In a 1929 case, a pacifist was refused citizenship because her "cosmic consciousness of belonging to the human family" prevented her from committing to "take up arms" against America's enemies. She lost in the Supreme Court, but Justice Holmes strenuously dissented: "If there is any principle . . . that more imperatively calls for attachment than any other it is the principle of free thought—not free thought for those who agree with us but freedom for the thought that we hate."[22] That later became the court's majority view.

During World War II, certain public schools expelled students for refusing to salute the American flag. To the court, the question was no longer whether the students were reliable citizens but whether the state had the power to force from anyone "an affirmation of belief and an attitude of mind." In *West Virginia State Board of Education v. Barnette* (1943), the court answered no. "If there is any fixed star in our constitutional constellation," wrote Justice Robert Jackson, "it is that no official . . . can prescribe what shall be orthodox in politics, nationalism, religion, or other matters of opinion." Invoking the Roman persecutions against Christians and the cruelties of the Inquisition, Jackson added, "Those who begin coercive elimination of dissent soon find themselves exterminating dissenters. Compulsory unification of opinion achieves only the unanimity of the graveyard."[23] That same day, in *Taylor v. Mississippi*, the court threw out sedition charges against several Jehovah's Witnesses, one of whom had said to others that "it was wrong for our President to send our boys across in uniform to fight. . . . These boys were being shot down for no purpose at all." Such remarks would likely have been enough to uphold a conviction during World War I, but no longer. Without creating a "clear and present danger to our institutions or our government," the comments, the court ruled, were protected "beliefs and opinions."[24]

These decisions are striking for how unremarkable they now seem. The prerogative to form and speak opinions, especially against government policies, is so woven into the Western political firmament that a free society is unimaginable without it. Yet it was not until the mid-twentieth century that the law effectively guarded the right to express such ideas. That is, if one was not of Japanese ancestry during World War II, in which case subversion was imputed and condemned. In 1942, Franklin Roosevelt issued the infamous Executive Order 9066, which, along with subsequent legislation, authorized the forced relocation of Japanese Americans to "internment," that is, concentration camps. The stated purpose was to prevent espionage and sabotage, to which these citizens were presumed to be inclined. More than a hundred thousand innocents were imprisoned, and the Supreme Court blessed the whole damn scheme. This shameful episode did not explicitly involve freedom of speech, but the question was woven into it because an entire segment of the population was effectively silenced.

The Cold War bred pervasive fears of Communists subverting American society; with those fears came renewed attacks on freedom of political belief. In 1948, the government prosecuted twelve leading Communists for conspiracy to violate the provisions of the Smith Act, which made it a crime to teach or advocate, or to organize any group that teaches or advocates, the violent overthrow of any government in the US. The defendants had taught standard Marxist-Leninist doctrine as set forth in texts such as *The Communist Manifesto*. None of the defendants had advocated, much less planned or caused, any violence, but inconvenient facts rarely matter in an atmosphere thick with paranoia. In *Dennis v. United States* (1951), the Supreme Court upheld the convictions, holding that the defendants' actions amounted to a conspiracy and "preparation for revolution," and thus a clear and present danger to the country.[25] More than 120 Communists were indicted after *Dennis*—not for any acts they had committed but for what they thought and believed.

The Court returned to its senses somewhat with *Yates v. United States* (1957), after some less prominent Communists were charged for teaching Marxism-Leninism.[26] This time, the convictions were overturned. The Court engaged in fancy rhetorical footwork to do so, making a thin distinction between advocacy of illegal action (bad) and advocacy of beliefs and ideas (not bad). Nevertheless, the right result was reached, and Smith Act prosecutions against Communists stopped. Finally, in 1969, the court set the prevailing standard for incendiary speech. The controversy involved a Ku Klux Klan rally in Ohio, during which its leader called for violence against "niggers," "Jews," and those who support them. He was charged under a World War I–era "syndicalism" prohibition criminalizing the advocacy of violence, and under then-current law he should have lost. After all, he had advocated for the commission of crimes not just as an idea, but also in fact. Yet the court held that unless the advocacy of violence incites "imminent lawless action," the First Amendment protects it, no matter how despicable it is.[27]

Anti-war speech returned to the fore with the intense resistance to the Vietnam War and the conscription of hundreds of thousands of men to fight it. Julian Bond, a prominent African American civil rights leader who had been elected to the Georgia legislature, was denied his seat because he had endorsed statements supporting draft resisters. In 1966, citing *Yates*, the Supreme Court ruled unanimously that his previous statements were protected, and he should not have been deprived of his seat.[28] Two years later, Dr. Benjamin Spock, the respected author of a best-selling baby-care guide, was sentenced to prison for urging defiance of the draft laws. At a large anti-war demonstration in Boston, Spock and others had collected many of the demonstrators' draft cards. A few days later, they made a media event of "returning" the cards to the government, whereupon they were arrested.[29] In a sharp defeat for the government, their convictions were overturned on appeal. And in 1968, an impudent young man named Paul Cohen strode into the Los Angeles courthouse wearing a jacket on which were scrawled the words "Fuck the Draft." He was convicted for disturbing the peace with offensive conduct, but the Supreme Court reversed. "One man's vulgarity is another's lyric," the court ruled, and one cannot "forbid particular words without also running a substantial risk of suppressing ideas in the process."[30]

This was also the period when two of the crown jewels of American press freedom, *New York Times v. Sullivan* and *New York Times v. United States* (the Pentagon Papers case), were handed down, giving the press broader protections than it had ever enjoyed. *Sullivan* arose in 1960, after an advertisement appeared in the *Times* soliciting contributions for Martin Luther King Jr.'s civil rights campaign. The ad made accusations of brutality against the Montgomery, Alabama, police, which were false in some respects. A city commissioner sued the *Times* for libel and—no surprise, with a friendly local judge and jury—was awarded $500,000 in damages. In reversing the award, the court stressed the country's "commitment to the principle that debate on public issues should be uninhibited, robust, and wide-open, and that it may well include vehement, caustic and sometimes unpleasantly sharp attacks" on government officials. Criticism of public officials, the court added, "does not lose its constitutional protection because it is effective," and false statements are "inevitable in free debate." To force government critics to guarantee that their remarks are true would intolerably limit public debate. To win a libel suit after *Sullivan*, a public official needs to show that the accused person either knew the challenged statements were false or acted with "reckless disregard" as to whether they were true or false.[31] In practice, this standard has been almost impossible to meet, and its application has been extended to derail libel suits by most famous people.

The Pentagon Papers case decided whether the government could stop the *Times* and *Washington Post* from publishing a large batch of leaked, classified documents concerning US involvement in the Vietnam War. The government's motivation in squelching publication was understandable: the documents revealed decades of incompetence and outright deception in the way the war was managed and publicly represented. Weighing government claims to secrecy against both the papers' value to an informed citizenry and the First Amendment's prohibition of prior restraints, the court held in 1971 that publication could proceed. In a concurring opinion, Justice Hugo Black wrote: "The government's power to censor the press was abolished so that the press would remain forever free to censure the government . . . and [to] bare the secrets of government and inform the people." The government could not use the courts to halt publication of news, as doing so would "wipe out the First Amendment." Far from condemning the *Times* and the *Post*, Black wrote that they should be commended for doing "precisely that which the founding fathers hoped and trusted they would do."[32]

Well, not exactly. The Founding Fathers' ideas about freedom of speech and the press likely did not go that far, but some hyperbole can be excused in the Supreme Court's determination to clear barriers to a truly free press—even a defunct one more than 150 years old. *Sullivan* declared that the 1798 Sedition Act was a "restraint . . . on criticism of government" and as such had been effectively invalidated in the "court of history." After these and similar decisions, it appeared that the progression starting with Spinoza, Milton, Cato, and Wilkes and continuing through Paine, Mill, Holmes, and Brandeis was nearing completion. Public figures could rarely block scrutiny or embarrassment; the people had a right to be informed about government decisions and misdeeds; and one's ability to express one's political views was protected by the law.

As momentous as these and other court opinions have been in marking protections for the press and dissent, they did not diminish the powerful censorious impulses that made them necessary in the first place. Public officials hate being exposed and embarrassed no less nowadays than in the time of George III, and many will still stop at little to halt the publication of unwelcome news or ridicule. Nowhere has this been more starkly demonstrated than by Donald Trump, whose efforts to silence criticism have been relentless.

"CAN'T BE LEGAL": PRESENT-DAY ATTACKS ON SPEECH AND DISSENT

The Trump administration appears to be the first to force White House employees to sign free-speech-trampling nondisclosure agreements

(NDAs). These agreements would likely be upheld if they kept only classified information under wraps, but they range much further than that. Adapted from the contracts Trump used to muzzle employees in his private business, some versions of the NDAs threatened aides with millions of dollars in penalties for disclosing virtually anything they saw or heard in the White House, even when they decided to write works of fiction. No court would uphold them against a First Amendment challenge. But the legality of the documents was not the point—the threat to aides of fines and costly litigation was. Former senior aide Omarosa Manigault Newman was sued in arbitration when she published *Unhinged*, a tell-all book about her brief White House tenure. Her NDA, signed when she worked on the 2016 Trump presidential campaign, included a promise never to "disparage or demean" Trump, his family, or any of their companies. As of May 2020, the Trump campaign was hounding her with more than four hundred alleged "counts" of violating the NDA. Another ex-aide, Cliff Sims, wrote the self-explanatory *Team of Vipers: My 500 Extraordinary Days in the Trump White House*. In 2019, after the Trump campaign initiated an arbitration against him, he asked a court to invalidate his NDA under the First Amendment. His book, like *Unhinged*, is still available.

Newman and Sims were ready to do battle with Trump and his lawyers, but other White House ex-employees with stories to tell undoubtedly were not. The administration's determination to silence critics within government reached beyond the White House. In 2018, approximately *two million* federal workers were formally directed not to use the words "resistance" or "impeachment" when discussing Trump at work.[33] Again, the legality of a measure such as this is highly dubious, but the intimidation value is not.

Trump's willingness to attack anyone questioning his character or competence was not news, and neither was it new for public officials. Approximately two dozen states still have "criminal libel" laws on the books, with penalties ranging from fines to lengthy jail terms. Even though these zombie statutes are unconstitutional relics, they remain effective tools for local officials to criminalize criticism—and nothing is too petty. In 2010, a Kansas man was charged after he put a sign on his lawn accusing a town administrator of ignoring a water drainage problem. A New Hampshire man was arrested in 2018 for writing on

Facebook that a policeman who gave him a traffic citation was "dirty" and the local police chief "covered up" the matter.[34] About twenty criminal libel prosecutions are brought each year, and many result in convictions. Even without invoking criminal libel laws, local officials take action when they object to how they are depicted. In 2018, a South Carolina police union challenged the inclusion on a school's reading list of *The Hate U Give*, an award-winning young adult novel dealing with racially motivated police brutality. The union claimed that the book is "almost an indoctrination of distrust of police."[35] It has been banned in several places.

Trump's strident verbal attacks on his media critics were leveled so often that much of the public eventually stopped paying attention—at least those who didn't already believe the press is the "enemy of the people." While most of the comments were forgotten, they and some very tangible actions against his perceived media enemies have collectively "dangerously undermined truth" and chilled critical reporting, as a 2020 report by the Committee to Protect Journalists concludes.[36] According to a lawsuit filed by PEN America, a nonprofit association of writers and media professionals, about one-third of its members avoided reporting on certain topics out of concern over potential retaliation, and more than half believed criticism of the administration would put them at risk.[37] Disfavored reporters such as CNN's Jim Acosta were barred from the White House; threats to revoke the broadcast licenses of TV networks were made for airing an ad that highlighted the deficiencies of Trump's response to the coronavirus pandemic; actions were taken to raise postal rates to target Amazon, whose CEO, Jeff Bezos, is the majority shareholder of the *Washington Post*; and an antitrust action was filed to challenge a merger between AT&T and Time Warner, whose subsidiary is CNN.

The full impact of such efforts will take time to gauge. The courts beat back the most egregious of them. The antitrust action failed, as did the administration's attempt to bar Acosta from the White House. It is also likely that the Trump campaign's libel lawsuits against CNN, the *Washington Post*, and the *New York Times*—all filed in 2020 over articles suggesting his re-election campaign was open to assistance from Russia—will collapse under the weight of *Sullivan* and other decisions. In March 2020, a federal judge greenlighted the PEN America lawsuit, which seeks to have the court declare that some of Trump's actions have violated the First Amendment. So far, the center is tentatively holding, and despite considerable headwinds, news outlets should continue breaking stories about misfeasance in the Trump adminstration and subsequent ones.[38]

Trump's hopes for a world in which he could hold office while enjoying immunity from derision by the citizenry had little chance of coming true. When the comedy television program *Saturday Night Live*, which frequently ridiculed him, broadcast a sketch in 2017, based on the film *It's a Wonderful Life*, that conjured a world without him as president, he tweeted that the program was "unfair," "can't be legal," and should be "tested in the courts."[39] Fortunately for Trump, it was not tested—because he would have lost if it had been. That same year, he blocked several people from his Twitter account after they criticized him on it. One was blocked after tweeting: "To be fair, you didn't win the WH; Russia won it for you." The courts held that the account was used as a public forum for speech, and Trump's blocking of critics based on their viewpoints violated bedrock First Amendment principles.[40]

Perhaps most far-fetched were Trump's frequent equations of opposition, scrutiny, and even lack of adulation with treason.[41] He leveled the charge against members of Congress who did not clap when he spoke; against the *New York Times* for reporting that Russia was making digital incursions into the United States; and against congressional Democrats for investigating his campaign's ties to Russia. However, the high crime of treason—which is punishable by death in the US—consists of assisting the country's enemies. Only in the more troubled reaches of Trump's imagination does it amount to saying or doing something the president does not like. That is not to say, however, that his accusations do not have terrifying effects. While no court would have entertained Trump's veiled calls for the death penalty against his critics, some of his supporters felt quite differently. Those who criticized Trump were often viewed as traitors who, by questioning him, lost their right to live.

After Trump shared images on Twitter promoting violence against CNN, a supporter mailed explosive devices in 2018 to CNN and to some of Trump's prominent Democratic Party antagonists. That that same year, a man pleaded guilty to making death threats, using phrases borrowed from Trump speeches, against *Boston Globe* journalists after the paper denounced Trump's attacks on the media. And in 2017, a law professor and former Obama administration official named Rosa Brooks published an article in the journal *Foreign Policy* that speculated about whether top military personnel would follow Trump's orders should he be found insane. The piece was picked up by the extreme-right *Breitbart News*, which accused Brooks of calling for a military coup. The gush of death threats began immediately, many accusing her of treason: "I Am Going to Cut Your Head Off . . . Bitch!" screamed one email. Others threatened to hang, shoot, deport, or imprison her. "You're a fucking cunt! Piece of shit whore!" read another message.[42] Thankfully, Brooks was not physically attacked.

THE PRICE OF JOURNALISM AROUND THE WORLD

News reporting was never a safe profession, and it is not becoming safer. The 2018 killing of the Saudi *Washington Post* contributor and US resident Jamal Khashoggi, who was sawed to pieces in the Saudi consulate in Istanbul, was stunning in its brutality, but not surprising from the Saudi regime. What made the murder even more galling was the American failure to condemn it or take action in response. In fact, Trump vetoed three congressional resolutions to halt arms sales to Saudi Arabia the following year. Such actions send a loud signal that even in the US, the lives of journalists are to be valued against business relationships, and if enough money is at stake, their fates will be overlooked. But even without the tacit consent of the American government, press censorship around the world is routinely accomplished with the simple expedient of eliminating reporters. In a 2018 report, *Killing the Messenger*, the International News Safety Institute documented seventy-three journalist killings worldwide that year, just seven of which resulted in legal proceedings.[43]

Regimes around the world use a variety of stratagems short of death to keep nosy journalists on the defensive. Investigative reporters in Italy are often monitored by authorities and sued for criminal libel, a conviction for which can bring up to six years in jail. The investigative tools used against reporters, including wiretaps, are the some of the same don't-sweat-the-civil-rights-details enforcement measures used against organized crime. In 2015, the Sicilian crime reporter Piero Messina published a piece alleging that a prominent doctor had made threatening remarks to a public official about the daughter of a murdered anti-Mafia prosecutor. At the resulting libel trial, Messina was confronted with transcripts of his private phone calls. "When a journalist discovers that he's under investigation in this way," Messina said, "he can't work anymore." Between 2012 and 2017, Italian journalists faced about three dozen such lawsuits. Another Italian reporter, Francesco Viviano, claims that he has been wiretapped, searched, or interrogated by authorities upwards of eighty times.[44]

Brazilian prosecutors charged the American journalist Glenn Greenwald with cybercrimes in 2020 after he published explosive stories confirming that a judge had colluded with prosecutors to imprison a popular leftist politician, thereby enabling the election of Jair Bolsonaro. (The judge, Sérgio Moro, became Bolsonaro's minister of justice.) Greenwald's reporting was based on anonymously sourced, hacked cell-phone messages. After the case against Greenwald drew broad international condemnation, and given Greenwald's previous clearance of wrongdoing in the hacking, the charges were dismissed. For the moment, publishing illegally obtained messages in Brazil does not make a journalist part of a "criminal organization," as the charges against Greenwald stated. However, Moro's and Bolsonaro's animosity toward Greenwald remains white-hot, and as of March 2020, the dismissal is on appeal.[45]

Greenwald is a respected journalist and a resident of Brazil, and as such still enjoys protections under Brazilian law. However, the designation of "journalist" is a distinct hazard in other jurisdictions, where newsgathering is closely monitored and the risks of reporting stories such as those published by Greenwald run high. In Egypt, Russia, and elsewhere, operators of social media accounts with a few thousand or more followers or monthly visitors are required to register as journalists, which magnifies their exposure to retaliation for spreading news challenging government policies or practices. Russia pioneered the tactic in 2014, with a law requiring blogs with more than three thousand monthly visitors to register with the state as media outlets.

Pointedly, the same Russian law also made bloggers liable for the "accuracy" of their content—all in a legal environment in which criticism of the government is often labeled false or extremist.[46]

Greenwald's travails raise another issue: the extent to which a journalist may bring to light purloined materials without bearing responsibility for the theft. In 2014, Greenwald and others won a Pulitzer Prize for reporting on a cache of confidential documents showing massive global cybersurveillance by the US, while Edward Snowden—the whistleblower who stole the materials and leaked them to Greenwald—was charged with espionage. Another publisher of stolen government documents, Julian Assange, is in serious legal jeopardy for publishing confidential US government materials on his WikiLeaks website in 2010. The materials were stolen by Chelsea Manning, an army intelligence analyst, who was given a lengthy sentence in a military prison for the theft. Should Assange be celebrated along with Greenwald as a journalist who brought important matters to the public, or is he a criminal along with Snowden and Manning? The answer, according to the US prosecutors who unsealed an indictment against Assange in 2019, is obvious: "Julian Assange is no journalist." Indeed, he deserves up to 175 years in prison under the Espionage Act.[47]

Assange is, to put it mildly, an unsavory individual, and his irresponsible release of the information exposed people to danger, but the indictment is still a travesty of press freedom. It seeks to criminalize what good investigative journalists do every day: soliciting, receiving, and publishing information governments want to keep secret. Conflating lawbreaking by a journalist's sources with the publishing of what the sources provide, as the indictment clearly does, shuts down a critical channel for whistleblowers to hold governments accountable. One need only reach back to the Pentagon Papers case to see how the law should be approaching the publication of newsworthy information, however obtained. Unless it can be shown that Assange assisted the hacking by Manning, the charges should be dropped.

THE INTERNET: BE CAREFUL WHAT YOU WISH FOR

Today's speech-protection doctrines took form in a slower and simpler world, where communication channels were few and vulnerable speakers sought to ward off the censorious excesses of governments. Whereas governing authorities then wielded the power to allow or forbid speech, censorship in the Internet era defies that model. Profit-driven private companies have become key gatekeepers for expression, and voices, far from being scarce, are now as plentiful as grains of sand. Online speech itself—its volume, its management, and its weaponization—has become a form of censorship. In such an environment, the twentieth-century idea that speech should be protected at all costs and encouraged to multiply may be doing more harm than good.

Recall the late medieval English marketplaces, which were the only places where news could be widely exchanged. Authorities controlled them to ensure that they alone spoke to the crowd. When the Peasants' Revolt exploded, it was no accident that rebels hijacked marketplaces to assert power and express grievances. Jump ahead seven centuries: the Internet has created, in the US Supreme Court's 2017 breathless estimation, *the* "modern public square," a "vast democratic forum" of "unlimited communication," and the "most important place . . . for the exchange of views." Unlike fourteenth-century king's bailiffs, the court enthused that anyone can now "become a town crier" and speak with "a voice that resonates farther" than ever before.[48] Echoing these characterizations, American law has thus far taken a largely hands-off approach to most Internet-based communications. What better way to let the Internet's marketplace of ideas flourish than to stay on the sidelines?

The problem is that the marketplace and public-square analogies are outmoded. Far from a gathering place where everyone's voice can "resonate," the Internet is more like an anthill, where an individual's speech is often trampled into silence before it is heard. Or perhaps it should be compared to a fixed wrestling match, where volumes of "cheap speech," as the scholar Tim Wu calls it, are deployed by one side to "attack, harass, and silence" the other.[49] The match is rigged because the promoters—Internet companies—favor the loudest, dirtiest fighters. False, hateful, and sensational speech holds users' attention, which in turn drives ad revenues. Algorithms amplify such messages, not because of their value to truth or public discourse, but because they generate money. When Facebook tries to satisfy profitable conservative constituencies by, for example, refusing to take down false stories before the 2016 US election or allowing certain of Trump's posts misstating basic facts about the coronavirus, the voting process, or civil rights advocates, and when platforms allow troll attacks that overwhelm minority views, terrorize speakers, and de-legitimate facts, the notion of a truth-revealing public forum becomes strained.[50]

The fact is that people on social media are not modern-day town criers, but mere users, to be baited and manipulated for the enrichment of others. "Clever implementation of persuasive technology created the illusion of user choice," writes the Silicon Valley venture capitalist and Facebook critic Roger McNamee, "making the user complicit in a wide range of activities that exist only for the benefit of the platforms. Some platforms, like Facebook, make it possible for third parties to exploit users almost at will, sometimes to the point of manipulation."[51] Once users are done posting, the platforms track them, recording and monetizing the stories they read and share, the sites they visit, and countless other details. "What concerns me," says law professor Kyle Langvardt, "is that we entrust a few unaccountable and self-interested tech companies to govern online discourse. It seems obvious . . . that this is an unacceptable way for a liberal society to do business."[52]

The pre-Internet rules against censorship evolved roughly along a dual axis, on which the interests of speakers and governments were balanced against each other. Today's censorship issues are multidimensional, involving not only these two sets of players but also the Internet companies and social media platforms that broker online speech, each pursuing its own imperatives. Most countries have put a variety of limits on the Internet platforms—for good, ill, or both at once—and the US is presently considering a number of restrictions. Autocratic jurisdictions such as China have adopted what the NGO Freedom House calls digital authoritarianism, whereas many European democracies are trying to force-feed a semblance of fairness and civility into online discourse. In other words, they are censoring to protect speech.

It didn't look this confusing at first; in fact, it all seemed pretty cool. As media "convergence" came over the horizon in the early 1980s, visionaries such as Ithiel de Sola Pool heralded a democratized, limitless communications environment. In his influential book *Technologies of Freedom* (1983), he looked forward to an age when "computers talk to computers," "demassified" media "serve individual wants," and "writing can become dialogue." As this "single system" matured, the rationale for the law's limits on the ownership of multiple media properties and requirement that broadcasters present multiple sides of issues (among other restrictions) would vanish. These rules had been justified by the scarcity of slots on the broadcast spectrum. In exchange for the few available licenses, broadcasters were required to serve the public interest. As such scarcity was disappearing, Pool reasoned, the rules were superfluous: "Computers, telephones . . . and satellites are technologies of freedom, as much as was the printing press," he declared. "Technology no longer needs control."[53]

The argument resonated. Broadcast media were deregulated, and the online world was fostered according to an "Internet freedom" agenda: it would be as unregulated as possible in structure, commerce, and what was said online. It was first believed that the Internet's decentralized nature made censorship impossible—Bill Clinton joked in 2000 that any such efforts by China would be "like trying to nail Jell-O to the wall"—but later administrations realized this was wrong.[54] They pushed what the law professor Jack Goldsmith calls a global "anti-censorship" principle. Huge amounts of money and effort were expended assisting individuals and groups in "circumventing politically motivated censorship," as Secretary of State Hillary Clinton put it in 2010.[55] The policy of ensuring the free flow of online speech and information was embraced as a way to subvert hostile dictatorships.

It worked—at first. With the active help of the US government, social media became an organizing tool for mass demonstrations in Iran following that country's 2009 election, and for the Arab Spring, which began in 2010 with the downfall of Tunisian president Zine El Abidine Ben Ali. *New York Times* columnist Nicholas Kristof characterized the "quintessential twenty-first-century conflict" as involving "government thugs firing bullets" against "young protesters firing 'tweets.'"[56] But repressive states resented the American-style Internet as a blunt instrument of imperialism. "Once the [Iran] protests quieted down," wrote the journalist Evgeny Morozov, Iranian officials "embarked on a digital purge of their opponents."[57] Over a remarkably short time, authoritarian regimes learned to suppress unwanted Internet activity. And China mastered the craft of nailing Jell-O to any wall it chooses. It developed elaborate mechanisms to bar unwanted news from abroad, control online discussion within its borders, and force Western companies to fall in line or lose access to its markets.

"SENATOR, WE RUN ADS": WHEN PROFIT PUMMELS SPEECH

Most media companies have long been private, profit-making enterprises. Have they skewed or killed important stories to placate advertisers? Yes, repeatedly. Would they champion a cause that would bankrupt their owners? Not likely. Yet even with this corruption, traditional news organizations have often been sharp thorns in the feet of governments. The highest function of the news, as the saying goes, is to speak truth to power, and time and again that goal has been met. However, Internet platforms have become virtual states unto themselves, but without the duties of states. No one voted for them, nor do we know exactly how they and their algorithms manage our speech. Yet they decide which of their billions of users will be heard and by whom, and which will not. That abuses occur countless times daily can be no surprise. They are built into the system.

It comes down to money—what the technology writer Charlie Warzel calls the "original sin" of Big Tech's prioritization of growth over the interests of users.[58] When an aging senator asked Facebook's Mark Zuckerberg in 2018 how the platform can be free to users, Zuckerberg replied (to snickers worldwide), "Senator, we run ads." He might have also explained to the befuddled politician that the ads don't work like those in paper publications: platforms curate and promote content for maximum "engagement," that is, the intensity and frequency with which users interact with them. Engagement is enhanced with divisive and controversial material, which the platforms often promote. Once users are engaged, the platforms assemble comprehensive dossiers on their interactions, buying patterns, prejudices and hatreds, even emotional states, which are in turn monetized with the sale of targeted advertisements. Until recently, Facebook allowed advertisers to target ads to the category "Jew haters." During a 2019 US measles outbreak, Facebook distributed anti-vaccination ads to pregnant women. "Platforms are . . . incentivized to permit and even to encourage the spread of extreme or controversial harmful speech, as it is likely to directly benefit them financially," write Jeff Gary and Ashkan Soltani.[59]

This has been called, among other things, the attention economy and surveillance capitalism, but the effect is the same: user engagement is snared with material that is "likely to be false, demagogic, conspiratorial, and incendiary," says law professor Jack Balkin, which appeals to the users' "fear, envy, anger, hatred, and distrust," and which is then turned to profit through the sale of the data such attention generates. Referring to Facebook, this creates what Balkin identifies as a "fundamental misalignment of incentives between its goals and the public's needs," and "an inherent conflict of interest with its end users and, indeed, with democracy itself."[60] In 2016, Facebook found that almost two-thirds of its extremist group "joins" resulted from its automated recommendation tools. Two years later, a Facebook internal study concluded, "Our algorithms exploit the human brain's attraction to divisiveness." If "left unchecked," the study warned, Facebook's practice would feed users "more and more divisive content in an effort to gain user attention and increase time on the platform." It was left unchecked.[61]

A 2018 *New York Times* investigation showed that Facebook executives had been so "bent on growth" that they ignored warning signs that the platform were also being used to disrupt the 2016 election, disseminate propaganda, and inspire global hate campaigns.[62] Policy staff sought to limit the platform's recommendations to legitimate news sources, but the proposal was rejected. And why wouldn't it be? According to a 2018 study, disinformation and fake news are shared 70 percent more often than factual stories, and spread roughly six times as fast.[63]

In the years following the 2016 US election, Facebook studied how its algorithms and prioritization of user engagement exacerbated division and polarization worldwide. The results were damning, but the research was largely shelved and efforts to mitigate the problems it exposed were weakened or scuttled.[64] Such revenue-reducing measures were anathema, as were other proposals to attenuate the hateful and false rhetoric coming from Trump. "The value of being in favor with people in power outweighs almost every other concern for Facebook," said David Thiel, a Facebook engineer who resigned in 2020, after the company refused to remove a post by Brazil's president, Bolsonaro, that denigrated the humanity of that country's indigenous population.[65]

The major social media platforms have taken steps to remove, deemphasize, or put warnings on harmful and false content, but the results are uneven at best. A 2018 Reuters investigation found that despite Facebook's commitment to combat hate speech against the Rohingya minority in Myanmar, hundreds of such items remained, some of which called them dogs, maggots, or rapists, and suggested they be exterminated.[66] When far-right American extremists used Facebook to exploit the coronavirus pandemic to promote a race war, Facebook was unable to prevent such pages from proliferating.[67] This is not surprising, given that as of January 2020, Facebook's third-party fact checkers were reviewing a paltry two hundred to three hundred articles in the US per month out of millions posted each day.[68] Its other content moderators, who number in the thousands worldwide, are often poorly trained to enforce Facebook's porous and opaque standards, which result in much hateful content remaining on the platform. (One group of content moderators, distressed over the amount of hate speech Facebook allows, bitterly referred to themselves as "algorithm facilitators.")[69] And even if Facebook could take down all the false and harmful posts, which is unlikely, its commitment to silencing such material runs against both the platform's internal design and the attitude of its majority shareholder and CEO.

In May 2020, Zuckerberg, looking to placate one of his best advertisers, said that Twitter was wrong to fact-check Trump's patently false posts, adding that digital platforms should not act as "arbiters of truth."[70] The following month, under the pressure of an advertiser boycott as well as employee discontent and threats from legislators, Facebook added additional measures to police content. But while it took down pages connected to a network of Trump-supporting racist insurrectionists, it did not remove a post by Trump himself about shooting Black Lives Matter marchers.[71] Even if it had, though, the same issues driving harmful content would remain. "The architecture of [Facebook]—its algorithmic mandate of engagement over all else, the advantage it gives to divisive and emotionally manipulative content—will always produce more objectionable content at a dizzying scale," writes Warzel.[72] This is true across all major platforms. "So long as platform profits rely on keeping users on-platform as long as possible," conclude Gary and Soltani, "controversial and harmful speech will continue to proliferate."[73] In August 2020, despite its public renewal of intention to remove hateful content, particularly by right-wing militias, Facebook left up a militia's page stating its members' intention to kill protestors in Wisconsin.[74]

Another result of the attention economy is that we now exist in filter bubbles online: users' beliefs and prejudices are intensified with a fire hose of sympathetic and often strident material, while inconsistent views are overwhelmed or diverted before users see them. "Platforms have little incentive to eliminate filter bubbles," explains McNamee, "because they improve metrics that matter: time on site, engagement, sharing."[75] That perpetual sense of indignation we feel on social media is exhausting, but it keeps us tethered to our laptops and phones. Every video we see and every story we read that confirms what we already believe—and tells us that the enemy is more diabolical than we think—is money in the bank for the platforms. In the process, the modicum of privacy that is a precondition for inquiry and expression is lost, and harassment and outright hate speech persist, whether spread by individuals or troll armies, living or bot.

Yet even with such problems, the Internet has become an indispensable component of contemporary life. The Faustian bargain we make each time we click "Accept" to one or another service's terms and conditions is tempting for the impressive package of benefits it can deliver and because, in the end, we often have no choice. To be offline can have the effect of leaving the world. Jurisdictions weighing these issues from a regulatory standpoint impose a mixture of shared cultural values and top-down realpolitik. The results differ profoundly.

THE WOLVES OF THE FREE MARKET: US LAW AND THE INTERNET

Nowhere is freedom of expression as safeguarded as in the US, and nowhere has online speech been more freewheeling. The First Amendment was already a high barrier against most government incursions, but in 1996, Congress built another rampart with Section 230 of the Communications Decency Act, a statute giving Internet companies and social media platforms additional and sometimes overlapping protections against liability. The law immunizes website operators from lawsuits for ads and most user-generated content, from political diatribes and videos of police brutality to vicious reviews of restaurants and plumbers. Thanks to Section 230, platforms can moderate their sites without the risk of being called to account for their users' and advertisers' false, hateful, or defamatory posts, and also amplify or take down posts, or even terminate user accounts, without legal exposure.

Section 230 is one of history's most significant enablers of speech, and like speech itself it is a mixed bag. Under its protection has emerged a social media environment reflective of the best and worst of its billions of inhabitants, and brimming with all the hatred, humor, creativity, and lies they can muster. The resulting "verbal cacophony," raised to an earsplitting volume by the platforms' division-driving algorithms, supercharges partisan political voices and infuriates the targets of online attacks. Democrats say the law helps to spread hate speech and right-wing disinformation and want more content taken down; Republicans argue it allows liberal-leaning platforms to "censor" conservative viewpoints and want less content removed. While proposals are bubbling up to eliminate or modify the law's liability shield, a divided Congress and the president must still agree on how, which is uncertain in the short term. For the present, American Internet censorship will continue to result less from legal constraints than from the individual platforms' patchwork of evolving, conflicting, and inconsistently enforced content moderation policies.

Section 230 was spurred in part by a crooked financial firm, Stratton Oakmont (made famous by its founder's memoir, *The Wolf of Wall Street*, and Martin Scorsese's eponymous film adaptation). In 1995, Stratton sued a now-forgotten Internet service provider (ISP), Prodigy, for libel for anonymous messages posted on one of its boards that accused Stratton of bad behavior. In ruling against Prodigy, a New York court held that because the ISP moderated its users' postings and had deleted other posts it found inappropriate, it was acting as a "publisher" of the accusations, and as such had legal exposure for libels against Stratton. Congress—intent on fostering a "vibrant and competitive free market" for the Internet "unfettered by . . . regulation," and worried that rulings such as the one against Prodigy would create a disincentive for the nascent industry to remove harmful content— adopted Section 230.[76] Under cover of this statute, sites have been able to manage online operations without having to evaluate every one of the countless posts that appear each day, while at the same time amplifying and profiting from those posts, even the hateful and obnoxious ones, with strategic ad placements.

The courts have applied Section 230 widely, striking down challenges both when sites remove user content and when they leave it up. In 2019, for example, a federal appellate court in New York held that the law even bars claims of civil terrorism. Some Israeli victims of attacks by Hamas (designated a terrorist organization in the US) alleged that Facebook had enabled the aggression by providing Hamas with a platform to promote terrorism around the world. The Court came down squarely for Facebook. In its view, providing "communications services" to Hamas, as Facebook had done, "falls within the heartland" of Section 230's protections. "So, too," the court held, "does Facebook's alleged failure to delete content from Hamas members' Facebook pages."[77] Put another way, Facebook was free to take down such content, but it bore no responsibility for choosing not to. Another court invoked the law in 2020 to dismiss Congressman Devin Nunes's $250 million lawsuit against Twitter, which was based on some parody accounts ridiculing him that had been posted by a "cow." Nunes accused Twitter of keeping the accounts up to harm conservatives such as himself, but the court said the platform's alleged political bias was irrelevant. Section 230 immunizes Twitter from exposure for what its users post, even from degradations coming from an account purportedly managed by a farm animal.[78]

Section 230's chief beneficiary to date has been Donald Trump, who built his political career on Twitter's and Facebook's willingness to carry his false and defamatory messages—something they never would have done without the immunity granted by the law. Yet, days after Twitter added fact-checking labels to some of Trump's May 2020 messages attacking mail-in voting, Trump turned on Twitter, and social media generally, with an executive order taking direct aim at Section 230.[79] The order is largely a stream-of-consciousness mish-mash of complaints about anti-conservative online bias, and its proposals were widely ridiculed by legal scholars as untenable. But like other Trump attacks on the media, legal effectiveness wasn't the real goal. The order was clearly meant to intimidate social media companies into refraining from interfering with his election-year communications strategy.

(Twitter and Facebook continued labeling Trump's false pre-election posts about voting, although they did so slowly and sporadically.)

The executive order also spurred a raft of legislative and other proposals to modify or reduce Section 230's protections. Which of them, if any, will become law is impossible to say; nor is it likely that the more aggressive ones would survive First Amendment challenges. But whether Section 230 is "doomed," as law professor Eric Goldman said in June 2020, or will merely be tweaked, it appears that what some call the Wild Wild Web may already be taming somewhat, even without legislative action. Within two days in late June 2020, the usually undisciplined Reddit banned thousands of forums for hate speech, Amazon-owned Twitch suspended Trump's official account for hateful conduct, and YouTube banned a number of far-right political figures.

Many of the attacks on the social media platforms' Section 230 immunity appear to be displaced complaints about the weakness of US political institutions generally. Never before has a president been such a source of division and misinformation. As there was no way to effectively call him to account for such speech, the impulse is to attack the channels through which Trump and similar divisive figures communicate. In a well-functioning political system, we would not get to the point where the platforms were forced to act as guardrails of unmoored government actors. The platforms share responsibility for the profusion of online misinformation and hatred, but it is a mistake to cast them as democracy's last line of defense. As the tech writer Casey Newton observed, "Trump is a problem the platforms can't solve."[80]

The Constitution raises its own formidable shield against content interference on the Internet. The First Amendment bars the government from censoring most speech of private citizens, but it also allows private companies to enforce their own speech restrictions. Like private schools, malls, or newspapers, Internet platforms are free to set their own rules on what may be said, amplified, or deleted. The platforms' efforts to represent themselves as free speech champions make for good public relations, but they are not such champions and have no obligation to be. Hundreds of millions of times each year, their employees and algorithms muscle speech around, promoting preferred voices and burying others. Individual users who post are thus protected against censorship by the government, but not by the plat-

forms themselves. By the same token, the platforms are constitution-
ally immune from government meddling if what they are doing can be
classified as speech, and what constitutes *speech* in this context can be
surprisingly broad.

In 2014, a federal district court characterized the burying of search
results by a search engine as protected political speech under the First
Amendment. The case was brought by a group of pro-democracy
advocates against Baidu.com, the giant Chinese search engine, for
blocking pro-democracy messages, videos, and similar content from
its search results. The court concluded that Baidu's algorithm, which
was evidently set to remove such materials on instructions from the
Chinese government, constituted an editorial judgment about which
political ideas to promote, which the Constitution protects.[81] Another federal district court held that Google's ranking of search results
is First Amendment speech, and so neither the government nor the
courts can question how it, or other search engines, goes about doing
so: "PageRanks are opinions—opinions of the significance of particular web sites as they correspond to a search query."[82]

The First Amendment also bars government officials from censoring private citizens on their own websites. As discussed earlier, Donald
Trump learned this when the courts stopped him from blocking people on his Twitter account. They were unmoved by Trump's assertion
that he held the account in his personal capacity. As the account was
used, it was a designated public forum, so Trump could not suppress
unwelcome viewpoints on it. Trump is not alone in using social media
accounts for political purposes and then blocking critical views. His
fellow Republican, Governor Larry Hogan of Maryland, was forced
to stop blocking and deleting criticisms on his social media accounts;
liberal congressperson Alexandria Ocasio-Cortez has been sued for
doing the same thing.

The rulings just discussed did not come from the Supreme Court,
and First Amendment law is nothing if not dynamic. Until Congress
and the court weigh in on the multiple ongoing issues raised by censorship on the Internet, there will be many open questions. But for
now, the dual protections of the First Amendment and Section 230
of the Communications Decency Act have fostered the world's most
vibrant, if often chaotic and misinformation-saturated, online speech

environment. Nothing on the Internet exists in isolation, however, and the US is not immune to the much more intrusive approaches of other jurisdictions.

FAT FINES AND FIREWALLS: INTERNET REGULATION IN EUROPE AND ELSEWHERE

"We are afraid of Google," wrote Mathias Döpfner, CEO of the German media group Axel Springer, in 2014, because it threatens "our values, our understanding of the nature of humanity, our worldwide social order and, from our own perspective, the future of Europe."[83] It is not just Google, with its near-saturation market share of Internet searches, that worries Döpfner and other Europeans: it is the hegemony of giant American Internet companies over the online ecosystem. Regulators there have not been shy about flexing their muscles to crack it. Apple was fined more than €13 billion for dodging taxes in France and Ireland, and more than €1.1 billion for price fixing; European regulators fined Google €2.4 billion for abusing its market power with regard to searches. In 2018, European authorities also slapped burdensome data and disclosure and privacy rules on all firms handling the personal information of EU citizens. All those pop-up notices and emails people get about privacy policies and cookies? They can thank the European General Data Protection Regulation for that. It doesn't stop there. In 2020, Germany's top court, the Federal Court of Justice, upheld a broad antitrust ruling against Facebook related to its harvesting of user data, which the *New York Times* called a "direct shot" at the platform's business model.[84]

Freedom of expression in Europe is prized in theory, but there are substantial limits, particularly online. For example, the European Union has embraced the "right to be forgotten," which allows citizens to demand that a search engine not link to pages with embarrassing personal information when their names are searched, even if the delinked information is accurate. There is, evidently, much to forget. Between 2014 and 2020, Google received 900,000 requests to delink 3.5 million URLs. These included search results showing a Dutch surgeon's suspension for medical negligence, which a court forced Google in 2019 to remove. That same year, the European Court of Justice refused France's demand to impose its delinking orders worldwide, but the court reached an opposite result in the context of libel. It forced Facebook to remove postings globally that called the Austrian politician Eva Glawischnig-Piesczek a "corrupt oaf," "lousy traitor," and "fascist."[85] Such remarks would hardly raise eyebrows in many countries, but they do in Austria—and now they are barred everywhere. Facebook complained that the ruling undermines the rights of individual countries to set their own speech standards, but its objections were ignored. For Internet companies, and to the detriment of users in more tolerant jurisdictions, the price of doing business internationally is that censorship decrees in one country could apply elsewhere or worldwide.

In the wake of the disinformation–saturated 2016 Brexit referendum and US election, European governments moved to force online Internet companies to purge disinformation from their platforms. A 2018 German law requires networks with more than two million members to take down fake news within twenty-four hours of notification or face fines of up to €50 million, and a 2018 French law allows authorities to order the deletion of false online information that could affect elections. In Germany, the Network Enforcement Act, or the NetzDG, targets a laundry list of "obviously illegal" materials. French legislators were more precise in defining fake news as "inexact allegations or imputations, or news that falsely report[s] facts, with the aim of changing the sincerity of a vote."[86] In 2018, the EU also arm-wrestled the major platforms into signing a "voluntary" agreement to abide by broad guidelines to address fake news, particularly as it relates to elections.

As well intentioned as such efforts are, they are censorship, with all the attendant risks that "good" expression will be squelched along with the "bad," and that speech will be chilled generally. Given that the Internet companies face severe financial consequences if they make a wrong call, they are incentivized to over-police speech. The German law soon came under review for causing the removal of too much content, while Twitter refused to carry the French government's own advertisements encouraging the electorate to vote, claiming such political ads were now forbidden. And as the platforms use both human labor and artificial intelligence to comply with a welter of conflicting national laws, as well as to apply their own ever-shifting standards, mistakes are inevitably made.

On the amusing side is Facebook's 2018 deletion of a small-town newspaper's posts quoting the US Declaration of Independence, on account of its reference to "merciless Indian Savages" (the posts were soon restored). More troubling is the removal from YouTube of thousands of videos showing atrocities and war crimes in Syria, which were painstakingly collected and verified by human rights advocates. The videos have been useful to investigators, advocates, and journalists but were ensnared by the platform's automated tools designed to remove extremist content. In one instance, the entire channel of the Violation Documentation Center, a human rights monitoring group, was removed, with its 32,000 videos.[87]

YouTube worked to restore the mistakenly deleted videos, but there is no such good faith in the censorship schemes of authoritarian governments. Under the pretense of combating fake news, online dissent has been widely suppressed. In 2017 alone, seventeen countries, including Belarus, Egypt, and Malaysia, passed or proposed laws outlawing fake news. While Russia's law is perhaps the most obvious in its hypocrisy—criminalizing false reports along with "blatant disrespect" for authorities—other regimes have the same aims. Egypt jailed nineteen dissident journalists in 2018 on charges of false news, while two women who uploaded videos on Facebook describing incidents of sexual harassment against them and decrying government inaction, were arrested for spreading false rumors.[88] One of them received eight years in prison. Approximately five hundred websites have also been blocked, including those of prominent human rights organizations.[89] In 2019, Singapore adopted its own anti-fake-news law, backed by harsh criminal penalties and obligating online platforms to remove whatever the government considers false. There is little chance the law will not be used to suppress dissent—not in a country Reporters Without Borders ranks 151st out of 180 countries in terms of press freedom. Human Rights Watch called the law a "disaster for online expression by ordinary Singaporeans, and a hammer blow against the independence of many online news portals."[90]

The Egyptian law was again put to use during the early stages of the coronavirus pandemic, when the government arrested foreign and domestic journalists for spreading "false" rumors—that is, correct reports—about the virus's spread. Egypt isn't alone in its use of such laws. Turkish authorities arrested at least eight journalists for "spreading misinformation" about the virus, while a Cambodian teen was arrested for her fearful social media posts about the virus in her area, and a Thai man was threatened with five years in prison for complaining online about inadequate preventive measures at Bangkok's airport. And as Facebook sent many of its content moderators home for their safety and relied more on artificial intelligence to filter content, articles by reputable outlets such as *The Atlantic* and the *Times of Israel* were mistakenly taken down.

By far the worst censor of online speech is China, both in the scale, sophistication, and brutality of its suppression and in its expanding reach around the world. A dissection of every aspect of the Great Firewall, a catchall term for Chinese Internet censorship, is impossible in the context of this book. It's too vast and it evolves day by day. The Great Firewall restricts the lives and minds of China's eight hundred million web users in countless ways, governing what they see, say, and learn, judging every one of their keystrokes and clicks, and imposing a range of punishments for violating restrictions. It blocks a wide range of foreign and disapproved sites and posts, from many Western news sources to images of Winnie the Pooh (for the cuddly bear's supposed resemblance to President Xi Jinping). The "Internet police," as they are known, also pound on doors. In early 2020, one Li Yuchen posted an essay online complaining about censorship related to the coronavirus outbreak. He was taken from his house, interrogated for hours, and then forced to sign a statement disavowing his views and pledging loyalty to the Communist Party. The hero of his essay, the Wuhan ophthalmologist Li Wenliang, had raised an early alarm about the mysterious virus, only to be dragged to a police station and forced to confess to spreading false and "illegal" rumors. As of March 2020, Dr. Li, who died of the virus, was a censored topic.[91] (Dr. Li was posthumously exonerated.)

The Great Firewall also crosses borders, by deployment of malware against the global Chinese dissident community; by China's aggressive export of censorship and surveillance technologies to other countries; and by China's demand that foreign companies comply with its speech restrictions or risk exclusion from its massive market. Apple complies by removing publications such as the *New York Times* as well as the virtual private networks (VPNs) that let users circumvent the Firewall, including a VPN that allowed access to banned coronavirus-related news, and thousands of other apps from its Chinese app store.[92] The videoconferencing app Zoom buckled under as well, when it took down the accounts of several Chinese dissidents living abroad. Taiwan is absent on the Chinese websites of foreign airlines, and the NBA's lucrative Chinese opportunities were abruptly severed in 2019 after a team manager tweeted *one* message in support of the pro-democracy protests taking place in Hong Kong. (China is not alone in wringing free-speech concessions from Internet platforms. Facebook agreed in 2020 to censor dissidents' posts in Vietnam. The company said it is doing so "to remain available" there.[93])

The lure of doing business in China is enough to test the free-speech mettle of even the most libertarian of Internet companies, and they often fail. In 2005, Yahoo became what Goldsmith and Wu called an "agent of thought control for the Chinese government" in return for access to China. Yahoo agreed to robust censorship of its products, including the use of software filters blocking catchphrases such as "multi-party elections" and "Taiwanese independence" in its chat rooms, and blocking sites to which the government objected.[94] Yahoo also handed over email data that led to the jailing of Shi Tao, a Chinese journalist. A year earlier, Microsoft admitted that its Chinese blog-hosting service automatically blocked words such as "freedom" and "democracy." The Google search engine's brief presence in China ended in 2010, when Google shut it down in protest over government hacking and censorship. Google's free-speech principles wore thin, however. In 2018, reports surfaced that it was working with the Chinese government to reintroduce the search engine, this time in full compliance with China's censorship rules. The project, code-named Dragonfly, was set to go live in early 2019 but was shut down after a revolt erupted within the company.[95]

The rudiments of the Great Firewall were built in the 1990s by American companies. Cisco had developed filtering systems that targeted employees who surfed the Internet for personal reasons while on the job. By 1997, Beijing had passed its first laws criminalizing posts deemed harmful to the state, and many more followed. China had reason to be concerned: the Internet was proving to be a powerful antigovernment organizing tool. In 1998, a young software engineer became the first person tried for online political crimes after he sent thirty thousand Chinese email addresses to a US-based pro-democracy magazine. The following year, the spiritual-practice organization Falun Gong used email and cell phones to organize a large surprise demonstration outside the Communist Party's main compound. The gathering precipitated a severe persecution of Falun Gong and a new determination to control the Internet.[96]

In 2011, after the Chinese government locked down reports about a horrific high-speed rail crash, Weibo, a Chinese version of Twitter, lit up with photos of the wreckage and howls of outrage about bad planning and a cover-up of deadly mistakes.[97] The Weibo mobilization led to a rare moment of accountability for Chinese authorities, but Weibo's brief period as a platform for discussion and dissent—as well as any semblance of free speech on Chinese platforms—ended with Xi Jinping's accession to power in 2012. As the Great Firewall's blocking and surveillance technology steamed forward and Internet censorship was centralized and expanded, the range of acceptable on-line speech narrowed further. Millions of people were enlisted to assist in the cause of monitoring and censoring the Internet, and the number of people punished for violations soared.

In addition to outright suppression and punishment, China has (along with Russia) pioneered a form of reverse censorship, sometimes called flooding. This involves the use of Internet platforms to inundate a population with masses of distracting nonsense and propaganda, drowning out disfavored speech. As of 2016, two million people were employed to post about 448 million social media items per year, which a study found was intended to "distract the public and change the subject [from controversial topics to] cheerleading for China, the revolutionary history of the Communist Party, or other symbols of the regime."[98]

"When listeners have highly limited bandwidth to devote to any given issue, they will rarely dig deeply" for opposing opinions, explains

Wu. "In such an environment, flooding can be just as effective as more traditional forms of censorship."[99] When bot-driven fake news is smeared into the mix, along with torrents of messages attacking the credibility of legitimate information sources, truth is lost along with attention. Similar policies in Turkey aim to create "an ever-bigger glut of mashed-up truth and falsehood to foment confusion and distraction," observes the sociologist Zeynep Tufecki. The goal is less to persuade people to accept one or another narrative than to "overwhelm people with so many pieces of bad and disturbing information that they become confused and give up trying to figure out what the truth might be—or even the possibility of finding out what is true," she writes.[100]

Flooding is no less a scourge in the West. The American social media environment is deluged with distraction and misinformation, leaving people numb and disoriented. "Once, censorship worked by blocking crucial pieces of information," writes Tufecki. Now, "censorship works by drowning us in too much undifferentiated information, crippling our ability to focus."[101] A large part of the deluge of falsehoods about the coronavirus pandemic—much of it also spreading pro-Trump conspiracy theories and calling for an early end to quarantines—was driven by online trolls and bots.[102] As in China and Turkey, the relentless conspiracies and waves of falsehoods that back them (remember "Pizzagate" or "Obamagate," anyone?) are not intended to be convincing as much as wearying and overwhelming. So long as flooding is pushed by governments that see benefit in the confusion and distrust it produces, and so long as it is profitable to the platforms by increasing engagement, it will be a challenge for people to agree even on which way is up. Before the technologies of freedom went live, what news anchors said on the evening news was largely accepted as fact. There was consensus that the reputable media had checked facts and filtered out the crazy stuff. In the attention economy, the crazy stuff—the "flood of shit"—is the point.

Much of the daily work of Chinese online censorship is imposed on private Internet companies, which are overinclusive in their decisions, since there are rarely consequences for censoring too much, but potentially severe repercussions for erasing too little. Online censorship is also mostly privatized in the West. Under pressure from dozens of different sets of laws, as well as their own standards and economic imperatives, the platforms' censorship decisions are an admixture of tentative efforts at good citizenship and keeping the regulatory wolves away. In response to the coronavirus pandemic, they actively (if incompletely) took down or flagged posts with misinformation. After years of criticism for allowing so much harmful speech, Facebook convened an "independent" blue-ribbon "oversight board" in 2020 to rule on its decisions to remove or leave up content. How the board will actually function, how its decisions will square with the demands of regulators worldwide, and the effect its decisions will have across the vast platform remain to be seen. Perhaps the most vexing question is how a private company—one that profits from the speech it seeks to regulate—can credibly resolve the urgent and often subtle issues that arise when expression is suppressed. What would James Madison, John Stuart Mill, or Justice Holmes think of a corporation arrogating to itself the roles of lawmaker, judge, jury, and Supreme Court on this, the most important of rights?

While the West wrestles with these issues, China is helping foreign governments build firewalls of their own. As of 2018, China has trained representatives from at least thirty-six countries, all, according to Freedom House, intended to "create a network of countries that will follow its lead on internet policy."[103] Far from making authoritarianism impossible, as was hoped a quarter century ago, the Internet is moving it along.

"I FIND THAT OFFENSIVE": HATE, INCITEMENT, AND THE LIMITS OF TOLERANCE

Which has more value: one's freedom to voice vile opinions, or the peace of mind of those spoken about? Is one person's or group's taking offense enough to shut down speech that is addressed to everyone? Put still another way, if tolerance is a foundation for a free society, what should result when tolerance reaches its limit? These questions underlie every complaint against microaggressions, every removal of abusive remarks online, and every prosecution for hate speech. Is freedom possible when some may rob others of their dignity, or is degrading speech one of the bitter medicines a free society must swallow? There is no consensus in the West.

The US subordinates dignity to liberty of speech. It's practically a fetish. To give the First Amendment "breathing space," the Supreme Court tells Americans they "must tolerate" speech that is "insulting, even outrageous." Such speech is protected not just when it "may have an adverse emotional impact," but also, in some cases, *because* it is offensive.[104] European and other democracies do not always agree. Freedom of expression is invariably enshrined in their laws, but it gives way when what is expressed pulls at other critical values. Speech may be restrained when "necessary in a democratic society," according to Article 10(2) of the European Convention on Human Rights. Thus, in 2017, neo-Nazis freely marched in Charlottesville, Virginia, chanting "Jews will not replace us," while a few days earlier, in Berlin, two tourists were arrested for raising the Nazi salute in front of the Reichstag.[105] A German politician was also sentenced to prison for a 2010 speech denying the Holocaust—an offense to the "dignity of the Jews"—and a German poet was convicted in 1994 for degrading the human dignity of refugees in a poem that insulted asylum seekers.[106]

The two approaches seem mutually exclusive—US law values liberty of expression over feelings, and other democracies take the converse view—but the reality on the ground is more textured. The European courts struggle daily to balance free expression against other values, and in the process draw ever more elusive and contradictory lines around what is allowed. A higher German court reversed the conviction based on the anti-refugee poem because it did not see the poem as an assault on the human dignity of refugees; however, a few months later, two other German courts reached contrary results.[107] Had the poem been put on Facebook after the NetzDG law went into effect in 2018, Facebook would likely have been forced to remove it or face an enormous fine. And many Americans are not as resilient as their courts demand. A 2019 survey shows that half the American public believes that hate speech should be illegal.[108] These people can be ridiculed as hypersensitive, but they also can be seen as, in effect, wanting to adopt what amount to European standards—and they are doing so where they can. Hate and offensive speech is hurled around the US public arena, but it is often barred in the private sphere, particularly on campuses and by employers, and under broad pressure, certain social media platforms are attempting to seriously restrict its presence online.

As restrictions on offensive speech tighten, the question resurfaces as to whether censorship works at all. Have the laws reduced the quantum of hatred in the world, or are they as futile as speech repression has always been? In Germany, where anti-hate-speech enforcement is quite tough—Facebook had to hire 1,200 people to delete hateful posts there—the number of violent far-right hate crimes surged from about 1,200 in 2017 to 1,664 in 2018.[109] Would that grim tally have been higher absent the hate-speech laws? We cannot know. A 2015 report by Norwegian researchers suggests that filtering out controversial expression may *increase* the risk of extremist violence, while an Australian study found that the country's laws reduced expressions of hatred in mediated outlets, but not on the streets.[110] In the end, our attitudes toward such laws will likely depend on whether we are the ones targeted by offensive speech.

We pick up the American path toward the toleration of hateful speech in 1836, when South Carolina senator John C. Calhoun, offended by aspersions in abolitionist literature against slave owners, successfully demanded a ban on antislavery petitions in Congress because they were, among other things, "injurious" to his and other slave owners' feelings. Early in the twentieth century, African American and Jewish groups had some success in pushing for the censorship of films and other materials depicting them with degrading stereotypes. W. E. B. du Bois and the National Association for the Advancement of Colored People led a campaign to suppress the 1915 hyper-racist blockbuster *The Birth of a Nation*, allowing that it was "dangerous to limit expression" but stressing that "without some limitations civilizations could not endure."[111] These and other efforts resulted in a series of film-censorship laws and general prohibitions against so-called group libel. Most government film censorship was held to be unconstitutional in 1952, but that same year the Supreme Court allowed a group libel conviction against a white Chicago man who had circulated a scurrilous petition against African Americans who were moving into white neighborhoods. The law under which he was charged barred speech that asserted the "depravity, criminality, unchastity, or lack of virtue of any class of citizens."[112]

Despite this decision, group libel never became a viable tool to protect groups from verbal attack, as it and related doctrines were neutralized under the relentless push to free up public discussion. In 1978, the courts affirmed the right of neo-Nazis to march in uniforms through the Chicago suburb of Skokie, Illinois, where forty thousand Jews—seven thousand of them Holocaust survivors—lived in the village of seventy thousand.[113] In 1992, the Supreme Court unanimously struck down a law against putting a burning cross or swastika anywhere "in an attempt to arouse anger or alarm on the basis of race, color, creed, or religion."[114] And in 2011, the court sided with a hate group that picketed the funeral of a gay soldier killed in Iraq, brandishing signs saying "God Hates Fags" and "Thank God for Dead Soldiers." "Such speech," the court held, "cannot be restricted simply because it is upsetting or arouses contempt."[115]

The European policy toward hate speech reflects the "paradox of tolerance" theory of the Austrian-born British philosopher Karl Popper. In *The Open Society and Its Enemies*, he wrote that "unlimited tolerance must lead to the disappearance of tolerance. If we extend unlimited tolerance even to those who are intolerant . . . then the tolerant will be destroyed, and tolerance with them. . . . We should claim the *right* to suppress [intolerance] if necessary even by force."[116] Popper published this in 1945, with Europe suffering enough intolerance to last a millennium. As Europe forged a new society out of the war's ruins with expansive human rights, it carved out exceptions to prevent a resurgence of deadly extremism. The European Court of Human Rights (ECHR) has not hesitated to punish expressions of hatred or bigotry. "It may be considered necessary," it affirmed in 2006, "to sanction or even prevent all forms of expression which spread, incite, promote or justify hatred based on intolerance."[117]

Hate and offensive speech is restricted aggressively in Germany, where Article 1 of its Basic Law states: "Human dignity shall be inviolable. To respect and protect it shall be the duty of all state authority." Every right, including freedom of expression, is subordinated to that. Hateful or insulting speech need not risk inciting violence to be proscribed; the law will step in when there is a generalized threat to an individual's or group's dignity. It is under this standard that Nazi symbols and salutes, Charlottesville-type marches, and extremist parties are banned. As with any censorship policy, however, it is subject to expansion beyond its original objective. In 2019, for example, a man was convicted for posting a picture of SS chief Heinrich Himmler with a swastika in a blog. Neither the German court nor the ECHR was troubled over the fact that the blogger had not used the image to support Nazism but instead to dramatize his frustrations with the government's mistreatment of migrant children, including his own daughter. The courts held that without a clear statement that the blogger rejected Nazi ideology, the use of the image as an "eye-catching device" was criminal.[118]

Censorious excesses—sometimes in good faith but overreaching, other times hateful in themselves—mark other European hate-speech enforcements. In 2008, the septuagenarian former sex kitten and animal-rights activist Brigitte Bardot was convicted and heavily fined for inciting racial hatred. Her crime consisted of writing a public letter in which she protested the ritual slaughter of sheep during a Muslim feast, complaining about "this population that is destroying us."[119] In Britain, a man was convicted for aggravated hostility toward a religious group after putting a poster in his window that showed the World Trade Center in flames along with the words "Islam out of Britain—Protect the British People." The ECHR upheld the conviction, finding that the poster was incompatible with the values of tolerance and social peace. A French man was also convicted for publishing a cartoon depicting the World Trade Center attack, this time with a caption expressing a contrary sentiment: "We have all dreamt about it . . . Hamas did it!" The ECHR again upheld the conviction, noting the cartoon's "solidarity" with the attack.[120] And in 2012, a young British Muslim man was convicted for a "racially aggravated" intemperate Facebook post against the UK military's presence in Afghanistan, saying British soldiers should "Die & Go to Hell!" The police spokesman said the youth "didn't make his point very well and that is why he has landed himself in bother."[121] The anti-Muslim prejudice infusing a prosecution such as this, and the classism against those who don't make their points "very well," is impossible to miss.

As the last example shows, hate-speech laws, like many actions against fake news, are also deployed against expressions of dissent. France has been rather touchy about protests against its business relations with Israel, so when twelve activists entered a supermarket in 2009 and applied stickers with anti-Israel slogans to vegetables imported from that country, they were convicted of hate speech. This case never reached the ECHR, but any expectations that the court would reliably distinguish dissent from hate speech are misplaced. True, the court reversed a fine against a man who held up a sign in 2008 calling France's president Nicolas Sarkozy a *con* ("jerk"), but that was an easy call; Sarkozy himself had used the term against a citizen.[122] But in 1999, after a Turkish newspaper republished two letters complaining about Turkey's brutal suppression of Kurdish nationalists, its owner was convicted of "disseminating propaganda against the indivisibility of the State and provoking enmity and hatred among the people." Amazingly, the European Court found that the conviction did not violate the newspaper's right to freedom of expression.[123]

Despite such troubling outcomes, Europe has of late redoubled its efforts against hate and offensive speech, especially online. The 2016 voluntary "Code of Conduct," discussed earlier regarding fake news, requires the signatory platforms to police themselves for hate speech, but that was evidently not enough. Claiming that existing law has "not gone far or fast enough" to keep online users safe, the UK Parliament is considering legislation to impose a "duty of care" on large platforms to prevent an extensive series of "online harms," including speech that is perfectly legal when voiced offline. A single regulator would define and enforce the duty, with substantial civil and possibly criminal penalties awaiting violators. The scheme has been roundly criticized by free-speech advocates as a ham-handed effort at "legislating for cultural change."[124] Germany's 2018 NetzDG law (on which the UK initiative is partially based) requires that major platforms take down hate speech within twenty-four hours or face large fines.[125]

If only the most corrosive posts were removed through these processes, they might be defensible, but they also appear to have removed a fair amount of legitimate expression. During the first week NetzDG was in place, Twitter deleted both a racist tweet by a far-right political party and a humorous reaction to the tweet by the satire magazine *Titanic*, as well as *Titanic*'s entire account.[126] Such over-inclusive responses are built into a process in which platforms have little time to analyze a huge volume of complaints (there were a half million about Twitter posts in 2018) under a variety of standards, and when a mistaken call can bring punitive sanctions. Since social media platforms also use algorithms to analyze and delete content, the deletions risk sweeping across borders. As law professor Danielle Keats Citron put it, "As companies alter speech rules and speech operations in a wholesale way (rather than retail via country), then the strictest regime prevails. . . . This is a considerable threat to free expression."[127]

Salman Rushdie knows a thing or two about the degree of hatred the offended can direct against their offenders. In 1992, while in hiding as the Ayatollah Khomeini's fatwa exhorted "brave Muslims"[128] to murder him, he published a story that read in part:

> We, the public, are easily, lethally offended. We have come to think of taking offence as a fundamental right. We value very little more than our rage, which gives us, in our opinion, the moral high ground. From this high ground we can shoot down at our enemies and inflict heavy fatalities. We take pride in our short fuses. Our anger elevates, transcends.[129]

The 1988 book that sparked the fatwa, *The Satanic Verses,* caused certain opportunistic religious leaders to stoke reprisals that included nearly two dozen deaths, scores of injuries, and the firebombing of bookshops. The book's translators were stabbed, shot, or killed in Japan, Italy, and Norway. Yet Rushdie's publisher stood firm in its support of the book, and Prime Minister Margaret Thatcher, despite Rushdie calling her "Maggie the Bitch" and "Mrs. Torture" in the book, refused to consider banning it.

In the years since the Rushdie affair, after murderous violence exploded in 2005 in response to twelve cartoon caricatures of the Prophet Muhammad in a Danish magazine, and in the long shadow of the 2015 massacre at the Paris offices of *Charlie Hebdo* for its visual depictions of the Prophet, Rushdie's observation of "lethal offense" has been borne out. As the writer Kenan Malik sharply observes, "The fatwa has effectively been internalised" in the West—and not just by religious fanatics.[130] For many on the left, he notes, "free speech is as likely to be seen as a threat to liberty as its shield." It has been transformed from an inherent good to an inherent problem because of its potential for offense, which has often been enough to justify suppression. "What has emerged," writes Malik, "is an auction of victimhood, as every group attempts to outbid all others as the one feeling the most offended."[131] The result is the suppression of all manner of speech.

The Danish cartoons were republished widely by newspapers and magazines, but the Swedish government shut down a website that posted some of them, and editors of student newspapers around the world were sacked for republishing them. Meanwhile, Berlin's Deutsche Oper closed a 2006 production of Mozart's *Idomeneo* because of its depiction of the Prophet; not long afterward, London's Royal Court Theatre canceled production of an adaptation of Aristophanes's *Lysistrata* set in the Islamic paradise. And after Yale University Press cravenly removed the Danish cartoons from a 2009 book about the controversy, called *The Cartoons that Shook the World*, Index on Censorship removed the images from its own magazine, where they were to accompany an article in which Yale's censorship was criticized.[132]

Perhaps most striking, in 2018, the European Court affirmed the conviction of an Austrian woman who had called the Prophet a pedophile when referring to his child bride. The court imposed a "duty" on speakers, when discussing "objects of veneration," to avoid remarks that are "gratuitously offensive." The woman's comments were likely to put "religious peace at risk," and thus "went beyond the permissible limits of an objective debate."[133] Whatever the "permissible limits" of debate may be, or whether or not any debate must be "objective," it appears that the court's actual concern was retaliation against the comments. By caving in to this fear, the court internalized the fatwa for the entire EU.

Offense to "objects of veneration," be they flags or religious symbols, is not grounds for government censorship in the US, but it is still useful to opportunistic politicians. In 1999, New York City's mayor Rudolph Giuliani smelled race-baiting advantage when the *Sensation* art exhibition arrived at the Brooklyn Museum from London. The show included a painting by the Black artist Chris Ofili, *The Holy Virgin Mary*, which depicts an African Madonna in brightly colored clothing. Although no one would notice without looking closely, bits of elephant dung are used to make up the image as are tiny photographs of female genitalia. Declaring the painting "sick stuff" that "offends me" and stating that the public should not support "vicious, horrible, biased attacks on religion," Giuliani made a public relations event of cutting the museum's funding and threatening to evict the century-old institution from its building unless the painting was removed. A judge brought Giuliani's clumsy attempt at censorship to a quick end, and the painting can now be viewed at New York's Museum of Modern Art—but the mayor's demagogic point was still made.[134]

The *Holy Virgin Mary* imbroglio affirmed well-established US prohibitions on the censorship of offensive speech. However, private employers can shut down offensive speech, and they do so often. One cannot be fired on the grounds of gender or race, but an employee's expressed opinions about these subjects are fair game. Google famously terminated an employee in 2017 after he circulated a memo stating that women were inferior to men in jobs such as engineering. The memo violated Google's employee conduct rules, said Google's CEO, "by advancing harmful gender stereotypes."[135] The engineer's memo was distributed at work, but even speech off the job can jeopardize one's employment. A white supremacist who marched in the Charlottesville demonstration that same year learned this firsthand when he returned to sell hot dogs at the Berkeley, California, restaurant where he worked and found himself out of a job. Also in 2017, a Yale University dean was placed on leave after she posted comments on Yelp that called certain restaurant patrons "white trash" and "low class folks."

The Yale dean should have known better. Just two years earlier, the campus had erupted after a lecturer questioned the school's advice to students to avoid "culturally unaware or insensitive" Halloween costumes. (The lecturer soon left the school.)[136] Rarely in the US or UK is speech more rigorously evaluated for offense than on college campuses, and few issues have delighted the libertarian and right-wing press more than the excesses of campus speech restrictions. Many such rules are indeed misguided, as are endless grandstanding warnings about "student Stasi" toppling freedom of expression and complaints that we have raised a crop of emotional hemophiliacs unable to coexist with controversy. In fact, the goals of campus speech rules are not much different than those purportedly pursued by Mayor Giuliani or vindicated routinely by employers and European courts. As Justice

Holmes recognized in 1925, "Every idea is an incitement."[137] If college students are "snowflakes" who melt under the heat of unwelcome words, that is cause not to ridicule a generation but for introspection as to what has led to this state of affairs.

Some of the speech restrictions at American colleges are indeed puerile. For example, Northeastern University prohibits students, on and off campus, from sending "offensive" or "annoying" materials online, while Sonoma State University requires students to report "any incidents of intolerance, injustice, or incivility."[138] At Purdue University, in 2008, a student was found guilty of racial harassment for reading the book *Notre Dame vs. The Klan* in public. (The book actually celebrated student battles against the Klan, but someone saw the cover and found it offensive.)[139] Such standards should be embarrassing for the schools. Yet the overall trend toward such micromanaging of speech is in decline. A report by the Foundation for Individual Rights in Education found a 50 percent decrease from 2009 to 2020 in the number of American colleges earning its most restrictive "red light" rating.[140] As for the "deplatforming" of controversial speakers at colleges that gets so much attention, it occurs far less often than news coverage implies. A BBC survey of 120 UK universities found just six canceling speakers from 2010 to 2018 because of what the speakers were anticipated to say,[141] while in 2018, American college administrations disinvited eleven speakers[142]—not good, but also not enough to man the freedom-of-speech barricades.

For the most part, freedom of expression is as vital or as impaired on campuses as it is elsewhere. A 2018 YouGov poll found that UK students are no more hostile to free speech nor do they want speakers banned more often than anyone else.[143] This comports with the results of a parliamentary inquiry from the same year, which found that while "there have been . . . incursions" on UK campuses, "press accounts of widespread suppression of free speech are clearly out of kilter with reality."[144] In the US, the economist Jeffrey Sachs showed in 2018 that there has been no generational shift in tolerance toward speech.[145] None of this, however, has minimized the drumbeat of complaints that free speech generally, and conservative voices in particular, are under siege by leftist campus intellectuals and their media confederates. It is an easily digested and galvanizing issue, and it is part of a broader trend by which right-wing politicians, activists, and corporations have co-opted the cause of freedom of speech for their advantage.

At the 2019 conclave of the Conservative Political Action Conference, Donald Trump took up the cause by announcing an executive order withholding federal aid from colleges unless they guarantee "free inquiry." When he later signed the order, he framed it as imperative to allow challenges to the "rigid, far-left ideology" prevalent on campuses.[146] His commitment to "cherish and protect the First Amendment" did not stop his administration from later threatening to pull funding from two universities for teaching "the positive aspects of Islam" in their joint Middle East Studies program, but no matter. He had tossed some tasty red meat to conservatives, and the narrative of victimization by the Left was advanced. It goes beyond campuses. Trump's son Donald Jr. advocated the dismantling of the "technology giants," which he called "the greatest threat to free speech and our democracy today" because they "deplatform people at the behest of liberals."[147] This grievance was leavened into a threat when the president tweeted that the "radical left" is in "total command" of the major Internet platforms. "The administration," he continued, "is working to remedy this illegal situation."[148] The result was the executive order attacking Section 230 of the Communications Decency Act.

Assuming the role of a free-speech martyr is also part of the far-right toolkit in Europe. The veteran extremist politicians Marine Le Pen of France and Geert Wilders of the Netherlands have both routinely mounted (and often lost) vigorous free-speech defenses to charges for calumnies against minorities and immigrants. In doing so, they convert their messages of hatred into complaints of victimization, which in turn stoke the fears that drive their appeal. Carrying this stratagem forward, the young Danish politician Rasmus Paludan, who advocates the expulsion of Muslims from Demark, put himself on the political map by marching into Muslim neighborhoods and burning copies of the Qur'an, then posting videos of the confrontations on his YouTube channel. Central to his appeal are his convictions in Denmark for hate speech and his repeated assertions that he is merely protecting his own freedom of expression as well as that of his (white, non-Muslim) countrymen.[149] By the same token, the US white supremacist group Proud Boys has framed its public provocations as "free-speech rallies," while in 2019, an American psychotherapist specializing in "converting" homosexuals teamed up with a far-right Christian group to challenge New York City's ban on gay conversion therapy in court on free speech grounds.[150]

WEAPONIZING FREE SPEECH

New York withdrew its ban on gay conversion therapy before the lawsuit could proceed far, because the city council feared the city would lose the case. "I don't want to be someone giving in to these right-wing groups," explained a gay member of the city council, "but the Supreme Court has become conservative."[151] Such worries were justified. Under the protection of an increasingly right-wing Supreme Court, the First Amendment has, over the past several decades, gone from a shield protecting dissenters and the weak to a sword to advance the interests of the moneyed and powerful, who have used it to tip elections with limitless corporate spending and to justify antigay discrimination, restrictions on labor unions, and attacks on the regulation of guns, pharmaceuticals, and tobacco. In the words of Justice Elena Kagan, conservatives are "weaponizing the First Amendment."[152]

While these changes exasperate the Left, the fact is that the law should shift with the zeitgeist. Liberals were naïve to think that the doctrines they pushed for would not one day be deployed to their adversaries' advantage. The past century's significant gains in civil and minority rights all involved sharp revisions to existing law, and once new doctrines are established, they are not controlled by those who first advocated for them. What has reshaped the modern speech landscape at its core, however, has been its invasion by a horde of creatures that do not eat, bleed, or hold opinions as living human beings do, but nevertheless have laid claim to their rights to free expression. That corporations do so with money—and not to "speak" but to bulldoze the terrain of ideas for their own bottom lines—has upended many of the foundational assumptions behind free expression. The grant to corporations of broad free speech protections has de facto prioritized profits over the rights of people to speak and be informed. A comprehensive 2015 study found that, in the US, "corporations have increasingly displaced individuals as direct beneficiaries" of free-speech rulings.[153]

The progression toward the law's embrace of corporate free-speech rights is long, but we can begin in 1907. President Theodore Roosevelt, stung by a scandal involving insurance money flowing into his campaign, signed the Tillman Act to choke off corporate money from politics. That and similar state laws were challenged in court, primarily by beer brewers who claimed they had a free-speech right to spend money to convince people to vote against ballot measures to ban alcohol sales. The courts disagreed. One held that corporations "are not citizens," and that spending money to influence elections, like the right to vote, was the prerogative of natural people. "The time has not come and probably never will come," the court said, to give these rights "to the artificial beings known as corporations."[154] Corporations had rights to property and to engage in commerce, but not to the liberties of individuals such as freedom of speech.

The idea that entities should not share the personal liberties of human beings endured for decades, but several decisions chipped at the distinction. In the 1930s, Louisiana's populist governor Huey Long battled the state's big-city newspapers when they opposed his plans to tax oil companies; the conflict soon metastasized into a bitter grudge match. Long set out to tax the papers out of existence, but his scheme fell apart in the Supreme Court. In *Grosjean v. American Press Co.* (1936), the court affirmed that the newspapers had First Amendment rights, and that the tax grossly interfered with them. Good enough, but the newspapers were also corporations, and in upholding their rights against a vindictive autocrat, the court also took a big step toward normalizing corporate liberty rights. "For the first time," writes law professor Adam Winkler, the Supreme Court held that "corporations have the right to freedom of speech and of the press."[155]

A key turning point resulted from, of all things, a push by Public Citizen, a consumer advocacy group founded by the anti-corporate activist Ralph Nader. In *Virginia State Board of Pharmacy v. Virginia Citizens' Consumer Council* (1976), it challenged a ban on the advertising of drug prices, which prevented patients from finding bargains without going from pharmacy to pharmacy. Nader's group argued that the ban impeded the flow of important information to consumers. The court agreed, and in handing Public Citizen a win, it also augmented speech protections for advertising and commercial speech. The impetus of the decision was the right of ordinary people to be informed, but it was later used against their interests: it would be invoked against restrictions on tobacco, liquor, and casino advertising, and requirements by dairy producers to disclose synthetic growth hormones. Later, looking back ruefully on the corporate weaponization of *Virginia State Board of Pharmacy*, Nader called it "one of the biggest boomerangs in judicial cases ever."[156] In 1976, liberals also pushed for the *Buckley v. Valeo* decision, which struck down certain limits on political spending on free-speech grounds. These cases and others begat *Citizens United v. FEC* (2010), which smashed many limitations on corporate spending to influence elections, and did so in the cause of corporate freedom of speech. Corporations not only have the right to engage in political speech, the court held, but they may "speak" by spreading around as much money as they wished, so long as the expenditures are not formally "coordinated" with campaigns.

Citizens United and subsequent rulings released a flood of corporate money into American politics, which is bad enough. But the embrace of corporate free-speech rights has had other effects as well. The year after *Citizens United*, the court found that pharmaceutical and data mining companies had a free-speech right to harvest doctors' prescribing records from pharmacies to help them hawk drugs, even without the doctors' consent. The court held that there is a "strong argument that prescriber-identifying information is speech."[157] Building on that, Internet service providers are filing lawsuits claiming a First Amendment right to sell their customers' browsing histories and other sensitive data without first obtaining the customers' consent.[158] Most alarmingly, ExxonMobil asserted its newfound First Amendment rights to defend itself against state investigations regarding its alleged defrauding of investors about the risks of climate change.[159] In future cases alleging massive corporate deceptions, large businesses will likely continue, in the words of the legal scholar Morgan Weiland, "using the First Amendment as a weapon, seeking to constitutionalize potentially fraudulent speech."[160]

Fortunately for the fossil fuel industry, the US government has also censored climate change information. The George W. Bush administration impeded the release of accurate and timely information to the media, the public, and Congress about climate change and the effects of greenhouse gases.[161] The Trump administration expanded the information lockdown. The phrases "climate change" and "greenhouse gas emissions" were blacklisted from many government press releases and publications; the Environmental Protection Agency removed a section of its website containing critical climate-change information; and dozens of studies regarding the effects of climate change were buried. Maria Caffrey, a scientist working on sea level and storm surge projections, lost her job at the National Park Service in 2019 after she refused to remove references to human-caused climate change from her report.[162]

To keep track of the constant suppression of knowledge concerning climate change, the Sabin Center for Climate Change Law and the Climate Science Legal Defense Fund jointly created an online "Silencing Science Tracker." As of April 20, 2020, the site lists nearly five hundred instances of such censorship since Trump came to power. The most recent entry concerning climate change involved the government's inserting misleading language into at least nine different scientific reports a few days after it had paused a six-year study of measures to reduce climate-related flood risks to New York and New Jersey. Evidently it is better *not* to prepare than to acknowledge that there is a problem.

The censorship and undermining of climate science under the Bush and Trump administrations contributed to widespread refusals among many Americans to accept plain, verified facts. In certain filter bubbles, the dismissal of scientific findings—even those with urgent, widespread public health implications—has become a way to assert one's "freedom" from the perceived intrusions of liberal politics and unwanted constructions of reality. As of June 2020, a similar partisan divide had arisen in the US over whether to accept the dangers of coronavirus contagion. "If Trump doesn't worry about it," said an Alabama woman whose father watches Fox News, "then my parents don't worry about it." The woman's father also believes global warming is a hoax, and characterizes concerns about the pandemic as "climate change 2.0."[163]

In these contexts, censorship may have had its deadliest effects yet. Under a haze of uncertainty over whether truth is even knowable, the resort for many is to put their faith in a leader they regard as strong. What could go wrong?

AFTERWORD

As this book went to press, censorship-related news—information lockdowns worldwide about the coronavirus; agitation by members of the US Republican Party against social media platforms for "censoring" conservative voices; China's co-opting of the Zoom communications platform to stifle dissent outside its borders; torrents of misinformation unleashed to confuse the American electorate about the Black Lives Matter movement; and more—was coming in so fast and furious that this book would never have been finished if I hadn't called an arbitrary halt to the intake of information. That is quite something for a work that begins with a Roman execution and includes Byzantine iconoclasm, the American Civil War, and the suppression of gay- and Communist-themed films during the Weimar Republic.

One of the benefits of writing a book of history is that the core events have already taken place. Once the relevant sources have been absorbed, the aim is to explain the facts and place them in a coherent, hopefully illuminating narrative. There are always competing interpretations, but absent new evidence, the underlying story will not change significantly. However, a book about censorship—even one that mostly concerns past rather than contemporary events—presses against the assumption that a reliable account can be told at all. Because the core process at work is the suppression of ideas and information, there persists the nagging doubt that the book does not sufficiently account for what was *not* said, what was expressed and then buried, which important speakers have vanished. To write about a subject as opaque as censorship in history feels like chasing a vacuum; once it is captured, only silence is revealed. The objects of the story, after all, have disappeared.

This is all especially true in the present day, as the volume of suppressed speech surges and basic assumptions about what censorship is, and how it is accomplished, are transforming. The very vehicles of speech, and speech itself, are now used to silence voices, while decisions as to what speech to allow are increasingly directed by IT engineers who are more concerned with developing profitable online products than managing their platforms responsibly. And the cause of free speech, so often the province of the dispossessed against moneyed and established interests, has steadily become the latter's clarion call. As Catharine MacKinnon put it about the First Amendment, "Legally, what was . . . a shield for radicals, artists and activists, socialists and pacifists, the excluded and the dispossessed, has become a sword for authoritarians, racists and misogynists, Nazis and Klansmen, pornographers and corporations buying elections."[1] She overstates the matter a bit but gets the mechanics right. In many important ways, restraints on censorship have come to be used to protect ingrained hierarchies of wealth and privilege rather than marginalized voices.

Such a fluid environment makes it impossible to divine which of today's roiling controversies will bring lasting change, which will be neutralized by political or technological developments, and which will simply evaporate. An example is the controversy over social media censorship. While Donald Trump's attacks on Section 230 of the Communications Decency Act, one of the pillars of speech protections on social media, lost momentum with his election loss, the issues exploded anew in January 2021, when Twitter banned him, along with seventy thousand QAnon accounts, following a pro-Trump attack on the US Capitol building. The immediate results were a drop in online misinformation, the migration of extremist content to the web's darker reaches, and bitter criticism of "Big Tech" and Section 230 from almost all corners. But even if Section 230 survives intact in the short term, the push to substantially restrict online speech may well bear fruit. It is useless to guess how that will occur. Indeed, the entire course of online speech regulation has defied prediction. Who, after all, would have imagined even a decade ago that a private tribunal assembled and financed by a thirty-six-year-old billionaire's company,

Facebook, would have the power to pass judgment—on a transnational basis—on some of the day's most important speech issues?

Yet despite the uncertain outcomes that any historical juncture presents, written text, spoken words, and images continue to terrify, as they always have. "The power of speech operates in ways that are not fundamentally different from ordinary actions in the everyday world," observes Robert Darnton,[2] and when speech threatens, denigrates, embarrasses, or kicks the shins of accepted verities, the impulse to stop it is as urgent today as it has ever been. When such speech is directed against those who wield power, only firm legal barriers can prevent them from censoring it, and such barriers in the West are of relatively recent vintage. The extent to which today's broad rights to speak out against government or report governmental misconduct will endure is anyone's guess.

While censorship is no less a spectacle of power now than in earlier times, it is even more futile. We cannot know how many destroyed texts were entirely lost over the centuries, but, as this book has shown, copies often survived, because the censoring authorities either kept them for themselves or could not track down all copies in circulation. Given the digitization of hundreds of millions of existing texts and the diffusion into the cloud of countless others as soon as they are composed, the channels for eliminating forbidden materials are closing. Even the tightest controls can often be circumvented. In 2020, the press-freedom group Reporters Without Borders managed to make a large cache of forbidden news stories available in heavily controlled countries such as China by routing it through the popular online game Minecraft. Banned news has also been embedded into pop songs and distributed through the online music service Spotify.[3] Authorities know about such tactics as well as anyone, yet they persist with their suppression efforts because they believe they must. It is not just speech they fear, but also the appearance of toleration. And once an aggressive stance toward speech has been taken—even a symbolic one—to abandon or soften it only makes matters worse.

The recent pushes to limit hate speech and offensive speech are both a testament to the power of words and an affront to the notion that speech, to the greatest extent possible, should be free. The plain fact is that people often have thoughts that are repugnant, immoral, or out of sync with the zeitgeist. When such thoughts are vented, *someone* within earshot (digitally or otherwise) is likely to feel pain, or perhaps be influenced to act badly. The post–World War II European experiment in balancing freedom of expression with limiting harmful speech does not seem to have worked as hoped. In February 2020, the Council of Europe raised an alarm over the sharp rise in anti-Semitic, anti-Muslim, and other racist hate crimes, as well as the advance of xenophobic politics.[4] In light of these findings, the council's secretary general, Marija Pejčinović Burić, urged, "We must stop the dissemination of toxic rhetoric from racist extremists which strikes at the very heart of our democracies."[5]

Burić may be right. To embrace free expression without regard to its consequences can be irresponsible. However, policing speech too aggressively risks exactly the kind of overbearing exercise of state power that spells the end of a free society. Balancing these two evils, I return to George Orwell's observation from the 1940s: "If liberty means anything, it means the right to tell people what they do not want to hear."[6] The elimination of harmful rhetoric protects the well-being of some in the short term, but no evidence shows it also eliminates the darkness behind the words. Speech can indeed cause harm, just as any other misdirected action. But if this book has made any point, it is that striking at speech to eliminate a dangerous idea is not only ineffective—it will cause worse mischief in the long run.

ACKNOWLEDGMENTS

This book was completed with a lot of help—from the many scholars on whose work I relied, from the direct assistance and guidance of others, and from two first-rate publishing teams that gave me a solid platform on which to do my work.

No work of scholarship is unique in itself. My book builds on the labors of others, without whose insights and innovations my efforts would have been impossible. Among them are John Barrell, Paul Boyer, Monica Braw, Ernst Cassirer, Zechariah Chafee, Michael Kent Curtis, Robert Darnton, Thomas Emerson, Jack Goldsmith, Robert Justin Goldstein, Charles Hedrick, Nat Hentoff, Rebecca Knuth, Elisabeth Ladenson, Leonard Levy, Catharine MacKinnon, Kenan Malik, George Orwell, Julian Petley, George Roeder, Dirk Rohmann, Alexander Rubel, Fredrick Siebert, Geoffrey Stone, Zeynep Tufekci, Adam Winkler, and Tim Wu. These are just a few of the masters on whose shoulders I stand.

Helping to shape my halting efforts and providing sage editorial help were Mitchell Albert and Charlie McCann, as well as Kirsten Janene Nelson.

On the business side has been my tireless agent, Andrew Stuart, whose support and advocacy I will always treasure, and the incomparable Joanna Green and Susan Lumenello at Beacon. At Saqi, I relied on the brilliant Lynn Gaspard. Lynn must also take much of the credit (if none of the blame) for this book, as the whole thing was her idea.

And every day was made possible by my children, Lawrence, Claire, and Grey, whose sad fate is to put up with me during these projects, and by my wife, Jennifer, the great love of my life.

NOTES

INTRODUCTION

1. See, generally, Rebecca Knuth, "China's Destruction of the Libraries in Tibet," in *Lost Libraries: The Destruction of Great Book Collections Since Antiquity*, ed. James Raven (Basingstoke, UK: Palgrave Macmillan, 2004), 247–60.

2. Rebecca Knuth, *Libricide: The Regime-Sponsored Destruction of Books and Libraries in the Twentieth Century* (Westport, CT: Praeger, 2008), 169, 183, 190.

3. Lois May Chan, "The Burning of the Books in China, 213 B.C.," *Journal of Library History* 7 (1972): 107.

4. Jing Liao, "A Historical Perspective: The Root Cause for the Underdevelopment of User Services in Chinese Academic Libraries," *Journal of Academic Librarianship* 30 (2004): 112.

5. Quoted in Simon Leys, *Broken Images: Essays on Chinese Culture and Politics*, trans. Steve Cox (New York: St. Martin's, 1979), 44.

6. Will Durant, *The Story of Civilization 1: Our Oriental Heritage* (New York: Simon & Schuster, 1942), 697.

7. Carrie Gracie, "Qin Shi Huang: The Ruthless Emperor Who Burned Books," *BBC Magazine*, October 15, 2012, https://www.bbc.com/news/magazine-19922863, accessed June 22, 2020.

8. George Orwell, *Nineteen Eighty-Four* (New York: Signet, 1950), 40.

9. George Orwell, "The Prevention of Literature," in *The Orwell Reader: Fiction, Essays, and Reportage* (San Diego, CA: Harcourt Brace Jovanovich, 1984), 371.

10. J. H. Plumb, *The Death of the Past* (Harmondsworth, UK: Pelican, 1969), 34.

11. *Guatemala: Memory of Silence/Tzinil Na Tabal: Report of the Commission for Historical Clarification—Conclusions and Recommendations* (Washington, DC: CEH 1999), 29–30, https://assets.documentcloud.org/document/357870/guatemala-memory-of-silence-the-commission-for.pdf; Comité pro Justicia y Paz de Guatemala, *Human Rights in Guatemala* (Geneva: World Council of Churches, 1984), 18, quoted in Antoon de Baets, *Censorship of Historical Thought: A World Guide, 1945–2000* (Westport, CT: Greenwood Press, 2002), 29.

12. Robert A. Kahn, *Holocaust Denial and the Law: A Comparative Study* (New York: Palgrave Macmillan, 2004), 57.

13. R. v. Zundel, 2 SCR 731 (1992).

14. West Virginia State Board of Education v. Barnette, 319 U.S. 624 (1943).

15. Susan Benesch, "But Facebook's Not a Country: How to Interpret Human Rights Law for Social Media Companies," *Yale Journal on Regulation Online Bulletin* (2020): 86, https://digitalcommons.law.yale.edu/cgi/viewcontent .cgi?article=1004&context=jregonline.

16. Henry Louis Gates Jr., Anthony P. Griffin, Donald E. Lively, Nadine Strossen, Robert C. Post, and William B. Rubenstein, *Speaking of Race, Speaking of Sex: Hate Speech, Civil Rights, and Civil Liberties* (New York: New York University Press, 1994), 42.

17. Elizabeth Dwoskin and Nitasha Tiku, "Facebook Employees Said They Were 'Caught in an Abusive Relationship' with Trump as Internal Debates Raged," *Washington Post*, June 5, 2020, https://www.washingtonpost.com/technology /2020/06/05/facebook-zuckerberg-trump.

18. Frederick Schauer, "The Ontology of Censorship," in *Censorship and Silencing: Practices of Cultural Regulation*, ed. Robert C. Post (Los Angeles: Getty Research Institute, 1998), 147; Ruth Gavison, "Incitement and the Limits of the Law," in Post, *Censorship and Silencing*, 43–44.

19. Rae Langton, "Subordination, Silence, and Pornography's Authority," in Post, *Censorship and Silencing*, 261.

20. Michael Holquist, "Corrupt Originals: The Paradox of Censorship," *PMLA* 109 (1994): 14–25; Robert C. Post, "Censorship and Silencing," in Post, *Censorship and Silencing*, 1–12.

21. Durant, *The Story of Civilization I*, 697.

22. F. G. Bailey, *Gifts and Poison: The Politics of Reputation* (New York: Schocken Books, 1971), 294.

23. "The Trial of John Tutchin at the Guildhall of London, for a Libel, in T. Bayly Howell et al., *A Complete Collection of State Trials and Proceedings for High Treason . . .*, vol. 14, 5th ed. (London: Printed by T. C. Hansard for Longman et al., 1816–28), 1128, https://babel.hathitrust.org/cgi/pt?id=uc1 .31175029419234&view=1up&seq=576.

24. Nix v. Germany, ECHR (2018).

25. Brian Winston, *Messages: Free Expression, Media and the West from Gutenberg to Google* (London: Routledge, 2006), 53.

26. Orwell, "The Prevention of Literature," 372, 378.

CHAPTER 1: HELPING GOD ALONG

1. "Avodah Zarah 18a," *The William Davidson Talmud*, Sefaria: A Living Library of Jewish Texts, https://www.sefaria.org/Avodah_Zarah, accessed March 17, 2020.

2. Ernst Cassirer, *Language and Myth*, trans. Susanne K. Langer (New York: Dover Publications, 1953), 59–60.

3. "The Creation Account of the Uitoto of Columbia, South America," in Internet Sacred Text Archive, http://www.sacred-texts.com/nam/sa/cau.htm, accessed March 17, 2020.

4. "Isis and the Name of Ra," Digital Egypt for Universities, University College London, 2003, https://www.ucl.ac.uk/museums-static/digitalegypt/literature /isisandra.html, accessed March 17, 2020.

5. Vere Gordon Childe, *Man Makes Himself* (Nottingham, UK: Spokesman, 2003), 93–94.

6. Dirk Rohmann, *Christianity, Book-Burning and Censorship in Late Antiquity: Studies in Text Transmission* (Waco, TX: Baylor University Press, 2017), 73; Elisabeth Ladenson, "Censorship," in *The Book: A Global History*, ed. Michael F. Suárez and H. R. Woudhuysen (New York: Oxford University Press, 2013), 177.

7. Catharine A. MacKinnon, *Only Words* (Cambridge, MA: Harvard University Press, 1993), 29.

8. Leviticus 24:10–23; Leonard W. Levy, *Blasphemy: Verbal Offense Against the Sacred, from Moses to Salman Rushdie* (Chapel Hill: University of North Carolina Press, 2009), 8.

9. Leviticus 24:16.

10. Isaiah 36–37.

11. Deuteronomy 4:15–18; Exodus 20:4–5.

12. Philip Alexander, "Reflections in Word Versus Image as Ways of Mediating the Divine Presence in Judaism," in *The Image and Its Prohibition in Jewish Antiquity*, ed. Sarah Pearce (Oxford, UK: Journal of Jewish Studies, 2013), 20; see also Hans J. L. Jensen, "Aniconic Propaganda in the Hebrew Bible, or: The Possible Birth of Religious Seriousness," *Religion* 47, no. 3 (2017): 399–407.

13. Jack Goody, *Representations and Contradictions: Ambivalence Towards Images, Theatre, Fiction, Relics, and Sexuality* (Oxford, UK: Blackwell, 1997), 37.

14. W. A. L. Elmslie, *Texts and Studies: The Mishna on Idolatry, ʾAboda Zara* (Eugene, OR: Wipf & Stock, 1911), 42, 67.

15. Elmslie, *Texts and Studies*, 53–67.

16. Elmslie, *Texts and Studies*, 26.

17. William Popper, *The Censorship of Hebrew Books* (New York: Knickerbocker Press, 1899), 2.

18. Robert Wallace, "The Power to Speak—and Not to Listen—in Ancient Athens," in *Free Speech in Classical Antiquity*, ed. Ineke Sluiter and Ralph M. Rosen (Boston: Brill, 2004), 222; see also Max Radin, "Freedom of Speech in Ancient Athens," *American Journal of Philology* 48, no. 3 (1927): 215, 221, 223–25.

19. Xenophon, *Memorabilia*, bk. 3, ch. 6, sec. 1, in *Xenophon in Seven Volumes*, vol. 4, trans. E. C. Marchant and O. J. Todd (Cambridge, MA: Harvard University Press, 1923); quoted in Wallace, "Power to Speak," 224.

20. Alexander Rubel, *Fear and Loathing in Ancient Athens: Religion and Politics During the Peloponnesian War* (New York: Routledge, 2014), 16.

21. Giulia Sissa and Marcel Detienne, *The Daily Life of the Greek Gods*, trans. Janet Lloyd (Stanford, CA: Stanford University Press, 2000), 169–70.

22. M. I. Finley, "Myth, Memory, and History," *History and Theory* 4, no. 3 (1965): 281, 283.

23. Plutarch, "Pericles," in *The Rise and Fall of Athens: Nine Greek Lives by Plutarch*, trans. Ian Scott-Kilvert (London: Penguin, 1960), ch. 32, sec. 2.

24. Rubel, *Fear and Loathing*, 70.

25. Rubel, *Fear and Loathing*, 155.

26. See, for example, Jacob Filonk, "Athenian Impiety Trials: A Reappraisal," *DIKE* 16 (2013), https://riviste.unimi.it/index.php/Dike/article/view/4290/4399.

27. Plato, *The Republic*, trans. A. D. Lindsay (New York: E. P. Dutton, 1957), 83–85.

28. Plato, *The Republic*, 73, 76, 395–397, 86, 104.

29. Plato, *Laws*, trans. Benjamin Jowett (Mineola, NY: Dover, 2006), 34.

30. Plato, *The Republic*, 386.

31. Plato, *The Republic*, 598, 602.

32. Plato, *Laws*, 700–701, 659.

33. Plato, "Theaetetus," in *Plato in Twelve Volumes*, vol. 12, trans. Harold N. Fowler (Cambridge, MA: Harvard University Press; London: William Heinemann, 1921), sec. 191a.

34. Tacitus, *Annals*, bk. 4, in *Complete Works of Tacitus*, trans. Alfred John Church and William Jackson Brodribb, ed. Sara Bryant (reprint; New York: Random House, 1942), ch. 35.

35. Livy, *The History of Rome*, bk. 25, ch. 1, trans. D. Spillan and Cyrus Edmonds (London: Henry G. Bohn; John Child and Son, Printers, 1849), 958.

36. Valerius Maximus, *Memorable Deeds and Sayings: One Thousand Tales from Ancient Rome*, trans. Henry John Walker (Indianapolis: Hackett, 2004), 6.

37. Eric Orlin, "Why a Second Temple for Venus Erycina?" in *Studies in Latin Literature and Roman History X*, ed. Carl Deroux (Brussels: Latomus, 2000), 77; Andreas Willi, "Numa's Dangerous Books: The Exegetic History of a Roman Forgery," *Museum Helveticum* 55, no. 3 (September 2003): 146, referenced in Daniel Sarefield, "Burning Knowledge: Studies of Bookburning in Ancient Rome," PhD diss., Ohio State University, 2004, 48.

38. Suetonius, "Julius Caesar," in *The Lives of the Twelve Caesars*, trans. John Carew Rolfe, Loeb Classical Library (London: Heinemann, 1913), sec. 75; see also Frederick H. Cramer "Bookburning and Censorship in Ancient Rome: A Chapter from the History of Freedom of Speech," *Journal of the History of Ideas* 6, no. 2 (1945): 157, 161.

39. Suetonius, "Augustus," in *The Lives of the Twelve Caesars*, secs. 51, 55–56.

40. David Potter, *Prophets and Emperors: Human and Divine Authority from Augustus to Theodosius* (Cambridge, MA: Harvard University Press, 1995), 95, 243n98.

41. Suetonius, "Augustus," sec. 31.

42. Tacitus, *Annals*, bk. 1, ch. 72, in Perseus Digital Library, http://www.perseus.tufts.edu/hopper/text?doc=Perseus%3Atext%3A1999.02.0078%3Abook%3D1%3Achapter%3D72.

43. Cramer, "Bookburning and Censorship," 170.

44. Cramer, "Bookburning and Censorship," 172–75; Dirk Rohmann, "Book Burning as Conflict Management in the Roman Empire (213 BCE–200 CE)," *Ancient Society* 43 (2013): 115, 130.

45. Cramer, "Bookburning and Censorship," 175.

46. Tacitus, *Annals*, bk. 4, ch. 34; Cassius Dio, *Roman History*, bk. 57, sec. 24, http://penelope.uchicago.edu/Thayer/E/Roman/Texts/Cassius_Dio/57*.html.

47. Tacitus, *Annals*, bk. 4, ch. 35, quoted in Cramer, "Bookburning and Censorship in Ancient Rome," 193.

48. Suetonius, "Caligula," in *The Lives of the Twelve Caesars*, sec. 16.

49. Cassius Dio, *Roman History*, bk. 57, sec. 24.

50. Tacitus, *Annals*, bk 4, ch. 69 in Perseus Digital Library, http://www.perseus.tufts.edu/hopper/text?doc=Perseus%3Atext%3A1999.02.0078%3Abook%3D4%3Achapter%3D69.

51. Tacitus, *Annals*, bk. 2, chs. 27–31, in Perseus Digital Library, http://www.perseus.tufts.edu/hopper/text?doc=Perseus%3Atext%3A1999.02.0078%3Abook%3D2%3Achapter%3D27.

52. Charles W. Hedrick, *History and Silence: Purge and Rehabilitation of Memory in Late Antiquity* (Austin: University of Texas Press, 2000), 165.

53. Suetonius, "Domitian," in *The Lives of the Twelve Caesars*, sec. 10; Jason A. Whitlark, *Resisting Empire: Rethinking the Purpose of the Letter to "the Hebrews"* (London: Bloomsbury, 2014), 45.

54. Tacitus, *Agricola*, trans. M. Hutton (Cambridge, MA: Harvard University Press, 1914), 28–29.

55. Pliny, *Letters and Panegyricus* (Cambridge, MA: Harvard University Press, 1975), 440–41.

56. Suetonius, "Domitian," sec. 23.

57. Lauren Hackworth Petersen, "The Presence of 'Damnatio Memoriae' in Roman Art," *Notes in the History of Art* 30, no. 2 (Winter 2011): 1–8.

58. Hedrick, *History and Silence*, 183.

59. Acts 19.

60. Gregory Nazianzen, "Oration 24," trans. Daniel Sarefield, quoted in Sarefield, "Burning Knowledge," 84–85; Rohmann, *Christianity*, 138–39.

61. Lactantius, *De mortibus persecutorum*, trans. J. L. Creed (Oxford, UK: Clarendon Press, 1984), 12.2, and Eusebius, *The Ecclesiastical History and The Martyrs of Palestine*, trans. H. J. Lawlor and J. E. L. Oulton, 2 vols. (London: Society for the Promotion of Christian Knowledge, 1927), 8.2.4, both quoted in Sarefield, "Burning Knowledge," 203; Rohmann, *Christianity*, 27–28.

62. "The Acts of Euplus," 1.1, 2.1–2, 3.2–3, from *The Acts of the Christian Martyrs*, trans. Herbert J. Musurillo (Oxford, UK: Clarendon Press, 1972), 310–19.

63. Michael Grant, *Constantine the Great: The Man and His Times* (New York: Scribners, 1994), 145–46.

1. Grant, *Constantine the Great*, 145, 170.

2. Socrates of Constantinople, "The Dispute of Arius with Alexander, His Bishop," bk. 1, ch. 5, in *The Ecclesiastical Histories of Socrates Scholasticus* (London: Henry G. Bohn, 1853), 5–6.

3. Gregory of Nyssa, "De deitate filii et spiritus sancto et In Abraham," *Patrologia Graeca* 46, col. 557, for shopkeepers on the *homousion*, in *Gregory*

of Nysa: The Minor Treatises on Trinitarian Theology and Apollinarism, ed. Volker Henning Drecoll and Margitta Berghaus, *Vigiliae Christianae* (supplements) 106 (Boston: Brill, 2011): 71–86, quoted in *Pagans and Christians in the Late Roman Empire: New Evidence, New Approaches (4th–8th Centuries)*, ed. Marianne Sághy and Edward M. Schoolman (Budapest: 2017), 59n2.

4. Rufinus of Aquileia, "Excerpt on the First Council of Nicaea," bk. 10, ch. 2, in *The Church History of Rufinus of Aquileia*, trans. Philip R. Amidon (New York: Oxford University Press, 1997), 9–10, quoted in Rohmann, *Christianity*, 33.

5. Eusebius, *Life of Constantine*, trans. Averil Cameron and Stuart G. Hall (Oxford, UK: Clarendon Press, 1999), and Timothy D. Barnes, *Constantine and Eusebius* (Cambridge, MA: Harvard University Press, 2006), cited by Sarefield, "Burning Knowledge," 220–23.

6. Levy, *Blasphemy*, 44.

7. Hypatios, trans. Daniel Sarefield, in Sarefield, "Burning Knowledge," 88, citing Callinicus, *Vita Sancti Hypatii*, ed. and trans. G. J. M. Bartelink (Paris: Éditions du Cerf, 1971), 43.8.

8. Saint Augustine, "Letter 185: Augustine to Boniface, tribune and count in Africa (417)—On the Treatment of the Donatists," in Vol. 4, *Fathers of the Church: St. Augustine: Letters*, trans. Wilfred Parsons (New York: Catholic University Press of America, 1956), 150–52.

9. Saint John Chrysostom, "Homily 1 on First Timothy" [1 Timothy 1:1, 2], https://www.newadvent.org/fathers/230601.htm.

10. Rohmann, *Christianity*, 291.

11. Ammianus Marcellinus, *History, Volume III: Books 27–31, Excerpta Valesiana*, trans. J. C. Rolfe, Loeb Classical Library 331, rev. ed. (Cambridge, MA: Harvard University Press, 1939), bk. 29, 211, para. 40.

12. Ammianus, *History*, 217.

13. Saint John Chrysostom, "Homily 38," in *The Homilies of Saint John Chrysostom . . . on the Acts of the Apostles, Part II: Hom. XXIX–LV* (Oxford, UK: John Henry Parker; London: F. and J. Rivington, 1852), 526.

14. Charlemagne, quoted in Peter Brown, *The Rise of Western Christendom*, 2nd ed. (Cambridge, MA: Blackwell, 2003), 429.

15. Saint Augustine appeared open to the use of reading "high" dramatic texts, while Saint Jerome admitted no exceptions in his condemnation of the stage.

16. Eric Berkowitz, *Sex and Punishment: Four Thousand Years of Judging Desire* (Berkeley, CA: Counterpoint, 2012), 102–3; see also John Wesley Harris, *Medieval Theatre in Context: An Introduction* (London: Routledge, 1992), 23–28.

17. Allardyce Nicoll, *Masks, Mimes and Miracles: Studies in the Popular Theatre* (New York: Cooper Square Publishers, 1963), 121.

18. Tertullian, "The Shows, or De Spectaculis," ch. 30, *Latin Christianity: Its Founder—Tertullian*, trans. S. Thelwall, vol. 3 of *The Ante-Nicene Fathers*, ed. Alexander Roberts and James Donaldson (Buffalo, NY: Christian Literature Publishing, 1881), 91.

19. Goody, *Representations and Contradictions*, 109–10; Harris, *Medieval Theatre in Context*, 31, 33, 34.

20. Harris, *Medieval Theatre in Context*, 40–44, 70.

21. Ernst Kitzinger, "The Cult of Images in the Age Before Iconoclasm," *Dumbarton Oaks Papers* 8 (1954): 85, 89.

22. Tertullian, "Idolatry: Origin and Meaning of the Name," ch. 3, in "Part II: On Idolatry," in *Latin Christianity: Its Founder—Tertullian*, 61.

23. Brown, *Rise of Western Christendom*, 375.

24. Kitzinger, "Cult of Images," 101, 107–8, 112–13.

25. Brown, *Rise of Western Christendom*, 375.

26. Brown, *Rise of Western Christendom*, 377–78.

27. Thomas F. X. Noble, *Images, Iconoclasm, and the Carolingians* (Philadelphia: University of Pennsylvania Press, 2013), 66.

28. Brown, *Rise of Western Christendom*, 380–81.

29. Robin Cormack, *Painting the Soul: Icons, Death Masks and Shrouds* (London: Reaktion Books, 1997), 46.

30. Popper, *Censorship of Hebrew Books*, 8.

31. Popper, *Censorship of Hebrew Books*, 7; see also Margaret Bald, *Literature Suppressed on Religious Grounds* (New York: Facts on File, 1998), 108; Judah M. Rosenthal, "The Talmud on Trial: The Disputation at Paris in the Year 1240," *Jewish Quarterly Review* 47, no. 1 (1956): 58; "Maimonidean Controversy," in *Encyclopedia Judaica*, Jewish Virtual Library, https://www.jewishvirtuallibrary.org/maimonidean-controversy, accessed May 28, 2020.

32. Kevin Guilfoy, "Peter Abelard (1079–1142)," *Internet Encyclopedia of Philosophy*, https://www.iep.utm.edu/abelard, accessed May 28, 2020; Bald, *Literature Suppressed on Religious Grounds*, 162–65; Constant J. Mews, "The Council of Sens (1141): Abelard, Bernard, and the Fear of Social Upheaval," *Speculum* 77, no. 2 (April 2002): 342–82.

33. Hans Thijssen, "Condemnation of 1277," *Stanford Encyclopedia of Philosophy* (Winter 2018), ed. Edward N. Zalta, https://plato.stanford.edu/archives/win2018/entries/condemnation; María Rosa Menocal, *Ornament of the World: How Muslims, Jews and Christians Created a Culture of Tolerance in Medieval Spain* (New York: Back Bay, 2002), 201–3; Malcolm de Mowbray, "1277 and All That: Students and Disputations," *Traditio* 57 (2002), 217–38.

34. Henry Charles Lea, *A History of the Inquisition of the Middle Ages*, vol. 1 (New York: Harper & Brothers, 1887), 324.

35. Levy, *Blasphemy*, 77–78; Bald, *Literature Suppressed on Religious Grounds*, 227–29.

36. Lea, *A History of the Inquisition*, 441–44; Ernst Cassirer, *The Individual and the Cosmos in Renaissance Philosophy*, trans. Mario Domandi (New York: Harper & Row, 1963), 107.

37. Giorgio Vasari, *Vasari's Lives of the Artists*, trans. Mrs. Jonathan Foster, ed. Marilyn Aronberg Lavin (Mineola, NY: Dover, 2005), 45.

38. Noah Charney, *The Museum of Lost Art* (New York: Phaidon, 2018), 109–10; Bald, *Literature Suppressed on Religious Grounds*, 53–55; Vasari, *Vasari's Lives of the Artists*, 146–50; Rachel Erlanger, *Unarmed Prophet* (New York: McGraw-Hill, 1987), 285; Felipe Fernández-Armesto, *1492: The Year Our World Began* (London: Bloomsbury, 2009), 125–33.

39. James Masschaele, "The Public Space of the Marketplace in Medieval England," *Speculum* 77, no. 2 (2002): 383–421.

40. R. B. Dobson, *The Peasants' Revolt of 1381* (London: Macmillan, 1970), 274.

41. Masschaele, "Public Space of the Marketplace," 417.

42. Courtney Stanhope Kenny, *Outlines of Criminal Law* (New York: Macmillan, 1907), 248–49; "The Historical Concept of Treason: English, American," *Indiana Law Journal* 35, no. 1, art. 4 (1959): 70–80; see also Sir Matthew Hale, *The History of the Pleas of the Crown*, vol. 1 (London: Printed by Nutt and Gosling for F. Gyles, 1736), 79; William T. Mayton, "Seditious Libel and the Lost Guarantee of a Freedom of Expression," *Columbia Law Review* 84, no. 1 (1984): 98–100.

43. *The Statutes: Revised Edition—Vol. 1. Henry III to James II, A.D. 1235–6–1685* (London: Printed by Eyre and Spotisswoode, 1870), 185.

44. James Fitzjames Stephen, *A History of the Criminal Law of England*, vol. 2 (London: Macmillan, 1883), 253.

45. Hale, *History of the Pleas of the Crown*, 110.

46. Robert P. Adams, "Despotism, Censorship, and Mirrors of Power Politics in Late Elizabethan Times," *Sixteenth Century Journal* 10, no. 3 (1979): 5–16.

CHAPTER 3: THE PRINTQUAKES OF THE SIXTEENTH AND SEVENTEENTH CENTURIES

1. Levy, *Blasphemy*, 72–73; Bald, *Literature Suppressed on Religious Grounds*, 191–93; Hilary Gatti, *Giordano Bruno and Renaissance Science: Broken Lives and Organizational Power* (Ithaca, NY: Cornell University Press, 2002), 18–20.

2. Paul F. Grendler, "Printing and Censorship," in *The Cambridge History of Renaissance Philosophy*, ed. Eckhard Kessler et al. (Cambridge, UK: Cambridge University Press, 1988), 25–28, 36–41.

3. Grendler, "Printing and Censorship," 41.

4. Robert Justin Goldstein, *Political Censorship of the Arts and the Press in Nineteenth Century Europe* (Basingstoke, UK: Macmillan, 1989), 34–35.

5. Haig A. Bosmajian, *Burning Books* (Jefferson, NC: McFarland & Company, 2012), 68–70; Christiane Anderson, "Polemical Prints During the Reformation," in *Censorship: 500 Years of Conflict*, ed. William Zeisel (New York: Oxford University Press, 1984), 35–36.

6. "Index Librorum Prohibitorum," in Derek Jones, ed., *Censorship: A World Encyclopedia* (London: Routledge, 2001), 4277.

7. Daniel P. Sheridan, "The Catholic Case: The Index of Prohibited Books," *Journal of Hindu-Christian Studies* 19, art. 8 (2006): 23.

8. Popper, *Censorship of Hebrew Books*, 52, 55–60, 84–87.

9. Goldstein, *Political Censorship of the Arts and Press*, 36.

10. Marcella Grendler, "A Greek Collection in Padua: The Library of Gian Vincenzo Pinelli (1535–1601)," *Renaissance Quarterly* 33, no. 3 (Autumn 1980): 386–416; Grendler, "Printing and Censorship," 52–53.

11. Charles Ripley Gillett, *Burned Books: Neglected Chapters in British History and Literature*, vol. 1 (New York: Columbia University Press, 1932), 23–24; Fredrick S. Siebert, *Freedom of the Press in England, 1476–1776: The Rise and Decline of Government Control* (Urbana: University of Illinois

Press, 1965), 45; Bald, *Literature Suppressed on Religious Grounds*, 21–22, 169–72.

12. Siebert, *Freedom of the Press in England*, 47; Hannibal Hamlin and Norman W. Jones, *The King James Bible After Four Hundred Years: Literary, Linguistic, and Cultural Influences* (Cambridge, UK: Cambridge University Press, 2010), 336.

13. "Tyndale's New Testament, 1526," British Library Collection Items, https://www.bl.uk/collection-items/william-tyndales-new-testament, accessed March 27, 2020.

14. Anderson, "Polemical Prints During the Reformation," 34–51.

15. "Richard Clough to Gresham, 21 August 1566, no. 668," *Calendar of State Papers: Foreign Series, of the Reign of Elizabeth, 1566–8*, ed. A. J. Crosby (Cambridge, UK: MacMillan & Co, 1871), 121–22.

16. Robert S. Miola, ed., *Early Modern Catholicism: An Anthology of Primary Sources* (Oxford, UK: Oxford University Press, 2009), 58–59.

17. Peter Arnade, *Beggars, Iconoclasts and Civic Patriots: The Political Culture of the Dutch Revolt* (Ithaca, NY: Cornell University Press, 2008), 92.

18. "The Royal Injunctions of Edward VI, 1547," in *Visitation Articles and Injunctions Vol. II, 1536–1557*, ed. W. H. Frere and W. P. M. Kennedy (London: Longmans Green & Company, 1910), 114, 126.

19. Goody, *Representations and Contradictions*, 115; William Dowsing, *The Journal of William Dowsing*, ed. C. H. Evelyn-White (Ipswich, UK: Pawsey and Hayes, 1885), 39.

20. Henry Dagge, *Considerations on Criminal Law* (Dublin: Printed for H. Saunders et al., 1772), 318.

21. John Reeves, *Reeves' History of the English Law: From the Time of the Romans to the End of the Reign of Elizabeth [1603]*, ed. W. F. Finlason, vol. 4 (Philadelphia: M. Murphy, 1880), 419–22; "The Historical Concept of Treason," 74–75; Mayton, "Seditious Libel," *Columbia Law Review*, 100–101.

22. Siebert, *Freedom of the Press in England*, 265.

23. "The Trial of John Twyn for High Treason," in *Cobbett's Complete Collection of State Trials and Proceedings . . .* , vol. 6, ed. T. B. Howell (London: Longman et al., 1816), 513–39, available at https://archive.org/details/googlebooks; Siebert, *Freedom of the Press in England*, 267.

24. Algernon Sidney, *The Arraignment, Tryal & Condemnation of Algernon Sidney, Esq. for High-Treason . . .* (London: B. Tooke, 1684), quoted in Thomas Salmon, *A New Abridgement and Critical Review of the State Trials*, vol. 1 (Dublin: Printed for R. Reilly, 1737), 471; for an online edition, see Early English Books Online, https://quod.lib.umich.edu/e/eebo.

25. Caroline Robbins, "Algernon Sidney's Discourses Concerning Government: Textbook of Revolution," *William and Mary Quarterly* 4, no. 3 (July 1947): 267–96, https://www.jstor.org/stable/1917334.

26. Lloyd E. Berry, ed., *John Stubbs's "Gaping Gulf": With Letters and Other Relevant Documents* (Charlottesville: University Press of Virginia, 1968), xv.

27. Berry, *John Stubbs's "Gaping Gulf,"* xxxiv, 148; Natalie Mears, "Counsel, Public Debate, and Queenship: John Stubbs's 'The Discoverie of a Gaping Gulf,' 1579," *Historical Journal* 44, no. 3 (September 2001): 629–50.

28. Judith Schenck Koffler and Bennett L. Gershman, "New Seditious Libel," *Cornell Law Review* 69, no. 4 (1984): 819–20; Mayton, "Seditious Libel," 103.

29. Siebert, *Freedom of the Press in England*, 271; "The Trial of John Tutchin . . . 1704," in T. Bayly Howell et al., *A Complete Collection of State Trials and Proceedings for High Treason . . .* , vol. 14, 5th ed. (London: Printed by T. C. Hansard for Longman et al., 1816–28), 1128.

30. Levy, *Blasphemy*, 110.

31. David S. Bogen, "The Origins of Freedom of Speech and Press," *Maryland Law Review* 42, no. 3 (1983): 432.

32. Siebert, *Freedom of the Press in England*, 280–81, 285–88.

33. "House of Lords Journal Volume 12: 18 December 1667," in *Journal of the House of Lords: Volume 12, 1666–1675* (London: 1767–1830): 173–76, British History Online, https://www.british-history.ac.uk/lords-jrnl/vol12/pp173–176#h3–0003.

34. Blackstone, *Commentaries on the Laws of England, Volume 4*, 151.

35. Margaret Jacob, "A New Consensus 1600–1700," in *Censorship: 500 Years of Conflict*, ed. William Zeisel (New York: Oxford University Press, 1984), 55.

36. Julian Petley, *Censorship: A Beginners Guide* (New York: Oneworld, 2009), 34.

37. Margaret Atwood Judson, *The Crisis of the Constitution: An Essay in Constitutional and Political Thought in England, 1603–1645* (New Brunswick, NJ: Rutgers University Press, 1949), 381.

38. Quoted in Leonard W. Levy, *Freedom of Speech and Press in Early American History: Legacy of Suppression* (New York: Harper & Row, 1963), 93; Siebert, *Freedom of the Press in England*, 193.

39. John Milton, *Milton's Areopagitica: A Speech for the Liberty of Unlicensed Printing*, ed. T. G. Osborn (London: Longmans, Green, 1873), 71; Siebert, *Freedom of the Press in England*, 196.

40. Baruch Spinoza, *The Political Works: The "Tractatus Theologico-Politicus" in Part and the "Tractatus politicus" in Full*, ed. A. G. Wernham (Oxford, UK: Clarendon Press, 1958), 572, 567, 566, 569, 572, https://issuu.com/bouvard6/docs/spinoza_-_theological_political_tre.

41. Bald, *Literature Suppressed on Religious Grounds*, 103.

42. Levy, *Freedom of Speech and Press*, 18.

43. Daniel Crown, "The Price of Suffering: William Pynchon and the Meritorious Price of Our Redemption," *Public Domain Review*, November 11, 2015, https://publicdomainreview.org/2015/11/11/the-price-of-suffering-william-pynchon-and-the-meritorious-price-of-our-redemption/#ref2; "erroneous," "unsound," and "heretical": see *Records of the Governor and Company of the Massachusetts Bay in New England*, ed. Nathaniel B. Shurtleff, vol. 4, part 1 (Boston: William White Press, 1854), 29–30.

44. Nat Hentoff, *The First Freedom: The Tumultuous History of Free Speech in America* (New York: Delacorte Press, 1988), 61–62.

45. Levy, *Freedom of Speech and Press*, 32–34.

CHAPTER 4: REVOLUTION AND CONTROL IN THE EIGHTEENTH CENTURY

1. "Cato" was the pseudonym of two Whig pamphleteers, John Trenchard and Thomas Gordon, whose essays, first published in London in 1720, were

widely read in England and the American colonies. The quote is taken from the 1721 pamphlet *Of Freedom of Speech: That the Same Is Inseparable from Publick Liberty.*

2. Goldstein, *Political Censorship of the Arts and Press*, 36–37.

3. John Trenchard and Thomas Gordon, "Cato's Letter No. 62," *Cato's Letters*, vol. 2, ed. Ronald Hamowy (Indianapolis: Liberty Fund, 1995), https://oll .libertyfund.org/titles/1238.

4. William Blackstone, *Commentaries on the Laws of England, Vol. 1* (Chicago: University of Chicago Press, 1979), 121, 262.

5. William Blackstone, *Commentaries on the Laws of England, Vol. 4* (Chicago: University of Chicago Press, 1979), 151–52.

6. Jonathan Swift, "Letter the Fifty-First," London, August 7, 1712, in *The Complete Works of Jonathan Swift . . .* , ed. Thomas Roscoe (London: Bell & Daldy, 1869).

7. Douglas O. Linder, "Trial Record: from Zenger's *A Brief Narrative of the Case and Trial of John Peter Zenger (1736),*" Famous Trials, www.famous -trials.com/zenger/89-record.

8. Siebert, *Freedom of the Press in England*, 384–89.

9. James Montgomery, *The Trial of James Montgomery for a Libel on the War . . .* (Sheffield, England: Printed by J. Montgomery, 1795); Kate Horgan, *The Politics of Songs in Eighteenth-Century Britain, 1723–1795* (London: Routledge, 2016), 165.

10. Peter D. G. Thomas, *John Wilkes: A Friend to Liberty* (Oxford, UK: Clarendon Press, 1996), 18–19.

11. Thomas, *John Wilkes*, 19, 26.

12. Edward Palmer Thompson, *The Making of the English Working Class* (New York: Pantheon Books, 1980), 88–90.

13. Levy, *Blasphemy*, 331.

14. "Thomas Paine: British Pamphleteer and Political Thinker, 1737–1809," in Jones, *Censorship*, 6504.

15. John Barrell, *Imagining the King's Death: Figurative Treason, Fantasies of Regicide, 1793–1796* (Oxford, UK: Oxford University Press, 2006), 234.

16. Barrell, *Imagining the King's Death*, 320–22.

17. Manoah Sibly, *The Genuine Trial of Thomas Hardy, for High Treason, at the Sessions House in the Old Bailey, from October 28 to November 5, 1794,* vol. 2 (London: Printed for J. S. Jordan, 1795), 33.

18. Erskine quoted in Barrell, *Imagining the King's Death*, 329.

19. Barrell, *Imagining the King's Death*, 509.

20. Barrell, *Imagining the Kings Death*, 515.

21. Barrell, *Imagining the King's Death*, 555.

22. Clyde Thogmartin, *The National Daily Press of France* (Birmingham, AL: Summa Publications, 1998), 15–16.

23. Malesherbes, *Mémoire sur la liberté de la presse* (Geneva: Éditions Slatkine, 1969), 300, quoted in Darnton, *Forbidden Best-Sellers*, xix.

24. Robert Darnton, *Censors at Work: How States Shaped Literature* (New York: Norton, 2015), 37.

25. Darnton, *Forbidden Best-Sellers*, 5.

26. Darnton, *Censors at Work*, 31, 49–50, n75.

27. Darnton, *Censors at Work*, 48, 53, n98.

28. Darnton, *Censors at Work*, 85.

29. Darnton, *Censors at Work*, 48, n72.

30. Denis Diderot, *Diderot's Selected Writings*, ed. Lester G. Crocker, trans. Derek Coltman (New York: Macmillan, 1966), 46.

31. Bald, *Literature Suppressed on Religious Grounds*, 91–95; Darnton, *Censors at Work*, 58–59.

32. Marie Ernest Raunié, ed., *Chansonnier historique du XVIIIe siècle* . . . , 10 vols. (Paris: A Quantin, 1879–84), 8:252–53, cited by Robert Purks Maccubbin, ed. *'Tis Nature's Fault: Unauthorized Sexuality During the Enlightenment* (Cambridge, UK: Cambridge University Press, 1988), 93.

33. Hugh Gough, *The Newspaper Press in the French Revolution* (1988; New York: Routledge, 2018), 98, n57.

34. Eugene Charlton Black, "The Eighteenth Century: Control and Revolution," in Zeisel, *Censorship: 500 Years of Conflict*, 69–71; Emmet Kennedy, *A Cultural History of the French Revolution* (New Haven, CT: Yale University Press, 1991), 321, 325.

35. Stanley J. Idzerda, "Iconoclasm During the French Revolution," *American Historical Review* 60, no. 1 (October 1954): 16–20.

36. Kennedy, *Cultural History of the French Revolution*, 219; Lynn Avery Hunt, *Politics, Culture, and Class in the French Revolution* (Berkeley: University of California Press, 1984), 63–66.

37. "Séance du 28 Nivôse," in *Gazette nationale ou le Moniteur universel*, no. 119 (January 18, 1794): 480 (http://fsu.digital.flvc.org/islandora/object/fsu%3A387417#page/Page+3/mode/1up), tr. in Idzerda, "Iconoclasm During the French Revolution," 21, n44.

38. Idzerda, "Iconoclasm During the French Revolution," 22–24.

39. *Procès-verbaux du Comité d'instruction publique de la Convention nationale*, II, 211.

40. Kennedy, *Cultural History of the French Revolution*, 225.

41. Levy, *Freedom of Speech and Press*, 21; Harold L. Nelson, "Seditious Libel in Colonial America," *American Journal of Legal History* 3, no. 2 (April 1959): 160–72.

42. Levy, *Freedom of Speech and Press*, 36–37; Isaiah Thomas, *The History of Printing in America: with a Biography of Printers* . . . vol. 2 (New York: Burt Franklin, 1874), 110–12. See also Clyde Augustus Duniway, *The Development of Freedom of the Press in Massachusetts* (New York: Longmans, Green, and Co., 1906), 98–102, 163–66.

43. Everett Joshua Edwards and Jeannette Edwards Rattray, *"Whale Off!": The Story of American Shore Whaling* (New York: Coward-McCann, 1956), 153–59.

44. Levy, *Freedom of Speech and Press*, 47–48.

45. Levy, *Freedom of Speech and Press*, 50–51.

46. "Trial Record . . . *John Peter Zenger*."

47. Bernard Bailyn, *The Ordeal of Thomas Hutchinson* (Cambridge, MA: Belknap Press of Harvard University Press, 1974), 376.

48. Livingston Rowe Schuyler, *The Liberty of the Press in the American Colonies Before the Revolutionary War* . . . (New York: T. Whittaker, 1905), 62.

49. Arthur M. Schlesinger, *Prelude to Independence: The Newspaper War on Britain, 1764–1776* (New York: Knopf, 1958), 139–48.

50. Alexander McDougall, "To the Betrayed Inhabitants of the City and Colony of New York," Department of History, Brooklyn College, City University of New York, 1769, http://academic.brooklyn.cuny.edu/history/burrows/NYC/Documents/McDougall.htm.

51. Levy, *Freedom of Speech and Press*, 177–79.

52. *Journals of the Continental Congress*, 4:18–20, January 2, 1776; Van Tyne Claude Halstead, *The Loyalists in the American Revolution* (New York: Macmillan, 1902), 66, 199, 327–29.

53. Robert W. T. Martin, *Government by Dissent: Protest, Resistance, and Radical Democratic Thought in the Early American Republic* (New York: New York University Press, 2013), 31–32.

54. "Act XCI: Divulgers of False News," in *The Statutes at Large: Being a Collection of All the Laws of Virginia*, vol. 2, ed. William Waller Hening (New York: Printed by R. & W. & G. Bartow, 1823), 109.

55. Leonard W. Levy, *Origins of the Bill of Rights* (New Haven, CT: Yale University Press, 2001), 103.

56. Pinckney himself argued to his state's ratification convention that "the general government has no powers but what are expressly granted to it; it therefore has no power to take away the liberty of the press." See Bogen, "Origins of Freedom of Speech and Press," 456–57.

57. Benjamin Franklin, "An Account of the Supremest Court of Judicature . . . (Sept. 12, 1789)," in *The Writings of Benjamin Franklin*, 10 vols., ed. Albert H. Smyth (New York: Macmillan, 1907), 67.

58. Levy, *Origins of the Bill of Rights*, 108–20; Levy, *Freedom of Speech and Press*, 233–38.

59. Zechariah Chafee, *Free Speech in the United States* (New York: Atheneum, 1969), 21–22. See also Alexander Meiklejohn, *Free Speech and Its Relation to Self-Government* (Clark, NJ: Lawbook Exchange, 2004), 17 (stressing the absolute language of the First Amendment, which "admits of no exceptions"); William T. Mayton, "Seditious Libel and the Lost Guarantee of a Freedom of Expression," *Columbia Law Review* 84, no. 1 (January 1984): 114.

60. Geoffrey R. Stone, *Perilous Times: Free Speech in Wartime from the Sedition Act of 1798 to the War on Terrorism* (New York: W. W. Norton, 2004), 42.

61. Stone, *Perilous Times*, 19.

62. Stone, *Perilous Times*, 37. See also Samuel Eliot Morison, *The Life and Letters of Harrison Gray Otis, Federalist, 1765–1848*, vol. 1 (Boston: Houghton Mifflin, 1913), 119.

63. "The Report of 1800, [7 January] 1800," *Founders Online*, National Archives, https://founders.archives.gov/documents/Madison/01–17–02–0202.

64. Hentoff, *First Freedom*, 82–83.

65. "5967: Newspapers, Prosecution of" in *The Jeffersonian Cyclopedia: A Comprehensive Collection of the Views of Thomas Jefferson . . .*, ed. John P. Foley (New York: Funk & Wagnalls, 1900), 638.

66. Koffler and Gershman, "New Seditious Libel," 827–28.

CHAPTER 5: CLASS WARFARE IN THE NINETEENTH CENTURY

1. John M. Merriman, "Contested Freedoms in the French Revolutions, 1830–1871," in *Revolution and the Meanings of Freedom in the Nineteenth Century*, ed. Isser Woloch (Stanford, CA: Stanford University Press, 2001), 187, 54.

2. Napoleon Bonaparte, "Napoleon I," in *Oxford Essential Quotations*, ed. Susan Ratcliffe (Oxford, UK: Oxford University Press, 2018), https://www .oxfordreference.com/view/10.1093/acref/9780191866692.001.0001/q-oro -ed6–00007762; Jones, *Censorship*, 3211.

3. *The Parliamentary Debates from the Year 1803 to the Present Time*, vol. 35 (Great Britain: T. C. Hansard, 1817), 584.

4. Donald Eugene Emerson, *Metternich and the Political Police: Security and Subversion in the Hapsburg Monarchy (1815–1830)* (The Hague: Springer, 1968), 116.

5. Karl Marx, *On Freedom of the Press and Censorship*, vol. 4, ed. Saul Padover (New York: McGraw-Hill, 1974), xiv. Von Bunsen quoted in *Rhyme and Revolution in Germany; A Study in German History, Life, Literature, and Character, 1813–1850*, ed., J. G. Legge (London: Constable, 1918), 176.

6. Marx, *On Freedom of the Press and Censorship*, 144.

7. Alex Hall, *Scandal, Sensation and Social Democracy: The SPD Press and Wilhelmine Germany 1890–1914* (Cambridge, UK: Cambridge University Press, 1977), 13.

8. Robert Justin Goldstein, *The Frightful Stage: Political Censorship of the Theater in Nineteenth-Century Europe* (New York: Berghahn Books, 2011), 82.

9. Robert Justin Goldstein, ed., *The War for the Public Mind: Political Censorship in Nineteenth-Century Europe* (Westport, CT: Praeger, 2000), 5.

10. Robert H. Keyserlingk, "Bismarck and Freedom of the Press in Germany, 1866–1890," *Canadian Journal of History* 11 (1976): 36.

11. Mariana Tax Choldin, *A Fence Around the Empire: Russian Censorship of Western Ideas Under the Tsars* (Durham, NC: Duke University Press, 1985), 63, 85.

12. *Pernicious Literature: Debate in the House of Commons: Trial and Conviction for Sale of Zola's Novels* (London: National Vigilance Assoc., 1889), 27.

13. *Daily Telegraph*, June 17, 1857, cited in M. J. D. Roberts, "Morals, Art, and the Law: The Passing of the Obscene Publications Act, 1857" *Victorian Studies* 28, no. 4 (Summer 1985): 614.

14. Richard Carlile, *The Report of the Proceedings of the Court of King's Bench . . .* (London: R. Carlile, 1822), 13, https://hdl.handle.net/2027/c001 .ark:/13960/t1pg27q1n.

15. Thomas Bowdler, ed., *The Family Shakspeare in One Volume* (London: Longman, Green, 1863), vii.

16. William Makepeace Thackeray, *Roundabout Papers and Denis Duval* (London: Macmillan, 1911), 67.

17. Joseph Wechsberg, *In Leningrad* (Garden City, NY: Doubleday, 1977), 69; Manolis Paraschos, "The Modern Greek Press," in *Modern Greek Studies Yearbook*, vol. 7, ed. Theofanis G. Stavrou (Minneapolis: University of Minnesota, 1991), 27.

18. Thompson, *Making of the English Working Class*, 639.

19. Joss Marsh, *Word Crimes: Blasphemy, Culture, and Literature in Nineteenth-Century England* (Chicago: University of Chicago Press, 1998), 19.

20. William Cobbett, *Cobbett's Political Register* 46, no. 9 (May 31, 1823): 513–14.

21. Marsh, *Word Crimes*, 20–21, citing *British Press*, October 15, 1819, 3.

22. Thompson, *Making of the English Working Class*, 832.

23. *Cobbett's Political Register* 35, January 27, 1820 (London: William Benbow, 1820), 760–61.

24. Richard Carlile, *The Battle of the Press, As Told in the Story of the Life of Richard Carlile*, ed. Theophila Carlile Campbell (London: Bonner, 1899), 297.

25. William Hone, *The Three Trials of William Hone . . .* (London: William Tegg & Co., 1876), 162, 76, 4.

26. Marsh, *Word Crimes*, 32–33.

27. Richard Carlile, *The Republican*, vol. 7 (London: R. Carlile, 1823), 683.

28. Richard Carlile, *The Republican*, vol. 1, nos. 2–16 (London: T. Davison, 1819), 17–18.

29. Thomas Paine, *The Age of Reason*, vol. 2 (London: R. Carlile, 1818), 12, 55–56, 82, https://play.google.com/books/reader?id=g3pbAAAAQAAJ&hl=en.

30. Carlile, *Report of the Proceedings of the Court of King's Bench*, 13, https://hdl.handle.net/2027/coo1.ark:/13960/t1pg27q1n; Carlile, *Battle of the Press*, 294, 281, 291.

31. Humphrey Boyle, *Report of the Trial of Humphrey Boyle . . .* (London: R. Carlile, 1822), 11, 15.

32. G. W. Foote, *The Freethinker*, v. 1, May 1881, p.1.

33. Edward William Cox, *Reports of Cases in Criminal Law Argued and Determined in All the Courts . . .* (London: Horace Cox, 1886), 238, http://bit.ly/2nZDg9x.

34. Marsh, *Word Crimes*, 8.

35. Cox, *Reports of Cases in Criminal Law*, 235.

36. John Stuart Mill, *On Liberty* (Kitchener, Ontario: Batoche Books, 2001), 49, https://socialsciences.mcmaster.ca/econ/ugcm/3ll3/mill/liberty.pdf.

37. Mill, *On Liberty*, 18–19, 45, 51.

38. For a fascinating discussion of this point, see Geert Van Eekert, "Freedom of Speech, Freedom of Self-Expression, and Kant's Public Use of Reason," *Diametros* 54 (2018): 118–37.

39. Mill, *On Liberty*, 14.

40. Mill, *On Liberty*, 36.

41. Leslie Stephen, "The Suppression of Poisonous Opinions," in *An Agnostic's Apology, and Other Essays* (London: Smith, Elder & Co., 1893), 274, 256, 255.

42. Stephen, "The Suppression of Poisonous Opinions," 284.
43. Marcelle Wong, "Censorship in Late Nineteenth-Century Britain," PhD diss., University of Edinburgh, 2009, 21n24.
44. Brynjolf Jakob Hovde, *The Scandinavian Countries, 1720–1865: The Rise of the Middle Classes*, vol. 2 (Ithaca, NY: Cornell University Press, 1948), 600.
45. Roger Price, *The French Second Republic: A Social History* (Ithaca, NY: Cornell University Press, 1972), 254.
46. Gerald Brenan, *The Spanish Labyrinth: An Account of the Social and Political Background of the Spanish Civil War* (Cambridge, UK: Cambridge University Press, 2014), 88.
47. Goldstein, *Political Censorship of the Arts and the Press*, 9–10.
48. Thomas Macaulay, *The Works of Lord Macaulay*, vol. 8 (London: Longmans, Green, 1866), 222, https://play.google.com/books/reader?id=Stiqj1h WAdgC&hl=en&pg=GBS.PA11.
49. Heinrich von Treitschke, *Sozialismus und seine Gönner* (Berlin: Reimer, 1875), 45.
50. John Gooch, *Armies in Europe* (London: Routledge, 2015), 57.
51. Goldstein, *Political Censorship of the Arts and the Press*, 39.
52. Roy Pascal, *From Naturalism to Expressionism: German Literature and Society, 1880–1918* (New York: Basic Books, 1973), 266; Goldstein, *War for the Public Mind*, 13–14n26.
53. Goldstein, *War for the Public Mind*, 14n25.
54. Mary Lee Townsend, "Language of the Forbidden: Popular Humor in Vormärz Berlin, 1819–1848," PhD diss., Yale University, 1984, 96, 261, cited in Goldstein, *Political Censorship of the Arts and the Press*, 43–44.
55. Lesley Chamberlain, *Ministry of Darkness: How Sergei Uvarov Created Conservative Modern Russia* (London: Bloomsbury, 2019), 203; Aleksandr V. Nikitenko and Helen Saltz Jacobson, *The Diary of a Russian Censor* (Amherst: University of Massachusetts Press, 1975), xii.
56. Goldstein, *Political Censorship of the Arts and the Press*, 134.
57. Paul Goldschmidt, *Pornography and Democratization: Legislating Obscenity in Post-Communist Russia* (London: Routledge, 2019), Kindle edition.
58. Goldstein, *War for the Public Mind*, 7 (italics in original).
59. W. E. Yates, *Theatre in Vienna: A Critical History, 1776–1995* (New York: Cambridge, 2005), 25.
60. Goldstein, *Frightful Stage*, 118, citing Victor Hallays-Dabot, *Histoire de la censure théâtrale en France* (1872).
61. *The Bookman: A Review of Books and Life*, vol. 3. (New York: Dodd, Mead, 1896), 27.
62. Zeisel, *Censorship: 500 Years of Conflict*, 71.
63. Napoleon Bonaparte, "Letter of October 1812," quoted in Robert Netz, *Histoire de la censure dans l'édition* (Paris: PUF, 1998), 6; J. Holland Rose, "The Censorship Under Napoleon I," *Journal of Comparative Legislation and International Law* 18, no. 1 (1918): 63.
64. Rose, "The Censorship Under Napoleon I," 62–63, in part citing Napoléon, *Correspondence*, xi, 472.

65. "France: 1815–1881," in Jones, *Censorship*, 3216–17; Thomas J. Cragin, "The Failings of Popular News Censorship in Nineteenth-Century France," *Book History* 4 (2001): 49–80.

66. Goldstein, *War for the Public Mind*, 13.

67. Cragin, "Failings of Popular News Censorship," 53, 56–57.

68. Cragin, "Failings of Popular News Censorship," 64, 71.

69. Roberts, "Morals, Art, and the Law," 612–13.

70. Sydney Smith, "Proceedings for the Society of the Suppression of Vice," *Edinburgh Review*, 1809, reprinted in *The Works of the Rev. Sydney Smith* (Philadelphia: Carey & Hart, 1845), 291.

71. Roberts, "Morals, Art, and the Law," 609–10, citing in part *Parliamentary Papers*, 1857 (126, Session 2), IV, 503.

72. Regina v. Hicklin. L.R. 3 Q.B. 360 (1868).

73. Harry White, *Anatomy of Censorship: Why the Censors Have It Wrong* (Lanham, MD: University Press of America, 1997), 25.

74. *In the High Court of Justice, Queen's Bench Division, June 18, 1877, the Queen v. Charles Bradlaugh and Annie Besant* (London: Freethought Publishing Company, 1877), 157, 179.

75. Wong, "Censorship in Late Nineteenth-Century Britain," 113–15, citing William Coote.

76. George Astor Singer [pseud.], *Judicial Scandals and Errors* (Watford, UK: University Press Ltd., 1899), 34, quoted in Wong, "Censorship in Late Nineteenth-Century Britain," 129, 139–40.

77. J. Onwhyn, "The Question of Indecent Literature," *Lancet* (November 19, 1898): 1344–45.

78. William Coote, "Law and Morality," in *Public Morals*, ed. James Marchant (London: Morgan and Scott, 1902), 69–70.

79. Ladenson, *Dirt for Art's Sake*, 38.

80. Ladenson, *Dirt for Art's Sake*, 11, 45, 25–26; Gustave Flaubert, letter of January 16, 1857, Correspondance: Année 1857, Édition Louis Conard, https://flaubert.univ-rouen.fr/correspondance/conard/outils/1857.htm#:~:text=Si%20mon%20livre%20est%20mauvais,est%20un%20pi%C3%A9destal%20pour%20lui.

81. Ladenson, *Dirt for Art's Sake*, 84, 75, 80, 81.

82. Commonwealth v. Sharpless, 1 S. & R. (Pa.) 91 (1815); Commonwealth v. Holmes, 17 Mass. 335 (1821).

83. *People v. Richard Hobbes*, September 28, 1842 (Indictment Papers, CGS), cited in Donna I. Dennis, "Obscenity Prosecution and Their Consequences in Mid-Nineteenth-Century America," *SSRN Electronic Journal* (October 11, 2005), https://doi.org/10.2139/ssrn.813944, 18n58.

84. George Akarman, "The Seizure of Obscene Literature," letter to the editor, *New York Herald*, September 20, 1857, 8.

85. Paul S. Boyer, *Purity in Print: The Vice-Society Movement and Book Censorship in America* (New York: Scribner, 1968), 2; New York Society for the Suppression of Vice, *Second Annual Report*, vol. 2 (1876), 4.

86. Anthony Comstock, *Traps for the Young*, 3rd. ed. (New York: Funk & Wagnalls, 1883), 28.

87. New England Watch and Ward Society, *Annual Report*, 1890–91 (Boston: Office of the Society, 1891), cited in Boyer, *Purity in Print*, 21n55; Anthony Comstock, *Frauds Exposed* . . . (New York: J. H. Brown, 1880), 416.

88. Rep. Clinton Merriam, speech in House of Representatives, March 1, 1873, reprinted as "Obscene Literature," *New York Times*, March 15, 1873, 1.

89. Anthony Comstock, "Vampire Literature," *North American Review* 153, no. 417 (August 1891): 165–66.

90. Michael Kent Curtis, "The Curious History of Attempts to Suppress Anti-slavery Speech, Press, and Petition in 1835–37," *Northwestern University Law Review* 89, no. 3 (1989): 805, citing in part "Acts Passed at the Thirteenth Annual Session [November, 1831], 116–17 (Tuscaloosa, AL, 1832)," and "An Act to Suppress Incendiary Publication," 1936, VA Acts 44, 45.

91. Andrew Jackson, "Seventh Annual Message to Congress," in *A Compilation of the Messages and Papers of the Presidents 1789–1897*, vol. 2, pt. 3, ed. James D. Richardson (1896), 175; "Meeting of the Citizens of Albany," *Washington Globe*, September 10, 1835, 2; George Wolf, "Annual Message to the Assembly—1835," in *Pennsylvania Archives, Fourth Series; Vol. VI: Papers of the Governors* (Harrisburg: State of Pennsylvania, 1901), 243.

92. *Congressional Globe*, 24th Congress, 1st Session 75 (1836), 83, 120.

93. Kathy Hessler, "Early Efforts to Suppress Protest: Unwanted Abolitionist Speech," *Boston University Public Interest Law Journal* 7 (1998): 185–86.

94. Curtis, "The Curious History," 866–67.

95. Hentoff, *First Freedom*, 89–90.

96. Abraham Lincoln, "General Orders. No. 141," September 25, 1862, https://bit.ly/33vOjcl.

97. Stone, *Perilous Times*, 125.

98. E. N. Fuller, "Five Hundred Thousand More," *Newark Evening Journal*, July 19, 1864, quoted in James J. Magee, *Freedom of Expression* (Westport, CT: Greenwood Press, 2002), 91–92.

99. Abraham Lincoln, "To Erastus Corning and Others, [June 12] 1863," in *Collected Works of Abraham Lincoln, Vol. 6* (New Brunswick, NJ: Rutgers University Press, 1953), 266–67.

100. Kennedy v. Mendoza-Martinez, 372 U.S. 144 (1963).

101. Ambrose Burnside, "General Orders No. 90," *The War of the Rebellion: A Compilation of the Official Records of the Union and Confederate Armies* (Washington, DC: US Government Printing Office, 1902), 739–40.

102. Stone, *Perilous Times*, 105. Italics in original.

CHAPTER 6: TROUBLE IN MIND

1. George H. Roeder, *The Censored War: American Visual Experience During World War II*. (New Haven, CT: Yale University Press, 1995), 8.

2. Thomas I. Emerson, *The System of Freedom of Expression* (New York: Vintage Books, 1971), 16.

3. Kristina Rosenthal, "Banned Books: Alice in Wonderland," *From McFarlin Tower* (blog), University of Tulsa Special Collections, February 5, 2014, http://orgs.utulsa.edu/spcol/?p=3192.

4. Phillip Knightley, *The First Casualty: The War Correspondent as Hero and Myth-Maker from the Crimea to Iraq* (Baltimore: Johns Hopkins University Press, 2004), vii.

5. UN, "Universal Declaration of Human Rights," available at www.un.org/en /universal-declaration-human-rights, accessed May 1, 2020.

6. George Orwell, "The Freedom of the Press," *New York Times*, October 8, 1972, https://www.nytimes.com/1972/10/08/archives/the-freedom-of-the -press-orwell.html.

7. John Roberts, "The Development of Free Speech in Modern Britain," Speak- ers' Corner Trust, http://www.speakerscornertrust.org/5064/the-development -of-free-speech-in-modern-britain, citing Public Records Office, MEPO (Met- ropolitan Police) 2/1211, accessed May 13, 2020.

8. Nicole Albert, "Books on Trial: Prosecutions for Representing Sapphism in *Fin-de-Siècle* France," in *Disorder in the Court: Trials and Sexual Conflict at the Turn of the Century*, ed. George Robb and Nancy Erber (New York: New York University Press, 1999), 119, citing G. Garrigues, "Moulin Rouge," *La Vie théâtrale* 4 (January 25, 1907): 26; 123, 137n18.

9. New England Watch and Ward Society, *Thirty-Seventh Annual Report* (Bos- ton: Office of the Society, 1915), 5, https://books.google.com/books?id =xEgxAQAAMAAJ&pg=RA5-PA5; Commonwealth v. Buckley, 200 Mass. 346 (1909).

10. Gloria Feldt, "Margaret Sanger's Obscenity," *New York Times*, October 14, 2006, https://www.nytimes.com/2006/10/15/opinion/nyregionopinions /15CIfeldt.html.

11. Geoffrey Stone, "'Sex and the Constitution': Margaret Sanger and the Birth of the Birth Control Movement," *Washington Post*, March 24, 2017, https:// www.washingtonpost.com/news/volokh-conspiracy/wp/2017/03/24/sex -and-the-constitution-margaret-sanger-and-the-birth-of-the-birth-control -movement.

12. *May Irwin Kiss*, Edison Manufacturing Co., 1896, filmstrip, 20 seconds, Library of Congress, https://www.loc.gov/item/00694131, accessed May 13, 2020.

13. Petley, *Censorship: A Beginners Guide*, 47.

14. Gary Stark, "Cinema, Society and the State: Policing the Film Industry in Im- perial Germany," in *Essays on Culture and Society in Modern Germany*, ed. Gary D. Stark and Bede Karl Lackner (Arlington: University of Texas, 1982), 165.

15. Matthew Bernstein, *Controlling Hollywood: Censorship and Regulation in the Studio Era* (London: Athlone, 2000), 22.

16. Mutual Film Corporation v. Industrial Commission of Ohio, 236 U.S. 230 (1915).

17. "Britain: British Board of Film Censors/Classification, in Jones, *Censorship*, 1418–19.

18. Stark, "Cinema, Society and the State," 131, 136, 142.

19. Goldstein, *Political Censorship of the Arts and Press*, 188–91; Stark, "Cin- ema, Society and the State," 154.

20. Boyer, *Purity in Print*, 54.

21. Richard Meinertzhagen, *Army Diary, 1899–1926* (Edinburgh: Oliver & Boyd, 1960), 223–24.
22. Steffen Bruendel, "Othering/Atrocity Propaganda," in *1914–1918 Online: International Encyclopedia of the First World War*, ed. Ute Daniel et al. (Berlin: Freie Universität Berlin, 2014), https://doi.org/10.15463/ie1418.10397.
23. Samuel Hynes, *A War Imagined: The First World War and English Culture* (London: Pimlico, 1992), 96.
24. Rupert Brooke, *1914 and Other Poems* (London: Sidgwick & Jackson Ltd., 1915), 11, 13–14.
25. Ernst Jünger, *Storm of Steel* (New York: Penguin 2004), 5.
26. Thomas Mann, "Thoughts in War [Gedanken im Krieg]," in *Essays*, trans. H. T. Lowe-Porter (New York: Vintage, 1957), 193; Stefan Zweig, *The World of Yesterday: An Autobiography* (Lincoln: University of Nebraska Press, 1943), 223.
27. Woodrow Wilson, "Wilson's War Message to Congress," April 2, 1917, WWI Document Archive, last modified May 28, 2009, https://wwi.lib.byu.edu/index.php/Wilson%27s_War_Message_to_Congress.
28. Harold Brainerd Hersey, *When the Boys Come Home* (New York: Britton, 1919), 47, 203, 141, 119.
29. Boyer, *Purity in Print*, 56.
30. P. Wyndham Lewis, *The Ideal Giant—The Code of Herdsman—Cantelman's Spring-Mate* (London: Privately printed for the Little Review by Shield and Spring, [1917]), 44, https://hdl.handle.net/2027/uc1.c2767297.
31. Anderson v. Patten, 247 Fed. 382 (S.D.N.Y. 1917).
32. Boyer, *Purity in Print*, 62.
33. Hynes, *A War Imagined*, 101–2, 336, 350.
34. Wolfgang Mühl-Benninghaus, "German Film Censorship During World War I," *Film History* 9, no. 1 (1997): 75–76.
35. Stark, "Cinema, Society and the State," 157.
36. Mühl-Benninghaus, "German Film Censorship," 81.
37. Trevor Wilson, ed., *The Political Diaries of C. P. Scott 1911–1928* (London: Collins, 1970), 324.
38. Roy W. Howard, "Lloyd George Says: 'We Will Fight Germany to a Knockout,'" UPI Archives, September 29, 1916, https://upi.com/5183965.
39. "Policing the War Effort," New Zealand History, Ministry for Culture and Heritage, updated November 24, 2016, https://nzhistory.govt.nz/war/public-service-at-war/policing-the-war-effort#heading2, n2; "World War I: Germany and France," Jones, *Censorship*, 9473.
40. Knightley, *The First Casualty*, 91.
41. Knightley, *The First Casualty*, 99–100.
42. "World War I: Britain," Jones, *Censorship*, 9486.
43. Philip Gibbs, *Adventures in Journalism* (New York: Harper and Bros., 1923), 248–49.
44. Wilson, *Political Diaries of C. P. Scott*, 100.
45. Ernest Hemingway, *Men at War: The Best War Stories of All Time* (New York: Bramhall House, 1979), xiii.
46. "World War I: Germany," Jones, *Censorship*, 9476.

47. Philip Gibbs, *The Battles of the Somme* (Toronto: McClelland, Goodchild & Stewart, 1917), 21.

48. James Robert Mock and Cedric Larson, *Words That Won the War* (Princeton, NJ: Princeton University Press, 1939), 100.

49. Knightley, *First Casualty*, 139–40.

50. "World War I: France," Jones, *Censorship*, 9479.

51. Deian Hopkin, "Domestic Censorship in the First World War," *Journal of Contemporary History* 5, no. 4 (1970): 158.

52. George Coppard, *With a Machine Gun to Cambrai: A Story of the First World War* (London: Cassell, 1999), 35.

53. Hynes, *War Imagined*, 327; Ann Kramer, *Conscientious Objectors of the First World War: A Determined Resistance* (Barnsley, UK: Pen & Sword History, 2013), 220.

54. "Eberhard Focke, Arrested German Official," New Zealand History, Ministry for Culture and Heritage, last updated April 21, 2016, https://nzhistory.govt.nz/media/photo/eberhard-focke.

55. Michael S. Sweeney, *Secrets of Victory: The Office of Censorship and the American Press and Radio in World War II* (Chapel Hill: University of North Carolina Press, 2003), 23.

56. Paul L. Murphy, *World War I and the Origins of Civil Liberties in the United States* (New York: Norton, 1979), 53, cited in Stone, *Perilous Times*, 137, 153.

57. Stone, *Perilous Times*, 154–57.

58. "Address by Governor Harding," *Proceedings of the Twenty-Fourth Annual Session* (Iowa City: Iowa State Bar Association, 1918), 171.

59. James R. Mock, *Censorship: 1917* (Princeton, NJ: Princeton University Press, 1941), 32.

60. Sweeney, *Secrets of Victory*, 25.

61. Pub. L. 65–24 (1917).

62. Pub. L. 65–150 (1918).

63. US House of Representatives, Committee on the Judiciary, "Wartime Sedition Act," *Hearings 1963*, vol. 1 (Washington, DC: Government Printing Office, 1963), 17, 16; US Department of Justice, *Interpretation of War Statutes Bulletin, No. 106* (Washington, DC: Government Printing Office, 1917), 8–9, 13, 16–17.

64. Chafee, *Free Speech in the United States*, 54.

65. US House of Representatives, Committee on the Judiciary, "Wartime Sedition Act," 16.

66. Chafee, *Free Speech in the United States*, 10, 55; Michael Inman, "United States v. 'The Spirit of '76,'" New York Public Library, July 30, 2014, https://www.nypl.org/blog/2014/07/30/us-v-spirit-76; United States v. Motion Picture Film "The Spirit of '76," 252 F. 946 (S.D. Ca. 1917).

67. Stone, *Perilous Times*, 224.

68. "Anarchists' Attacks Fail to Terrorize Government," *Philadelphia Inquirer*, June 4, 1919; A. Mitchell Palmer to H. H. Hayhow, February 18, 1920, quoted in Hentoff, *First Freedom*, 112–15.

69. Robert K. Murray, *Red Scare: A Study in National Hysteria, 1919–1920* (Minneapolis: University of Minnesota Press, 1955), 216n15.

70. Attorney General A. Mitchell Palmer on Charges Made Against Department of Justice by Louis F. Post and Others," *Hearings Before the Committee on Rules*, Sixty-Sixth Congress, Second Session, June 1, 1920 (Washington, DC: GPO), 27, https://hdl.handle.net/2027/umn.31951d03632177u.

71. Schenck v. U.S., 249 U.S. 47 (1919).

72. Debs v. United States, 249 U.S. 211 (1919).

73. Oliver Wendell Holmes and Harold Joseph Laski, *Holmes-Laski Letters: The Correspondence of Mr. Justice [Oliver Wendell] Holmes and Harold J. Laski, 1916–1935*, vol. 1 (Cambridge, MA: Harvard University Press, 1953), 217.

74. Abrams v. United States, 250 U.S. 616 (1919).

75. United States v. Rumely, 345 U.S. 41 (1953).

76. Whitney v. California, 247 U.S. 357 (1927).

77. James D. Steakley, "Cinema and Censorship in the Weimar Republic," *Film History* 11 (1999): 189–90.

78. Steakley, "Cinema and Censorship," 181–82, 187–88, 190–92n74; Franz A. Birgel, "Kuhle Wampe, Leftist Cinema, and the Politics of Film Censorship in Weimar Germany," *Historical Reflections/Reflexions Historiques* 35, no. 2 (January 2009): 41.

79. Birgel, "Kuhle Wampe," 43–48.

80. Birgel, "Kuhle Wampe," 48–50, 53.

81. "Platform of the National-Socialist German Workers' Party (February 24, 1920)," Jewish Virtual Library, https://www.jewishvirtuallibrary.org/platform-of-the-national-socialist-german-workers-rsquo-party.

82. "Nazi Germany, 1933–45," in Jones, *Censorship*, 3483.

83. World Committee for the Victims of German Fascism, *The Brown Book of the Hitler Terror and the Burning of the Reichstag* (London: Victor Gollancz, 1933), 193.

84. Petley, *Censorship*, 23–24; Christopher Isherwood, *Christopher and His Kind* (New York: Farrar, Straus & Giroux, 1976), 128–29.

85. *Der Angriff*, May 6, 1933, cited in World Committee for the Victims of German Fascism, *The Brown Book of the Hitler Terror*, 169.

86. Petley, *Censorship*, 24–25; Rebecca Knuth, *Libricide: The Regime-Sponsored Destruction of Books and Libraries in the Twentieth Century* (Westport, CT: Praeger, 2008), 56, citing (for Goebbels's speech) "The Burning of Books—II: Dr. Goebbels, Minister for Public Enlightenment and Propaganda, Delivers His Speech of Justification, May 10, 1933," in Louis L. Snyder, *Hitler's Third Reich: A Documentary History* (Chicago: Nelson-Hall, 1981), 121–22.

87. Knuth, *Libricide*, 86–91.

88. Sem C. Sutter, "The Lost Jewish Libraries of Vilna and the Frankfurt Institut zur Erforschung der Judenfrage," in *Lost Libraries: The Destruction of Great Book Collections Since Antiquity* ed. James Raven (Basingstoke, UK: Palgrave Macmillan, 2004), 222, 229, citing in part "Zum ersten Mal in der Geschichte: Judenforschung ohne Juden," *Illustrieter Beobachter* 18, April 30, 1942.

89. Lisa Z. Sigel, "Censorship and Magic Tricks in Inter-War Britain," *Revue LISA/LISA e-Journal* 11, no. 1 (May 30, 2013), par. 17, https://doi.org/10.4000/lisa.5211.

90. "Indecent Books," *London Times*, March 6, 1929.
91. "Censorship and Restriction of Liberty," *Parliamentary Debates*, House of Commons, vol. 342, no. 22 (December 1938): 1273, https://api.parliament .uk/historic-hansard/commons/1938/dec/07/censorship-and-restriction-of -liberty#column_1273.
92. D. W. Spring, *Propaganda, Politics, and Film, 1918–45* (London: Palgrave Macmillan, 1982), 122, cited in part in Petley, *Censorship*, 81–84.
93. "Censorship and Restriction of Liberty, " 1273.
94. "Britain, Anti-Nazi Films Political Censorship, 1933-39," in Jones, *Censorship*, 1410–16.
95. Richard Overy, *Why the Allies Won* (London: Pimlico, 2006), 297.
96. Orwell, "The Freedom of the Press."
97. Nicole Moore, "Censorship," *Oxford Research Encyclopedia of Literature* (December 2016), https://doi.org/10.1093/acrefore/9780190201098.013.
98. D. H. Lawrence, *Sex, Literature, and Censorship* (New York: Viking, 1959), 125.
99. David Bradshaw, "*Ulysses* and Obscenity," British Library, "Discovering Literature: Twentieth Century, Ulysses," May 25, 2016, https://www.bl.uk /20th-century-literature/articles/ulysses-and-obscenity; United States v. One Book Called "Ulysses," 5 F.Supp. 182 (S.D.N.Y. 1933).
100. Ladenson, *Dirt for Art's Sake*, 172.
101. Andrew Graham-Dixon, "Rude Awakening," *Telegraph*, November 5, 2003, https://www.telegraph.co.uk/culture/art/3605916/Rude-awakening .html; Danielle Demetriou, "'Obscene' Art of DH Lawrence Goes on Show After 70-Year Ban," *Independent*, December 4, 2003, https://www .independent.co.uk/news/uk/this-britain/obscene-art-of-dh-lawrence-goes -on-show-after-70-year-ban-81065.html.
102. Radclyffe Hall, *The Well of Loneliness* (London: Penguin, 2015), 274, 568.
103. James Douglas, "A Book That Must Be Suppressed," *Sunday Express*, August 19, 1928.
104. Paul Fussell, *Wartime: Understanding and Behavior in the Second World War* (Oxford, UK: Oxford University Press, 1989), 288.
105. Sweeney, *Secrets of Victory*, 75.
106. John Steinbeck, *Once There Was a War* (New York: Penguin, 2007), 4–7.
107. Fussell, *Wartime*, 268.
108. Roeder, *Censored War*, 57.
109. Roeder, *Censored War*, 1, 10–15, 134, 161nn19, 21.
110. Glenn D. Hook, "Censorship and Reportage of Atomic Damage and Casualties in Hiroshima and Nagasaki," *Bulletin of Concerned Asian Scholars* 23, no. 1 (1991): 14, n8, 17, 19, nn14–16; "Wilfred Burchett: The Atomic Plague," Fair Observer, August 27, 2014, https://www.fairobserver.com /region/north_america/wilfred-burchett-atomic-plague-99732.
111. Greg Mitchell, "How Press Censorship Hid the Shocking Truth About Nagasaki A-Bomb 65 Years Ago," *HuffPost*, updated December 7, 2017, https://www.huffpost.com/entry/how-press-censorship-hid_b_675106.
112. John W. Dower, *Embracing Defeat: Japan in the Wake of World War II* (New York: Norton, 2000), 412–13.

113. Monica Braw, *The Atomic Bomb Suppressed: American Censorship in Occupied Japan* (Armonk, NY: M. E. Sharpe, 1991), 90–99.

114. Greg Mitchell, "The Great Atomic Film Cover-Up," *HuffPost*, May 25, 2011, https://www.huffpost.com/entry/for-veterans-day-the-grea_b_353270.

CHAPTER 7: SCREAMING AT THE CROWD IN THE CONTEMPORARY ERA

1. Bill Berkeley, *The Graves Are Not Yet Full* (New York: Basic, 2008), viii.

2. Samantha Power, "Bystanders to Genocide," *Atlantic*, September 2001, https://www.theatlantic.com/magazine/archive/2001/09/bystanders-to-genocide/304571.

3. "Interview: Samantha Power," *Frontline*, April 1, 2004, PBS, https://www.pbs.org/wgbh/pages/frontline/shows/ghosts/interviews/power.html.

4. R.A.V. v. City of St. Paul, 505 U.S. 377 (1992).

5. Josh Halliday, "Twitter's Tony Wang: 'We Are The Free Speech Wing of the Free Speech Party,'" *Guardian*, March 22, 2012, https://www.theguardian.com/media/2012/mar/22/twitter-tony-wang-free-speech.

6. Ryan Mac et al., "Growth at Any Cost: Top Facebook Executive Defended Data Collection in 2016 Memo—And Warned That Facebook Could Get People Killed," *BuzzFeed*, last updated March 29, 2018, https://www.buzzfeednews.com/article/ryanmac/growth-at-any-cost-top-facebook-executive-defended-data#.upw3jdyR8. The executive later said this statement did not reflect his true views.

7. Cohen v. California, 403 U.S. 15 (1971).

8. Sean Illing, "'Flood the Zone with Shit': How Misinformation Overwhelmed Our Democracy," *Vox*, February 6, 2020, https://www.vox.com/policy-and-politics/2020/1/16/20991816/impeachment-trial-trump-bannon-misinformation.

9. Campaign for Free Speech, "Majority of Americans Want to Scrap First Amendment, Polling Finds," October 23, 2019, https://campaignforfreespeech.org/free-speech-under-dire-threat-polling-finds; "Online Caravan Free Speech Survey," September 3–5, 2019, 1–2.

10. Claire Burke, "Polite Society: Why Are British Cities Banning Swearing?," *Guardian*, last modified February 3, 2020, https://www.theguardian.com/cities/2019/aug/07/polite-society-why-are-british-cities-banning-swearing-pspo?CMP=Share_iOSApp_Other.

11. European Court of Human Rights, Press Unit, "Hate Speech," fact sheet, March 2020, 1, citing Erbakan v. Turkey, https://www.echr.coe.int/Documents/FS_Hate_speech_ENG.pdf.

12. Michael Brown & Ors v. Members of the Classification Review Board of the Office of Film and Literature [1998] FCA 319 (24 March 1998), Federal Court of Australia, http://www7.austlii.edu.au/cgi-bin/viewdoc/au/cases/cth/federal_ct/1998/319.html.

13. Zeisel, *Censorship: 500 Years of Conflict*, 7–9.

14. Orwell, "The Prevention of Literature," 371.

15. Clóvis Moura, "Climate of Terror," *Index on Censorship* 4 (July 1, 1979): 8, https://doi.org/10.1080/03064227908532938.

16. "Censorship," in Thomas Benjamin, ed., *Encyclopedia of Western Colonialism Since 1450* (Detroit: Thomson Gale, 2007), 198, 200.

17. Shirley Eber, "Dror Green: The Train of Wonders," *Index on Censorship* 19, no. 10 (November 1, 1990): 18–19, https://doi.org/10.1080/03064229008534983.

18. "Censorship" and "Anata Toer Pramoedya" in *Encyclopedia of Western Colonialism*, 200–202; "Pramoedya Toer: Why You Should Know Him," *Al Jazeera*, February 6, 2017, https://www.aljazeera.com/indepth/features/2017/02/pramoedya-ananta-toer-170206053453639.html.

19. Robert D. McFadden, "Zhores Medvedev, 93, Dissident Scientist Who Felt Moscow's Boot, Is Dead," *New York Times*, November 16, 2018, https://www.nytimes.com/2018/11/16/obituaries/zhores-medvedev-dead.html.

20. Dominic Boyer, "Censorship as a Vocation: The Institutions, Practices, and Cultural Logic of Media Control in the German Democratic Republic," *Contemporary Studies in Society and History* 45, no. 3 (June 2003): 522, 530, 524, 528–29, 531–32.

21. Brandenburg v. Ohio, 395 U.S. 444 (1969).

22. United States v. Schwimmer, 279 U.S. 644 (1929).

23. *West Virginia State Board of Education v. Barnette*.

24. Taylor v. Mississippi, 319 U.S. 583 (1943).

25. Dennis v. United States, 341 U.S. 494 (1951).

26. Yates v. United States, 354 U.S. 298 (1957).

27. *Brandenburg v. Ohio*.

28. Bond v. Floyd, 385 U.S. 116 (1966).

29. Ian Shapiro, "He Was America's Most Famous Pediatrician. Then Dr. Spock Attacked the Vietnam Draft," *Washington Post*, January 5, 2018, https://www.washingtonpost.com/news/retropolis/wp/2018/01/05/he-was-americas-most-famous-pediatrician-then-dr-spock-attacked-the-vietnam-draft.

30. Cohen v. California, 403 U.S. 15 (1971).

31. New York Times v. Sullivan, 376 U.S. 254 (1964).

32. New York Times v. United States, 403 U.S. 713 (1971).

33. Charlie Savage, "Federal Employees Are Warned Not to Discuss Trump 'Resistance' at Work," *New York Times*, November 29, 2018.

34. "ACLU Files First Amendment Challenge to Criminal Defamation Law," ACLU, press release, December 18, 2018, https://www.aclu.org/press-releases/aclu-files-first-amendment-challenge-criminal-defamation-law.

35. Alison Flood, "South Carolina Police Object to High-School Reading List," *Guardian*, July 3, 2018, https://www.theguardian.com/books/2018/jul/03/south-carolina-police-object-to-high-school-reading-list.

36. "The Trump Administration and the Media," Committee to Protect Journalists, April 16, 2020, https://cpj.org/x/837b.

37. PEN American Center v. Donald J. Trump, Civil Action No. 18-cv-9433-LGS (S.D.N.Y.).

38. In a 2019 concurring opinion, Justice Clarence Thomas questioned Sullivan's validity, calling it and the decisions extending it "policy-driven decisions masquerading as constitutional law." McKee v. Cosby, 586 U.S. ___ (2019). While Thomas's opinion carries no immediate legal force, it may be a basis

for a later decision. Should that come to pass, it would be a body blow to First Amendment protections for the media that have been in place for nearly sixty years.

39. "'Democrat Spin Machine': Trump Says SNL 'Can't Be Legal' & Should Be Tried in Court System," *RT*, December 16, 2018, https://on.rt.com/9klu. See Jayme Deerwester, "Trump Tweets: 'Should Federal Election Commission and/or FCC' Look Into 'SNL'?," *USA Today*, March 18, 2019, https://amp .usatoday.com/amp/3199989002?__twitter_impression=true.

40. Knight First Amendment Inst. v. Trump, 928 F.3d 226 (2d Cir. 2019).

41. Eric Berkowitz, "Trump Likes to Charge His Opponents with Treason. He Is Echoing Europe's Worst Despots," *Washington Post*, July 23, 2019.

42. Rosa Brooks, "And Then the Breitbart Lynch Mob Came for Me," *Foreign Policy*, February 6, 2017, https://foreignpolicy.com/2017/02/06/and-then-the -breitbart-lynch-mob-came-for-me-bannon-trolls-trump.

43. Cardiff School of Journalism, *Killing the Messenger 2018*, report prepared for the International News Safety Institute, https://newssafety.org/fileadmin /Killing_the_Messenger_2018FINAL.pdf.

44. Ben Taub, "How Not to Solve the Refugee Crisis," *New Yorker*, July 24, 2017, https://www.newyorker.com/magazine/2017/07/31/how-not-to-solve-the -refugee-crisis?verso=true.

45. "Brazilian Prosecutors Appeal Judge's Order, Refuse to Drop Criminal Charges Against Journalist Glenn Greenwald," Freedom of the Press Founda- tion, March 3, 2020, https://freedom.press/news/brazilian-prosecutors-appeal -judges-order-refuse-to-drop-criminal-charges-against-journalist-glenn -greenwald/; Ernesto Londoño and Letícia Casado, "Glenn Greenwald Charged with Cybercrimes in Brazil," *New York Times*, January 21, 2020, https://www.nytimes.com/2020/01/21/world/americas/glenn-greenwald-brazil -cybercrimes.html.

46. Adrian Shahbaz, "Freedom on the Net 2018: The Rise of Digital Authoritari- anism," Freedom House, https://freedomhouse.org/report/freedom-net/2018 /rise-digital-authoritarianism.

47. Jon Allsop, "Espionage Charges Against Assange Are a 'Terrifying' Threat to Press Freedom," *Columbia Journalism Review*, May 24, 2019, https://www .cjr.org/the_media_today/julian_assange_espionage_act.php?utm_source =CJR+Daily+News.

48. Packingham v. North Carolina, 137 S.Ct. 1730 (2017), citing in part Reno v. ACLU, 521 U.S. 844 (1997).

49. Tim Wu, "Is the First Amendment Obsolete?," Knight First Amendment In- stitute, September 1, 2017, https://knightcolumbia.org/content/tim-wu-first -amendment-obsolete.

50. Craig Timberg, "How Conservatives Learned to Wield Power Inside Face- book," *Washington Post*, February 20, 2020, https://www.washingtonpost .com/technology/2020/02/20/facebook-republican-shift.

51. Roger McNamee, *Zucked: Waking Up to the Facebook Catastrophe* (New York: Penguin 2019), 251.

52. Kyle Langvardt, quoted in David L. Hudson Jr., "Free Speech or Censorship? Social Media Litigation Is a Hot Legal Battleground," *ABA Journal*, April 1,

2019, https://www.abajournal.com/magazine/article/social-clashes-digital -free-speech.

53. Ithiel de Sola Pool, *Technologies of Freedom* (Cambridge, MA: Belknap Press, 1983), 227, 230–31, 226, 6.

54. James Griffiths, "China Is Exporting the Great Firewall as Internet Freedom Declines Around the World," CNN, last updated November 2, 2018, https:// www.cnn.com/2018/11/01/asia/internet-freedom-china-censorship-intl/index .html.

55. Jack Goldsmith, "The Failure of Internet Freedom," Knight First Amendment Institute, June 13, 2018, https://knightcolumbia.org/content/failure-internet -freedom; Hillary Rodham Clinton, "Remarks on Internet Freedom," Newseum, January 21, 2010, https://2009-2017.state.gov/secretary/20092013clinton/rm /2010/01/135519.htm.

56. Nicholas Kristof, "Tear Down This Cyberwall!," *New York Times*, June 17, 2009, https://www.nytimes.com/2009/06/18/opinion/18kristof.html.

57. Evgeny Morozov, *The Net Delusion: The Dark Side of Internet Freedom* (New York: PublicAffairs, 2011), 10.

58. Charlie Warzel, "Big Tech Was Designed to Be Toxic," *New York Times*, April 3, 2019, https://www.nytimes.com/2019/04/03/opinion/facebook -youtube-disinformation.html.

59. Sean Burch, "'Senator, We Run Ads': Hatch Mocked for Basic Facebook Question to Zuckerberg," *The Wrap*, April 10, 2018, https://www.yahoo .com/entertainment/mark-zuckerberg-gives-orrin-hatch-quick-explainer -facebook-202404519.html; Jeff Gary and Ashkan Soltani, "First Things First: Online Advertising Practices and Their Effects on Platform Speech," Knight First Amendment Institute, August 21, 2019, https://knightcolumbia .org/content/first-things-first-online-advertising-practices-and-their-effects -on-platform-speech.

60. Jack M. Balkin, "How to Regulate (and Not Regulate) Social Media," Knight First Amendment Institute, March 25, 2020, https://knightcolumbia.org /content/how-to-regulate-and-not-regulate-social-media.

61. Jeff Horowitz and Deepa Seetharaman, "Facebook Executives Shut Down Efforts to Make the Site Less Divisive," *Wall Street Journal*, May 26, 2020, https://www.wsj.com/articles/facebook-knows-it-encourages-division-top -executives-nixed-solutions-11590507499?mod=searchresults&page =1&pos=2.

62. Sheera Frenkel et al., "Delay, Deny and Deflect: How Facebook's Leaders Fought Through Crisis," *New York Times*, November 14, 2018, https://www. nytimes.com/2018/11/14/technology/facebook-data-russia-election-racism .html?utm_campaign=The%20Interface&utm_medium=email&utm _source=Revue%20newsletter.

63. Soroush Vosoughi et al., "The Spread of True and False News Online," *Science* 359, no. 6380 (March 9, 2018): 1146–51, https://science.sciencemag .org/content/359/6380/1146.

64. Horowitz and Seetharaman, "Facebook Executives."

65. Elizabeth Dwoskin, Craig Timberg, and Tony Room, "Zuckerberg Once Wanted to Sanction Trump. Then Facebook Wrote Rules That

Accommodated Him," *Washington Post*, June 28, 2020, https://wapo.st
/3dZJXMH.

66. Steve Stecklow, "Why Facebook Is Losing the War on Hate Speech in Myanmar," Reuters, August 15, 2018, https://www.reuters.com/investigates
   /special-report/myanmar-facebook-hate.

67. Tech Transparency Project, "Extremists Are Using Facebook to Organize for
   Civil War amid Coronavirus," Campaign for Accountability, April 22, 2020,
   https://www.techtransparencyproject.org/articles/extremists-are-using-facebook
   -to-organize-for-civil-war-amid-coronavirus.

68. Chris Rodrigo, "Critics Fear Facebook Fact-Checkers Losing Misinformation
   Fight," *Hill*, January 20, 2020, https://thehill.com/policy/technology/478896
   -critics-fear-facebook-fact-checkers-losing-misinformation-fight.

69. Andrew Marantz, "Why Facebook Can't Fix Itself," *New Yorker*, October
   12, 2020, https://www.newyorker.com/magazine/2020/10/19/why-facebook
   -cant-fix-itself.

70. Tom McCarthy, "Zuckerberg Says Facebook Won't Be 'Arbiters of Truth' After Trump Threat," *Guardian*, May 28, 2020, https://www.theguardian.com
   /technology/2020/may/28/zuckerberg-facebook-police-online-speech-trump.

71. Davey Alba, "Facebook Bans Network with 'Boogaloo' Ties," *New York
   Times*, June 30, 2020, https://www.nytimes.com/2020/06/30/technology
   /facebook-ban-boogaloo.html.

72. Charlie Warzel, "Facebook Can't Be Reformed," *New York Times*, July 1,
   2020, https://www.nytimes.com/2020/07/01/opinion/facebook-zuckerberg
   .html.

73. Gary and Soltani, "First Things First."

74. Marantz, "Why Facebook Can't Fix Itself."

75. McNamee, *Zucked*, 126.

76. 47 U.S.C. §230 (b)(2).

77. Force v. Facebook, 943 F.3d 53 (2d Cir. 2019).

78. Kate Irby, "Devin Nunes Can't Sue Twitter over Statements by Fake Cow,
   Judge Rules," *Fresno Bee*, June 24, 2020, https://www.fresnobee.com/news
   /nation-world/national/article243664982.html.

79. White House, "Executive Order Preventing Online Censorship," May 28,
   2020, https://www.whitehouse.gov/presidential-actions/executive-order
   -preventing-online-censorship.

80. Casey Newton, "Trump Is a Problem Platforms Can't Solve," *Platformer*,
   October 5, 2020, https://www.platformer.news/p/the-covid-presidency-arrives
   -on-platforms; Charlie Warzel, "The Facebook-Twitter-Trump Wars Are Actually About Something Else," *New York Times*, October 18, 2020, https://
   www.nytimes.com/2020/10/18/opinion/ny-post-biden-twitter.html.

81. Jian Zhang v. Baidu.com, 10 F.Supp.3d 433 (S.D.N.Y. 2014).

82. Search King v. Google Technology, Inc., Case No. CIV-02-1457-M (W.D.
   Okla., May 27, 2003).

83. Mathias Döpfner, "An Open Letter to Eric Schmidt: Why We Fear Google,"
   Frankfurter Allgemeine Zeitung, May 25, 2016, https://www.faz.net/aktuell
   /feuilleton/debatten/mathias-doepfner-s-open-letter-to-eric-schmidt-12900860
   .html.

84. Adam Satariano, "Facebook Loses Antitrust Case in Germany over Data Collection," *New York Times*, June 23, 2020, https://www.nytimes.com/2020/06/23/technology/facebook-antitrust-germany.html.

85. Adam Satariano, "Facebook Can Be Forced to Delete Content Worldwide, E.U.'s Top Court Rules," *New York Times*, October 3, 2019, https://www.nytimes.com/2019/10/03/technology/facebook-europe.html.

86. Daniel Funke and Daniela Flamini, "A Guide to Anti-Misinformation Actions Around the World," Poynter, last updated August 13, 2019, https://www.poynter.org/ifcn/anti-misinformation-actions/#france.

87. Dia Kayyali and Raja Althaibani, "Vital Human Rights Evidence in Syria Is Disappearing from YouTube," *Witness* (blog), https://blog.witness.org/2017/08/vital-human-rights-evidence-disappearing-youtube, accessed May 15, 2020.

88. Shannon Van Sant, "Russia Criminalizes the Spread of Online News Which 'Disrespects' the Government," NPR, March 18, 2019, https://www.npr.org/2019/03/18/704600310/russia-criminalizes-the-spread-of-online-news-which-disrespects-the-government; Daniel Funke, "Egypt Is Jailing More Journalists on 'False News' Charges Than Anywhere Else in the World," Poynter, December 13, 2018, https://www.poynter.org/fact-checking/2018/egypt-is-jailing-more-journalists-on-false-news-charges-than-anywhere-else-in-the-world.

89. Shahbaz, "Freedom on the Net 2018."

90. "Singapore Fake News Law a 'Disaster' for Freedom of Speech, Says Rights Group," *Guardian*, May 9, 2019, https://www.theguardian.com/world/2019/may/09/singapore-fake-news-law-a-disaster-for-freedom-of-speech-says-rights-group.

91. Paul Mozur, "Coronavirus Outrage Spurs China's Internet Police to Action," *New York Times*, March 16, 2020, https://www.nytimes.com/2020/03/16/business/china-coronavirus-internet-police.html?searchResultPosition=1.

92. Jane Li, "A Keyboard Encryption App Used to Skirt Coronavirus Censorship Was Removed by Apple in China," *Quartz*, March 20, 2020, https://qz.com/1822127/encryption-app-to-avoid-coronavirus-censorship-removed-by-apple-in-china/; Alex Hern, "Apple Removes two podcasts from China store after censorship demands," *Guardian*, June 12, 2020, https://www.theguardian.com/technology/2020/jun/12/apple-removes-two-podcast-apps-from-china-store-after-censorship-demands.

93. James Pearson, "Facebook Agreed to Censor Posts After Vietnam Slowed Traffic," Reuters, April 21, 2020, https://www.reuters.com/article/us-vietnam-facebook-exclusive/exclusive-facebook-agreed-to-censor-posts-after-vietnam-slowed-traffic-sources-idUSKCN2232JX.

94. Jack Goldsmith and Tim Wu, *Who Controls the Internet? Illusions of a Borderless World* (New York: Oxford University Press, 2008), 10.

95. Kate Conger and Daisuke Wakabayashi, "Google Employees Protest Secret Work on Censored Search Engine for China," *New York Times*, August 16, 2018, https://www.nytimes.com/2018/08/16/technology/google-employees-protest-search-censored-china.html; Ryan Gallagher, "Google Employees

Uncover Ongoing Work on Censored China Search," *Intercept*, March 4, 2019, https://theintercept.com/2019/03/04/google-ongoing-project-dragonfly.

96. Elizabeth C. Economy, "The Great Firewall of China: Xi Jinping's Internet Shutdown," *Guardian*, June 29, 2018, https://www.theguardian.com/news /2018/jun/29/the-great-firewall-of-china-xi-jinpings-internet-shutdown.

97. James Griffiths, "Weibo's Free-Speech Failure," *Atlantic*, March 20, 2019, https://www.theatlantic.com/technology/archive/2019/03/what-went-wrong -chinas-weibo-social-network/584728.

98. Gary King, Jennifer Pan, and Margaret E. Roberts, "How the Chinese Government Fabricates Social Media Posts for Strategic Distraction, Not Engaged Argument," *American Political Science Review* 111, no. 3 (2017): 484, https://gking.harvard.edu/files/gking/files/how_the_chinese_government _fabricates_social_media_posts_for_strategic_distraction_not_engaged _argument.pdf.

99. Wu, "Is the First Amendment Obsolete?"

100. Zeynep Tufecki, *Twitter and Tear Gas: The Power and Fragility of Networked Protest* (New Haven, CT: Yale University Press, 2017), 231, 241.

101. Zeynep Tufecki, "Wikileaks Isn't Whistleblowing," *New York Times*, November 4, 2016, https://www.nytimes.com/2016/11/05/opinion/what-were -missing-while-we-obsess-over-john-podestas-email.html.

102. Bobby Allyn, "Researchers: Nearly Half of Accounts Tweeting About Coronavirus Are Likely Bots," NPR, May 20, 2020, https://www.npr.org/sections /coronavirus-live-updates/2020/05/20/859814085/researchers-nearly-half -of-accounts-tweeting-about-coronavirus-are-likely-bots; Thor Benson, "Trolls and Bots Are Flooding Social Media with Disinformation Encouraging States to End Quarantine," *Business Insider*, April 20, 2020, https:// www.businessinsider.com/trolls-bots-flooding-social-media-with-anti -quarantine-disinformation-2020-4.

103. Shahbaz, "Freedom on the Net 2018."

104. Shahbaz, "Freedom on the Net 2018."

105. Boos v. Barry, 485 U.S. 312 (1998), citing Hustler Magazine v. Falwell, 485 U.S. 46 (1988); FCC v. Pacifica Foundation, 438 U.S. 726 (1978).

106. "Two Chinese Tourists Are Arrested for Making a Hitler Salute in Germany," *Economist*, August 7, 2017, https://www.economist.com/gulliver /2017/08/07/two-chinese-tourists-are-arrested-for-making-a-hitler-salute-in -germany.

107. Pastörs v. Germany, European Court of Human Rights (ECHR) (2019).

108. Free World Centre, "Article 19—Germany: Responding to "Hate Speech," Country Report (London: Free World Centre, 2018), 59n109, https://www .article19.org/wp-content/uploads/2018/07/Germany-Responding-to-%E2 %80%98hate-speech%E2%80%99-v3-WEB.pdf.

109. Campaign for Free Speech, "Majority of Americans."

110. Jack Ewing and Melissa Eddy, "Far-Right Shooting Shatters an Already Fragile Sense of Security in Germany," *New York Times*, February 21, 2020, https://www.nytimes.com/2020/02/20/world/europe/germany-hanau-shisha -bar-shooting.html.

111. Enstad and Ravndal, "Hvorfor er det så mye mer høyreekstrem vold i Sverige?"; Katharine Gelber and Luke McNamara, "The Effects of Civil Hate Speech Laws: Lessons from Australia," July 29, 2015, *Law and Society Review* 49, no. 3 (September 2015): 631–64.

112. Gerald Horne and Charisse Burden-Stelly, *W. E. B. Du Bois: A Life in American History* (Santa Barbara, CA: ABC-CLIO, 2019), 79n340.

113. Beauharnais v. Illinois, 343 U.S. 250 (1952).

114. Meghan Keneally, "Skokie: The Legacy of the Would-Be Nazi March in a Town of Holocaust Survivors," ABC News.com, June 22, 2018, https://abcnews.go.com/US/skokie-legacy-nazi-march-town-holocaust-survivors/story?id=56026742

115. R.A.V. v. City of St. Paul, 505 U.S. 377 (1992).

116. Snyder v. Phelps, 562 U.S. 443 (2011).

117. Karl R. Popper, *The Open Society and Its Enemies* (Princeton, NJ: Princeton University Press, 1994), 627.

118. Erbakan v. Turkey, ECHR (2006).

119. Nix v. Germany, ECHR (2018).

120. "Brigitte Bardot Fined £12,000 for Racial Hatred After Claiming Muslims Are Destroying France," *Daily Mail*, June 3, 2008, https://www.dailymail.co.uk/tvshowbiz/article-1023969/Brigitte-Bardot-fined-12–000-racial-hatred-claiming-Muslims-destroying-France.html.

121. Antoine Buyse, "Judgment on Apology of Terrorism," *ECHR Blog*, October 2, 2008, http://echrblog.blogspot.com/2008/10/judgment-on-apology-of-terrorism.html.

122. Richard Seymour, "Azhar Ahmed—Charged with Treason over Facebook Comments?," *Guardian*, March 15, 2012, https://www.theguardian.com/commentisfree/libertycentral/2012/mar/15/azhar-ahmed-treason-army-facebook-comments.

123. "EU Court Criticizes France for Fining Man over Sarkozy Insult," Reuters, March 14, 2013, https://www.reuters.com/article/us-eu-france-sarkozy-idUSBRE92D0SV20130314.

124. Sürek v. Turkey, ECHR (1999).

125. "Online Harms White Paper," HM Government, April 2019, https://assets.publishing.service.gov.uk/government/uploads/system/uploads/attachment_data/file/793360/Online_Harms_White_Paper.pdf; Ruth Smeeth, "New 'Online Harm' Legislation Is a Threat to Free Speech," *Independent*, September 28, 2020, https://www.independent.co.uk/voices/online-abuse-hate-speech-legislation-government-b669750.html.

126. A French law modeled on NetzDG was mostly thrown out by a French constitutional court in 2020 as an impermissible limit on expression. Aurelien Breeden, "French Court Strikes Down Most of Online Hate Speech Law," *New York Times*, June 18, 2020, https://www.nytimes.com/2020/06/18/world/europe/france-internet-hate-speech-regulation.html.

127. Free World Centre, "Article 19—Germany."

128. Hudson, "Free Speech or Censorship?"

129. Fatwa against Salman Rushdie, last modified, April 1, 2013, Iran Data Portal, https://irandataportal.syr.edu/fatwa-against-salman-rushdie.

130. Salman Rushdie, "At the Auction of the Ruby Slippers," *Granta*, April 1, 1992.

131. Kenan Malik, "Shadow of the Fatwa," *Index on Censorship* 37, no. 4 (November 2008): 113, 117, https://doi.org/10.1080/03064220802519588.

132. Kenan Malik, *From Fatwa to Jihad: How the World Changed from "The Satanic Verses" to "Charlie Hebdo"* (London: Atlantic, 2017), 184.

133. Malik, *From Fatwa to Jihad*, 145–46, 150–51, 228–30.

134. E.S. v. Austria, ECHR (2018).

135. See Floyd Abrams, *Speaking Freely: Trials of the First Amendment* (New York: Penguin, 2005), Kindle ed., ch. 7.

136. Michael Grothaus, "Here Is Google CEO Sundar Pichai's Response to Employees About the Anti-Diversity Memo," *Fast Company*, August 8, 2017, https://www.fastcompany.com/40450156/here-is-google-ceo-sundar-pichais -response-to-employees-about-the-anti-diversity-memo.

137. Conor Friedersdorf, "The Perils of Writing a Provocative Email at Yale," *Atlantic*, May 26, 2016, https://www.theatlantic.com/politics/archive/2016 /05/the-peril-of-writing-a-provocative-email-at-yale/484418.

138. Gitlow v. New York, 268 U.S. 652 (1925).

139. "Spotlight on Speech Codes 2020," *Fire*, https://www.thefire.org/resources /spotlight/reports/spotlight-on-speech-codes-2020/#fr36, accessed May 13, 2020.

140. Greg Lukianoff and Jonathan Haidt, "The Coddling of the American Mind," *Atlantic*, September 2015, https://www.theatlantic.com/magazine /archive/2015/09/the-coddling-of-the-american-mind/399356.

141. "Spotlight on Speech Codes 2020."

142. Rachel Schraer and Ben Butcher, "Universities: Is Free Speech Under Threat?," BBC, October 23, 2018, https://www.bbc.com/news/education-45447938.

143. Lee C. Bollinger, "Free Speech on Campus Is Doing Just Fine, Thank You," *Atlantic*, June 12, 2019, http://bit.ly/32LrL5f.

144. Matthew Smith, "Are Students Really More Hostile to Free Speech?," YouGov, June 26, 2018, https://yougov.co.uk/topics/politics/articles-reports /2018/06/27/are-students-really-more-hostile-free-speech.

145. UK Parliament, "The Scale of the Problem," *Freedom of Speech*, March 27, 2018, items 37, 35, https://publications.parliament.uk/pa/jt201719/jtselect /jtrights/589/58906.htm.

146. Jeffrey Adam Sachs, "There Is No Campus Free Speech Crisis: A Close Look at the Evidence," Niskanen Center, April 27, 2018, https://www.niskanen center.org/there-is-no-campus-free-speech-crisis-a-close-look-at-the-evidence.

147. Maggie Haberman and Michael D. Shear, "Trump Signs Executive Order Protecting Free Speech on College Campuses," *New York Times*, May 21, 2019, https://www.nytimes.com/2019/03/21/us/politics/trump-free-speech -executive-order.html.

148. Donald Trump Jr., "Free Speech Suppression Online Builds Case to Break Up Big Tech," *Hill*, September 30, 2019, https://thehill.com/opinion /technology/463631-free-speech-suppression-online-builds-case-to-break -up-big-tech.

149. Donald Trump, Twitter, May 16, 2020, 4:56 a.m., https://twitter.com/real DonaldTrump/status/1261626674686447621, accessed May 27, 2020.

150. Nick Rigillo, "Convicted Racist Hits Danish Campaign Trail After Easter Riots," *Bloomberg*, updated May 4, 2019, https://www.bloomberg.com /news/articles/2019-05-03/a-convicted-racist-joins-list-of-candidates-in -danish-election

151. Jeffery C. Mays, "New York City Is Ending a Ban on Gay Conversion Therapy. Here's Why," *New York Times*, September 12, 2019, https://www .nytimes.com/2019/09/12/nyregion/conversion-therapy-ban-nyc.html.

152. Mays, "New York City Is Ending a Ban on Gay Conversion Therapy."

153. Janus v. American Federation of Employees, 138 S.Ct. 2448 (2018).

154. John C. Coates IV, "Corporate Speech and the First Amendment: History, Data, and Implications," University of Minnesota Law School, July 8, 2015, 223–24, http://hdl.handle.net/11299/183130.

155. United States v. United States Brewers' Assn., 239 F. 163 (W.D.P. 1916).

156. Adam Winkler, *We the Corporations: How American Businesses Won Their Civil Rights* (New York: Liveright, 2018), 255.

157. Adam Liptak, "How Conservatives Weaponized the First Amendment," *New York Times*, June 30, 2018, https://www.nytimes.com/2018/06/30/us /politics/first-amendment-conservatives-supreme-court.html.

158. Sorrell v. IMS Health, Inc., 564 U.S. 552 (2011).

159. Jon Brodkin, "ISPs Sue Maine, Claim Web-Privacy Law Violates Their Free-Speech Rights," *Ars Technica*, February 18, 2020, https://arstechnica .com/tech-policy/2020/02/isps-sue-maine-claim-web-privacy-law-violates -their-free-speech-rights.

160. John Schwartz, "Exxon Mobil Fights Back at State Inquiries into Climate Change Research," *New York Times*, June 16, 2016, https://www.nytimes .com/2016/06/17/science/exxon-mobil-fights-back-at-state-inquiries-into -climate-change-research.html.

161. Morgan N. Weiland, "Expanding the Periphery and Threatening the Core: The Ascendant Libertarian Speech Tradition," *Stanford Law Review* 69, no. 5 (May 2017): 1469.

162. See, for example, Tarek Maassarani, "Redacting the Science of Climate Change: An Investigative and Synthesis Report," Government Accountability Project, March 2007, https://ncac.org/wp-content/uploads/import /gap_report(1).pdf.

163. Jon Allsop, "The Trump Administration Is Suppressing Climate Science," *CJR*, August 7, 2019, https://www.cjr.org/the_media_today/trump_adminis-tration_climate_change.php; Helena Bottemiller Evich, "Agriculture Department Buries Studies Showing Dangers of Climate Change," *Politico*, June 23, 2019, https://www.politico.com/story/2019/06/23/agriculture-department -climate-change-1376413; Bill McKibben, "The Trump Administration's Solution to Climate Change: Ban the Term," *Guardian*, August 8, 2017, https://www.theguardian.com/commentisfree/2017/aug/08/trump -administration-climate-change-ban-usda.

164. Neela Banerjee and David Hasemyer, "Decades of Science Denial Related to Climate Change Has Led to Denial of the Coronavirus Pandemic," *Inside Climate News*, April 8, 2020, https://insideclimatenews.org/news/08042020 /science-denial-coronavirus-covid-climate-change.

AFTERWORD
1. Catharine A. MacKinnon, "The First Amendment: An Equality Reading," in *The Free Speech Century*, ed. Geoffrey R. Stone and Lee C. Bollinger (New York: Oxford University Press, 2019), 140.
2. Darnton, *Censors at Work*, 19.
3. Caleb Chen, "Activists in Minecraft Made a Digital Library to Bypass Government Censorship," *Privacy News Online*, March 24, 2020, https://www.privateinternetaccess.com/blog/activists-in-minecraft-made-a-digital-library-to-bypass-government-censorship, accessed June 20, 2020; Miriam Deprez, "Emojis, Minecraft and Spotify: How Citizens Are Beating the Censors," *Southeast Asia Globe*, May 4, 2020, https://southeastasiaglobe.com/press-freedom-beating-censors, accessed June 20, 2020.
4. Council of Europe, "Annual Report on ECRI's Activities Covering the Period from 1 January to 31 December, 2019," https://rm.coe.int/ecri-annual-report-2019/16809ca3e1.
5. Council of Europe, "News 2020," "Ultra-Nationalism, Anti-Semitism, Anti-Muslim Hatred: Anti-Racism Commission Raises Alarm over Situation in Europe," February 27, 2020, https://www.coe.int/en/web/portal/-/ultra-nationalism-anti-semitism-anti-muslim-hatred-anti-racism-commission-raises-alarm-over-situation-in-europe, accessed June 20, 2020.
6. George Orwell, "The Freedom of the Press," *New York Times*, October 8, 1972, https://www.nytimes.com/1972/10/08/archives/the-freedom-of-the-press-orwell.html.

INDEX

292